IN FAIRNESS TO CHILDREN
Working for Social Justice in the Primary School

by
Morwenna Griffiths and Carol Davies
with
Margret Cadman and Ann Dean

David Fulton Publishers
London

David Fulton Publishers Ltd
2 Barbon Close, London WC1N 3JX

First published in Great Britain by
David Fulton Publishers 1995

British Library Cataloguing in Publication Data

A catalogue record for this book is available from the British Library

ISBN 1-85346-341-8

Typeset by The Harrington Consultancy
Printed in Great Britain by BPC Books and Journals Ltd., Exeter.

Contents

Acknowledgements

We would like to acknowledge, with gratitude, the help of the following teachers, children and adult colleagues who helped in many ways: by contributing materials for this study, by giving up time to be interviewed at length, and by making suggestions about earlier drafts. We are especially grateful to:
A. Bewick, C. Brewster, A. Cotton, J. Cox, C. Lovett, C. Parish, P. Ross and T. Smith.

We would also like to acknowledge the help and cooperation of others, both adults and children, who should remain anonymous. We are thinking especially of the children in Carol Davies' classes, and of the other teachers in the school. We could not have done it without them, and we are grateful for their ideas, enthusiasm, criticism and patience – as well as for all the writing and drawings which they have given us permission to use.

Adrian Mitchell's poem 'Back in the Playground Blues' is taken from *On the Beach at Cambridge*, published by Allison and Busby, and reprinted by permission of the Peters, Fraser and Dunlop Group Ltd. None of Adrian Mitchell's poems are to be used in any examination whatsoever.

Preface

When we agreed to write this book, we both wondered what we had let ourselves in for. Wasn't full-time work enough? How would we get it done, along with everything else? Now that it *is* done – although it really *was* hard to find time and energy to do it, just as we thought – we are pleased it was written at the same time as trying to teach. It is addressed to busy teachers: we want them to find time to read it and, we hope, develop their own teaching and learning. So it is important that everything we discuss in the book actually took place as part of normal school life. When we had a complete first draft we gave it to another class teacher. Her comments made us feel we had got this right. She said that what had made it interesting for her was that it was not written by a 'should-do' but by a 'does-do'!...there will not be a teacher or a parent that doesn't believe in your experiences – we've all been there!

We wanted to write the book because we think ordinary classrooms and schools have so much to contribute to how fair life is for children, and to the chances they have to grasp all that education has to offer. We have also enjoyed the work we have done with children to improve fairness. We hope our readers will find the same is true for them.

Morwenna Griffiths and Carol Davies
Nottingham
July 1995

The Primary Curriculum Series

This innovative series is an ideal means of supporting professional practice in the post-Dearing era, when a new focus on the quality of teaching and learning is possible. The series promotes reflective teaching and active forms of pupil learning. The books explore the implications of these commitments for curriculum and curriculum-related issues.

The argument of each book flows in, around and among a variety of case studies of classroom practice, introducing them, probing, analysing and teasing out their implications before moving on to the next stage of the argument. The case study material varies in source and form – children's work, teachers' work, diary entries, drawings, poetry, literature, interviews. The vitality and richness of primary school practice are conveyed, together with the teacher expertise on which these qualities are based.

Series Editors

Mary Jane Drummond is Tutor in Education, University of Cambridge Institute of Education, and Andrew Pollard is Professor in the Faculty of Education, University of the West of England, Bristol.

Series Titles

ASSESSING CHILDREN'S LEARNING
Mary Jane Drummond
1-85346-198-9

COLLABORATIVE LEARNING IN STAFFROOMS AND CLASSROOMS
Colin Biott & Patrick Easen
1-85346-201-2

DEVELOPMENTS IN PRIMARY MATHEMATICS TEACHING
Anne Sawyer
1-85346-196-2

THE EXPRESSIVE ARTS
Fred Sedgwick
1-85346-200-4

THE HUMANITIES IN PRIMARY EDUCATION
Don Kimber, Nick Clough, Martin Forrest, Penelope Harnett, Ian Menter & Elizabeth Newman
1-85346-342-6

IN FAIRNESS TO CHILDREN – WORKING FOR SOCIAL JUSTICE IN THE PRIMARY SCHOOL
Morwenna Griffiths & Carol Davies
1-85346-341-8

LITERACY
Margaret Jackson
1-85346-197-0

PERSONAL, SOCIAL AND MORAL EDUCATION
Fred Sedgwick
1-85346-291-8

PRIMARY DESIGN AND TECHNOLOGY – A PROCESS FOR LEARNING
Ron Ritchie
1-85346-340-X

PRIMARY SCIENCE – MAKING IT WORK
Chris Ollerenshaw & Ron Ritchie
1-85346-199-7

WHOSE WRITING IS IT ANYWAY?
Gordon Taylor & Sylvia Warham
1-85346-360-4

Chapter 1

IN FAIRNESS TO CHILDREN

Improving schools and classrooms

Mosiah is a big boy for his 10 years, and is not far off average in achievement as regards the basic skills of English and Maths. He is popular with the other boys and he spends quite a lot of his time competing for position with them. He causes some trouble in the playground, but is not a particularly notorious troublemaker. He is on the brink of going on to the next stage of education, the secondary school. How will he get on there; and, indeed what are his chances of getting on well in his adult life?

On the face of it, you might think that he is all set, with no particular problems, academically or socially. Closer acquaintance disrupts this happy picture. When asked what he wanted to improve on in school, this is what he had to say:

> I want to improve on not talking but certain people in my class which I rather wouldn't want to include are encouraging me even more and arguing. One person causes all of the arguments.

His performance may be average, but it is clear he is a very intelligent boy, and could manage far better. He distances himself from his work and finds the authority of the teachers a problem, even though this year he has told his mother that he likes and respects his class teacher. He rarely contributes to class discussions, though when he does, the point is always thoughtful and relevant. The time he spends competing for position annoys him. He says that he feels he is pressured into it, but cannot easily help himself. Another factor which we must mention is that his head is cropped into fashionable 'lines' – he is of 'mixed race' with a white mother and a Jamaican father who is living in another city. He looks African Caribbean – notice that he has adopted an African Caribbean hairstyle – but says he hates Jamaica. The boys he plays with in school are as often white and Asian as black.

Have his primary schools (for he has been to several) been fair to him, educationally? Have they helped him gain rather than lose the self-esteem, self-confidence and openness to others which will enable him to live well and to contribute to the fairness of the various communities he lives in, both now and in the future? He is a very intelligent boy performing no better than average. Is the fact that he is so clearly under-achieving and at odds with the system and with himself, related to the fact of his mixed race, or his gender? If so, could the schools have done something about it? Could they help him resolve his complex identities, situated as he is between 'black', 'Caribbean', 'white', 'tough guy', 'sensitive and intelligent person', and, no doubt, other felt contradictions too? Surely a school or a classroom can only be fair if all the children are equally able to feel at home, and to do their best.

This book is about fairness to children – including ways in which they can learn to be fair to each other. It is therefore about all the variety of children to be found in British primary schools, boys and girls; black and white; rich and poor; rural and urban; Muslim, Christian, Jew and Hindu; with and without specific learning disabilities; and with and without emotional and behaviourial difficulties. It is written for children like Mosiah and all his various classmates, in the hope that together we all can find ways of improving fairness to children.

It is a book written from two perspectives. Sometimes we, Carol and Morwenna, talk as 'we' and sometimes each of us speaks for ourselves.[1] The book has been written with the help of many others: teachers, children, parents, advisers, governors, educational researchers. Their views appear during the course of the book. Especially important are some teachers and a governor who have discussed what they are trying to do to move their own schools in the direction of more fairness to children; these people are acknowledged on the title page, but not as themselves in the text. This has allowed them to be very open about their own schools: about their problems as well as their strengths.

Carol

As a classroom teacher working in the messy real world of the Primary school I recognize that feeling that 'it's been one of those days!'. It doesn't matter how experienced we teachers are; if we are honest we've all been there, and will probably be there quite a few more times in our careers.

They are the days that seem to pop up without warning so that despite the brilliantly planned lesson something is bound to go wrong. You know the kind of thing: you've planned a class lesson investigating division but when you arrive in your classroom you discover that workmen are there knocking down a partition with another room, making it impossible for anybody to work, let alone concentrate. Like most teachers I could tell some amazing tales of days spent trying to teach in difficult circumstances, stories which now seem comical but which originally left me harassed and drained. Indeed it is when these days occur that I often get quite emotional and irate to read about falling standards of teaching and learning and new initiatives to be introduced. I often wonder if some of the people who continually tell teachers how to teach could actually do better given the situations we are often faced with.

However, that isn't to say that we as teachers couldn't improve. I recognise that we are often faced with difficult circumstances but I also think that there is room for us to develop our own teaching, and I believe that teachers have a professional responsibility to evaluate practice continually and should search rigorously for ways to improve the teaching situation in which we all operate. After all, it is our own pupils and ourselves who are attempting to learn and teach in the real-life, messy world of the primary classroom, and, unlike many educationists suggesting reform who never see the inside of a classroom, we have a vast knowledge of what takes place in a classroom – the difficulties, the possibilities. Above all, we have a knowledge of our needs. If we want to improve practice and our educational environment then we should use the opportunities we have to do something about it rather than just criticising others who are trying to help.

Three principles of fairness

We are interested in creating the best possible learning environment for every individual child. As Carol has said, we are acutely aware that when we say 'best possible' we mean possible in the real-life conditions of schools, with all the various pressures they face, and the constraints they work under. We are also aware that the schools we work in are part of the wider community. In creating fair schools, we are also doing something towards creating a fair society. Schools where children are treated with fairness and justice and where they learn to treat others in the same way are an important part of the creation of a better world for everybody.

Some reasons for unfairness in school are easy to see. Some children come hampered by poverty, or from communities disadvantaged by their isolation or by their high levels of crime and vandalism. Some children are unable to relate their own cultural backgrounds to the environment they find in school. Some of them come with disabilities which make it difficult for them to learn. Girls and boys react to school differently: their achievements are different and so are the lessons they learn about themselves, personally and socially. These reasons are easy to see, but difficult to deal with. However, it is possible to deal with them, and it is the aim of this book to make some suggestions about how.

These suggestions are not – and could not be – simple tips about actions which would automatically work everywhere. Think of two schools within 10 miles of each other in the Midlands, each on the edge of a city. One of them is a primary school in a practically all-white council estate, where unemployment is at 50%. Only one black family, headed by an out-of-work single parent, lives there. The other is a nursery school in a working-class estate where most of the parents are in work. There is one black family: they are middle-class Africans, temporarily in some financial difficulty while the father studies for a higher degree. What should the primary school staff do about parents who see no point in helping with their children's education, since they feel there will be no work whatever the educational achievements? What should the nursery school do about the fact that the African family is thinking of moving to the inner city (a move they can ill afford) just to be with other black families – even though those other black people are unlikely to be Africans? Indeed, how should each school respond to the presence of their isolated black children? Just to be black is significant in a predominantly white setting – but this should not mask the large differences in culture and social background of the particular black children we describe.

Both of these schools, like all others in the UK, need to address issues of fairness for all their children, white and black, and coming from families both in and out of work. Both schools need to help each individual child grow up empowered to work out their own wants and needs in life – and also to have the skills, attitudes and knowledge to reach for them. There are principles the two schools can follow, but there are no easy answers for either of them.

Firstly, in our view, fairness – or social justice – is made up of two strands: one deals with the empowerment of individuals and the other deals with the righting of structural injustice, due to race, class, gender and special educational needs. These strands are interlinked, and attention to both is essential.

Secondly, there is no one right way of organising a school or classroom. As we point out below, in the section on 'fairness and social justice in practice', the process of organisation is as important as its end-result. As in all of primary education, the processes are crucial. They should never be thought of just as a means to some predetermined end-result; the process is just as important as the end. Finding one's own way through the many dilemmas presented by teaching and learning in primary classrooms is an essential part of establishing fairness. Treating people fairly is an important part of enabling them to behave fairly themselves. As Gandhi said: equality is not the end, it is the way.

Thirdly, there is no thought that the interests of the individual are sacrificed. Each individual is valuable, and recognised as an important valued part of the community as a whole. On the other hand, there is a recognition that no individual exists apart from the community. Thus the good of the community inevitably has implications for the good of the individual. There is no conflict between individual excellence and fairness to all. On the contrary, teaching which improves fairness and social justice is good for all children.

The three principles are derived from the values that underlie the commitment to fairness. These values are found in the best tradition of primary education in this country: care and respect for individuals, groupwork and co-operation, entitlement to a core academic and social curriculum, and using knowledge of the real home backgrounds of the children (rather than stereotypical presumptions about them).

We talk of 'the tradition of primary education' meaning a living tradition. The idealism found in the tradition is not just something that used to be relevant, in the good old days. Neither is it something that might become relevant in some distant golden future when present pressures let up a bit. Indeed, we want to emphasise that asking for attention to be given to fairness and justice, is not asking that something more be loaded onto already hard-pressed teachers and schools. It is not something else to be squeezed into an overstretched curriculum, nor yet another set of checklists or forms to be completed by teachers and managers. A glance forward to the chapter headings of this book shows what we mean. As they indicate, opportunities to work for fairness for all children and teachers are to be found in the everyday matters of establishing ground-rules in a classroom, of dealing with bullying and harassment, and of raising children's levels of achievement. Opportunities for more justice can be found in everyday decisions about school management, curriculum content, school trips, and home–school links. All of these are central and everyday concerns in any primary school. The examples we provide in the next section will show how these concerns are also concerns about fairness and justice.

Fairness and social justice in practice

It is a Thursday morning in November in a city centre in the Midlands. Traffic whirls by the big asphalt playground, which is empty at the moment, though through the fence you can see some small children playing on brightly coloured equipment in the nursery playground. Walk inside this city school, past the display of photographs of governors, teachers and helpers, past the corridors decorated with displays of autumn pictures, and go inside the nearest classroom. It is an ordinary classroom full of children getting on with their work. As you walk into the classroom, you notice that these Year 5 children are sitting grouped around tables, working more or less steadily at their maths scheme workbooks, while exchanging a few jokes and squabbling a bit over rights to rulers. Their teacher is also sitting at one of the tables counting out cardboard money with two of the children. A classroom helper is sitting with one of the children, who is counting on her fingers: no, wait a minute, she is not counting on her fingers so much as counting on her knuckles. Another child also has an adult all to himself: they are working quietly on counting straws into bundles of ten. Some of the children are isolated from the others, sitting on their own at desks, rather than working with the others.

This is a description of a real school, and it is so ordinary that it could almost be any primary school, anywhere in the UK. There would be differences in details, of course. The playground might be grassy. There might be no nursery. There might be fewer adults in the room. And so on. However, these are details: the picture is utterly normal.

The very normality of it disguises the many decisions that have been made which are intended to make it a fair place for children to learn, and which make it a fair place for the adults to work. Moreover, it is hard to see at a glance how fair it is. (Snapshot-style, observational checklists will not help much here.) The surface normality disguises not only the decisions that have been made but the attitudes and values which underlie them. However, we can point out some of the different ways that this classroom raises issues of fairness, which must be resolved for each situation – though not necessarily the same way every time.

One decision which teachers must make is how to seat the children. It is impossible to avoid the question of what tables the children should sit at and whether they should have any choice about it. When children are given 'free' choice, they still react to social pressures. They tend to sit in groups marked by class and gender divisions, and to a lesser extent, by race, especially where there are bilingual children who like to sit in groups of children with whom they share both languages. It is clear that children may learn more, increase their mutual understanding, and extend their range of ways of learning and living, given freedom from peer pressure. They are entitled to this experience; entitlement to a common curriculum is only fair. On the other hand, leaving children no free choice about their preferred modes of learning will reduce their chances of learning to voice their own preferences and act on them – the empowerment which is essential to fairness. They may learn more from choosing who to work with and how. There is a dilemma here for the teacher about entitlement and empowerment.

Teachers also need to decide how to distribute their own attention, and that of other adults in the class. The giving of teacher attention is a decision about fairness. It is obvious that some children should get more attention. What is less obvious is the basis for such a decision.

In the class we described there are two children receiving extra help. Yasmin is counting on her knuckles because she is newly arrived from Bombay, and that is how it is done there. Her grasp of number is very good, but she is having trouble with her maths work card, because her English is not yet fluent. The extra attention from the adult sitting with her means that her progress in number does not suffer unduly, while she learns more English. For instance, one-to-one, it is possible for the adult to notice that Yasmin uses her knuckles rather than her fingers to count, and to apply this information in helping her work out the sums. John, the child counting straws, needs extra help because his tolerance of frustration is so limited. He is statemented as having special educational needs; he and the rest of the class can get a chance to get on with their work only if his frustration is contained so he does not express it by rampaging through the room.

What about the rest of the children? The teacher needs to decide whether there is an equality of attention, measured in teacher time and in kinds of interaction (praise, reprimands, cognitive questions) across races, sexes, and social class. If there is not – and almost certainly there will not be – the reasons for inequality need to be evaluated. Possible reasons include needs (like special needs), merit (who deserves the attention), compensation (children who have so far lost out in life), and entitlement to certain minimum standards.

Each of these decisions is complicated by other considerations which affect them. Like all teachers, both of us have an idea of what standards of work and behaviour to expect of the children. We have different expectations of children according to their age and sex; but what about race and class? How far these expectations are fair ones is something else to be considered. Children need to feel respected and valued whatever their actual levels of ability, but on the other hand low expectations are known to hamper disadvantaged groups. Moreover it seems that few teachers, schools or LEAs have adequate policies about differentiation.[2]

Children themselves have views about all of these questions, and can be quite sophisticated in discussing the issues related to, for instance, seating and teacher expectations. (We explain in more detail in the next chapter.)

Treating children with respect requires an ethos of mutual respect and tolerance from all the members of the class, both adults and children. Such an ethos is based on mutual openness and trust, which is why we place an emphasis on trust as well as on achievement and learning. Trust is needed in a fair classroom, but it is also dependent on an even more basic need for safety. If bullying and harassment are rife, in or out of the classroom, children will be impeded in their learning. A fair community is impossible to set up where some of its members are abusing their power over others. All this is invisible to the casual observer of the classroom described above, but is essential, nevertheless.

Just as invisible and just as important, teachers also need to be treated fairly. Who decided on the maths scheme? Who chose the equipment? Will the head support the teacher when required? How will colleagues react when one of them is under particular stress? All of these issues are important, not only in themselves, but also because in the long run they affect the quality of the children's learning.

Even though all these examples show that questions of fairness are intertwined with everyday decision making in school, there still remains a feeling in many schools that 'We don't have time to do anything about equality and justice: we are too busy getting on with the main business of schools.' The following remarks are often heard in schools and out of them: 'We are interested in the personal development of individuals, not in changing society'; 'You should keep politics out of education'; or, 'We'd love to do something about equal opportunities but we are too busy keeping up with all the recent changes'. Remarks like these show that issues of fairness may be felt to be something of a luxury, something to be thought about and taken into account after the main aims of the school have been established. Sometimes there is more hostility. Some people think that issues of fairness and justice are an unwelcome distraction introduced into education by crusading, politically motivated groups like feminists or anti-racists, and that they should be resisted.

We are not saying that any of these views are particularly widespread – it is more likely that most people recognise the close connection between education and hopes of achieving a better society.[3] However, such views are powerful, and propagated by powerful sections of society, like some newspaper editors. More worryingly, they can be used to mask hostility to the aims of building fairer schools and communities. It is important therefore to acknowledge the power of such views – and to be ready with arguments and strategies to deal with them. We have given some already. We expand on them in Chapter 11, for those of our readers who would like a more detailed explanation about the meaning of fairness and social justice than we have so far given.

The beginning of our Fairness project

Morwenna

The Fairness project at Riverside[4] school began some years ago now, when we decided to work together on a topic roughly related to equal opportunities. The link between us has not been easy to maintain, given the pressure of school and university life. But somehow we have kept the project going, making changes in its direction from time to time, while keeping a sense of underlying principles, which we began by thinking of as 'equal opportunities', and, by now, think of more as 'fairness'. There are some strong reasons, on my side at least, for keeping the link intact and the project going.

My university day starts later and ends later than the school one. I teach a lot at weekends and late into the evenings. On the mornings I go into school, the alarm goes off very early, and at that point I often wonder why I am maintaining the link at all. (Carol is, understandably, less than sympathetic when I complain of the early start, when we meet in the classroom at just past 8.00! But I still complain.) By the time I am driving back to the University a few hours later, I remember exactly why I go in.

The sheer energy of the children is entirely delightful if you do not have to deal with it day in, day out, week in, week out. We think that the relationship means that I am a bit like a 'Grandmother', while Carol is 'Mum'. She is the secure but harassed centre of the class, while I drift in once a week and enjoy myself. On the other hand, I come in so often, that I do not disrupt anything: I am part of the furniture. The children seem to recognise quickly that I am not a student or a parent, but neither am I quite a teacher either.

There are professional reasons too, which keep me getting up early on cold, dark mornings. I spend my life teaching practising teachers, but at a distance, as they come on courses or ask me to take on short consultancies. I find coming regularly into a classroom and working alongside Carol is of great help in sorting out my ideas – and, of course, keeping my feet on the ground. (I often find myself referring to the work we do together, during my lectures and seminars.) The ideas that I most needed to sort out were related to my appointment to the University to lecture in Equal Opportunities. We began, therefore, by thinking what we might do to help the children's learning and improve equality of opportunity. The way that the project developed thereafter is described in three of the chapters of this book.

In a larger sense, too, this book is a result of our co-operation. Together we can use our own particular strengths. As Carol says, the contents of the book do not come from any University ivory tower, removed from the lively, real world of schools and children. I am aware that any ideas we have must be made to work in and around all the normal goings-on of a busy primary school, and they must take account of all the pressures that teachers and schools have felt over the last few years. At the same time, I am in contact with a range of schools and perspectives, as part of my normal teaching and research. So just as this book puts forward a view rooted in real schools, equally it is not just the view from school. I am able to help bring a wider perspective drawn from the contacts, reading and research which are also part of my job.

Carol

I think, for me, it began by accident. The first year I suppose I wanted to do something like I had done with Alison, 2 years before, when she and I had worked on PSE and human relations with the children. I knew that I had learnt something different and new from Alison, and had challenged myself. But at first, I had only a hazy understanding of what Morwenna and I were doing as a whole. Things dawned on me slowly. I'd realised I'd learnt something new, and that I was making improvements in my teaching. At that point I didn't know much theory – I've acquired some, now, but it's been the doing that's been the most important.

At the time I didn't have a clear understanding about it at all – but over the years it's been like walking through a fog which is slowly becoming less dense. I've been challenged; I've learnt things about education and about myself as a teacher. I'm not sure I'll ever make it to the clearing. I'm not sure that I'm worried about that. I'm glad that things are getting clearer for me – my philosophy of education is strengthening – but I don't want to get to the point that I'm so blinded by the light that I can no longer see.

Summary of chapters

We thought it would be helpful to readers if we included a summary of what is to be found in each chapter, so that if there was something they wanted to read first – or to skip – it would be easier for them to do so.

We begin the book by drawing on the Fairness project at Riverside school. This means that Chapter 2, 'Changing classrooms', roots the book firmly in the classroom. We show how it is possible to work towards empowering children to influence changes in the classroom. 'Increasing trust in the classroom' is the topic of Chapter 3. This extends the theme of Chapter 2; we emphasise the importance of trust as a prerequisite for co-operation and mutual learning, and so for improving the fairness towards children in school, and discuss some of the dilemmas that have arisen for us in trying to do so. Chapter 4 takes up a similar theme in relation to the whole school. It is called 'Learning in safety' and it considers the importance for all the children – regardless of their social background – of having the opportunity to go about the school without fear. We discuss issues of bullying and harassment in the school as a whole: not only in classrooms, but also in playgrounds, corridors and cloakrooms.

In Chapter 5 and 6 the focus moves from change and empowerment to learning and achievement. Chapter 5, 'Very fair work', discusses the possibilities of improving achievement at classroom and school levels. We begin by discussing the Fairness project introduced in Chapter 2 and 3, and also explain some other projects in different schools which focus directly on gender or race: masculinity and reading at Junior level; femininity and technology at Infant level; and Section 11 work for ethnic minority children. In Chapter 6, 'Self-identity, self-esteem and achievement', the focus moves to the implications of achievement in schools being used to sort and grade children, with all that means for groups of people who have been 'marginalised' as a result of their gender, race or social class.

In Chapter 7, 'Changing schools', we continue to consider the whole school, but move from the focus on children to concentrate on the teaching staff and *their* empowerment. The focus of the chapter is on the whole school: the teachers, their relation to management, and the effect all this has on the learning of the children. We use the example of a school responding to the Dearing Report on the curriculum. We turn our attention to more detailed issues about the curriculum in Chapter 8, which is called 'Curriculum Planning: trips and topics'. Here we discuss the issues involved in making sure that every individual has access to a breadth of curriculum through trips and topics, and is able to benefit educationally from them. We use case studies of Riverside school trips to Warwick Castle and to York.

A continuing theme throughout the book is the importance – and difficulty – of improving communication between home and school, and between the local community and school. The theme is addressed for parents and schools in Chapter 9, 'Getting closer to home'. We begin with examples of individual children and go on to a case-study of a nursery school getting to know and work with its Asian parents. Chapter 10, 'Right up your street', extends the theme by describing some work at Riverside, undertaken with the help of a small grant from the Greater Nottingham Education Business Partnership, in which links with the local community as a whole were expanded.

In Chapter 11, 'A framework for change', we explain the underlying rationale behind the kinds of change advocated in the book as a whole. We discuss some of the theory behind reflective action research which underpins the work described in this book. We also look again at the meaning of fairness and social justice in schools. The book ends, as it should, with some views from the children with whom we are now working most closely: the Year 3 and Year 4 children in Carol's present class at Riverside school.

Chapter 2

CHANGING CLASSROOMS

Improving the learning of children: improving the learning of teachers.

We had a lot to learn. (One of the pleasures as well as one of the trials of teaching is that you never know it all.) We began the Fairness project (which we first mentioned in the last chapter) with reasonably clear ideas about what we would do, at least in the short term, but it did not take long for the children to overturn them, and teach us how well they could take responsibility for the direction of the project as a whole. As this class moved on, we continued to learn from the next one, and the next, changing our own ideas about how to improve the children's learning, and about what was needed if the classroom was to be a place that was fair to them all.

One of the children in that first class was Mosiah, the child we described at the beginning of Chapter 1. He brought a fund of intelligent knowledge about himself and how he might continue to develop, together with strong ideas about how he ought to be treated by authority. He remained sceptical about the worth of the Fairness project – a valuable attitude in itself. Parveen was much more enthusiastic. Her life in class revolved round her close friendship with two other Asian girls, one of them very assertive, sometimes aggressive. Parveen liked to please her friends and her teachers: she worked hard to work out her own needs and deal with them. Suzie had some difficulty in understanding what we were getting at. She was not achieving average standards academically (like many white working class girls, she had not found school easy). However she was well above average in her ability to co-operate with other children, willingly taking the most unhappy and difficult children into her group and dealing with them. We learnt a lot from all of these children about how they set about trying to improve their learning. As the years have gone by, we have learnt more about the way different individuals, in all their cultural and social diversity, respond to being asked to examine their own processes of learning, and in the process we have also learnt a lot more about acting in fairness to children.

We use what we learnt from the Fairness project in a number of the following chapters, to ground the issues we discuss. In this chapter we look at what it taught us about working together with the children for change, with a focus on empowerment. In the next chapter, we look at what it taught us about the importance of trust, as a prerequisite for any work meant to improve fairness in classrooms and schools. In Chapter 5, we pick up on the content, rather than on the processes, as we consider children's learning and how to improve it.

Morwenna[1]

Early beginnings

When I first met Carol it was early one February. In January I had approached the Head and it had been arranged that I should meet both Carol and her class, at the end of that month. We began by trying to identify a project to work on during the second half-term. Group work emerged as an issue that interested both of us. She had previously been involved in some PSE and Human Relations work with groups in the class, and had found it valuable. I was interested in possible gender, race or class aspects to group work. I thought, for instance, that it might be interesting to do some group work in science or technology (for instance, egg-race activities) since, I thought, boys might be bad at group work, and girls at science or technology, and we could work on both areas simultaneously.

We began introducing the work to the children at the beginning of February, towards the end of the first half-term. We started the day with a class brainstorm and discussion about the problems of group working, ways of solving problems of group working, and how to choose a group to work with. The children were then set a task of designing a room and making a model of it. They had first to choose groups, and then to set ground-rules for themselves (expressed as contracts). Finally they had to plan the task before starting on it.

I observed the participation patterns during the class discussion, and also the way the children managed choosing groups. I wrote up these observations and sent them to Carol[5].

Excerpts from Morwenna's journal

Participation patterns: The discussion was dominated by girls, especially Chris and, later, Jill. ...The discussion was dominated by whites, who participated more obviously than the Asians. ...Even the ones who seemed a bit out of it may have been participating more than was apparent: for instance, Mosiah suddenly 'woke up' and said something relevant and worthwhile, and then nothing more. Thomas appeared very interested too, and was with the discussion as was clear from his quiet comments. ...Some of the white girls were quite non-participative: Beth for instance was only concentrating on getting through the session, I think. ...Boys were far more vociferous than girls about not wanting to work with the other sex, but they seemed unable to say why. (Does the class ethos prevent them being rude to each other in sex/race terms?) Not all the boys felt like this: the ones who did were the ones who seemed to be trying to work in gangs.

Choosing Groups: Given the slight feeling against mixed sex on the part of some boys, Thomas and Qasim were not quite sure they wanted to be seen to be choosing girls, but on the other hand they rather wanted to. A delicate negotiation followed with Juliet and Poppy, with quite a lot of sensitive help from the two girls. ...While there was obviously feeling around mixing sexes, I could see none around mixing ethnic groups. I checked this later on looking at the finished groups, and could see no sign of difficulty as reflected in the composition of the groups.

We met and discussed all these observations. At this stage we thought we would continue to concentrate on group working. However, it was here that the project took its first unexpected turn. Drawing on the detailed observations, we wondered if perhaps the children needed to think what their *individual* learning goals were, rather than have us prescribing class goals, which were unlikely to match individual needs. My observations on the participation of various groups in group discussions show some of the complexities. For instance, I noted that girls dominated the class discussion – but this fact masked another fact, that these girls were all middle class, and almost all white. The four Asian girls and the three white, working class girls contributed far less. Again, I noted how differently the boys reacted to being in mixed-sex groups. In such a mixed -class as this, groups like 'boys' or 'Asians' or 'middle class', were not homogeneous at all.

In effect we were moving from us working *for* the children, in the assumptions that we knew their needs, to working *with* them. As a result, we were also moving from thinking of equal opportunities work being primarily about the needs of, for example girls as a group, or Asians as a group. We were shifting our ideas towards empowering children of all groups to work out how they each might best achieve what they needed and wanted from schooling. In this we did not lose sight of the importance of race, class, and gender factors (each of which will influence a child's perception of what is to be gained from schooling). So as well as seeing a child as an individual with their[6] particular needs and wants, we remained alert to how their being a member of a particular social group affected their ability to make best use of their schooling.

Third beginning

On the first Monday of the new half-term we arranged a brief class discussion about methods of working. We began by asking the children why they thought they needed to work in groups at school, and what ways of learning worked best. I explained what I had noticed during the observations I had been making, sometimes mentioning individuals. During the discussion it became clear that many children were just as interested in improving their ability to work on their own as in getting better at co-operating in groups. One powerful reason for this seemed to be their understandable concern that they would be moving up to secondary school soon, where they thought they would be asked to do even more individual work than they had in the primary school.

We were both convinced by the children's arguments, and agreed we should include 'working on your own' as well as 'working in a group' as part of what we were aiming at. We had come even further from the starting place; this was a third beginning to our project. As a result of the first stage of close observation of the class, we had come to see that the children needed to identify individual goals, and now, again, from listening carefully to the children, we saw that they might well want to include individual and class learning among the individual goals they were to identify at the end of the week.

As a result each child completed a 'learning contract' using a proforma designed by Carol. Since they had shown an interest in individual and class discussions as well as in group work they were encouraged to include any of these in their answers. The proforma was headed 'My Goal' and we assured the children that we were the only people who would know what each one of them had written (*see* Figure 2.1).[7]

By now, we had realised the significance of including the children in as much of the project as possible: they had helped us decide on the issues we should investigate, and the goals that should be set. They were now to help in collecting observations – *not* just as pairs of eyes or ears, but also in deciding what to observe and why. To begin with it was we who designed the questionnaires, though this was to change as the children became more familiar with their construction. We used the responses of the children in their learning contracts as a basis for the questions we asked. The first one was about 'asking the teacher' (Figure 2.2).

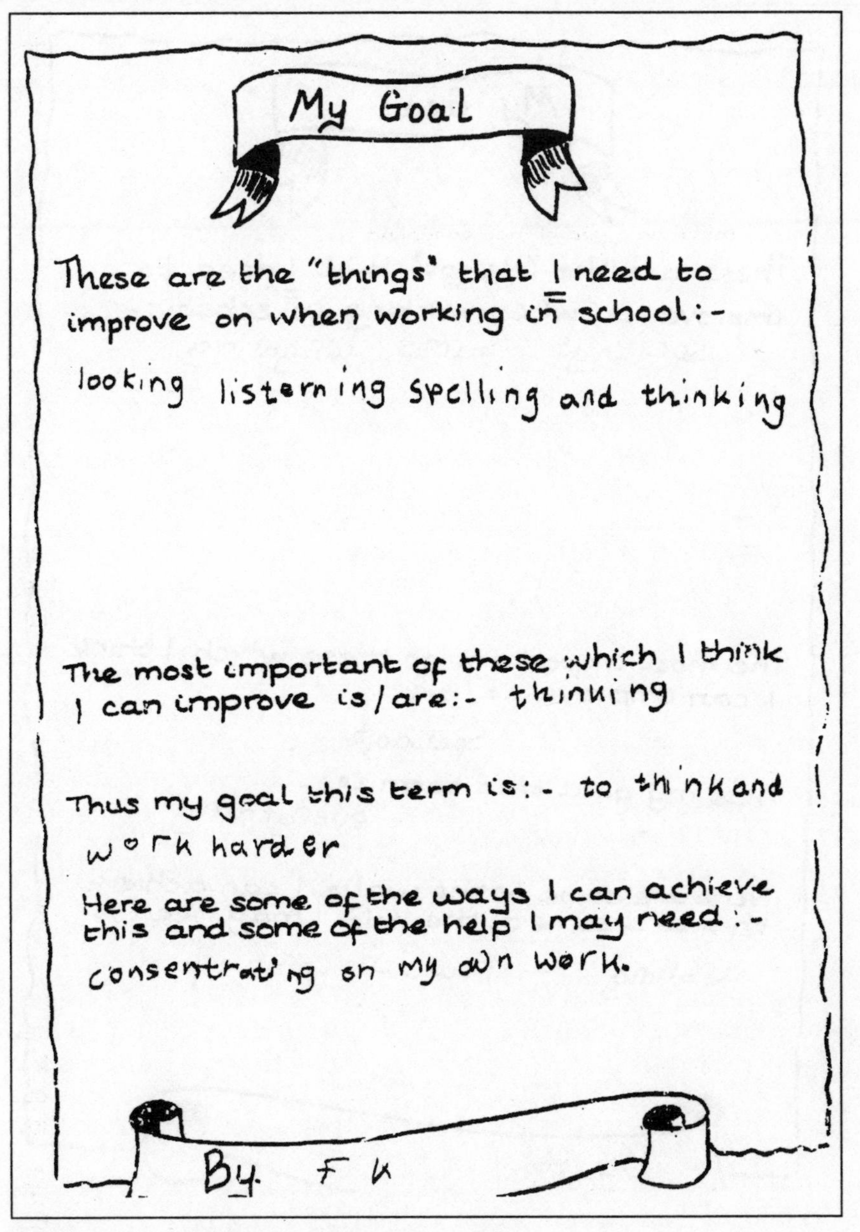

Figure 2.1 Examples of learning contracts

After the children had tried using the first questionnaire, we used their comments on its design to devise two more. We made sure that the learning goals that each child had set for themselves were addressed by at least one of the questionnaires. The other two were called 'Talking to friends', and 'Getting on with work' (Figures 2.3 and 2.4).

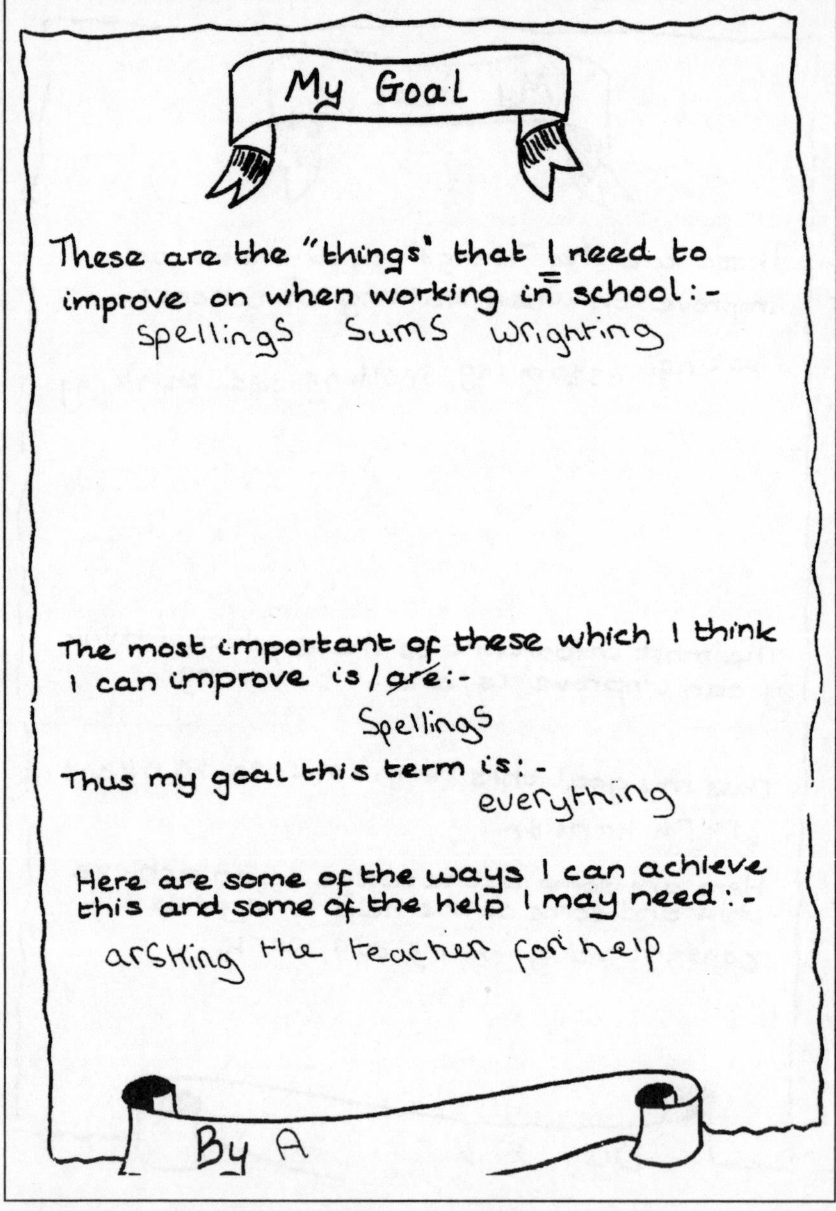

Figure 2.1 Examples of learning contracts

Over the next few weeks the children tried out the questionnaires, filing them in their own individual folders, rather than giving them in for someone else to think about. Results were analysed by means of class discussion which revealed what had been learned. Suggestions were made about the research tools themselves. The second part of the discussion focused on action to be taken.

Asking the teachers :

Name:

Activities:

<u>I asked a teacher</u>

For a spelling ('How do you spell...?)
☐☐☐☐☐ ☐☐☐☐☐ ☐☐☐☐☐ ☐☐☐☐☐ ☐☐☐☐☐

To find resources (Where is....? Can I have....?)
☐☐☐☐☐ ☐☐☐☐☐ ☐☐☐☐☐ ☐☐☐☐☐ ☐☐☐☐☐

To ask permission
☐☐☐☐☐ ☐☐☐☐☐ ☐☐☐☐☐ ☐☐☐☐☐ ☐☐☐☐☐

To find out what work to do next
☐☐☐☐☐ ☐☐☐☐☐ ☐☐☐☐☐ ☐☐☐☐☐ ☐☐☐☐☐

Because I finished my work, and I wanted to see if it was right
☐☐☐☐☐ ☐☐☐☐☐ ☐☐☐☐☐ ☐☐☐☐☐ ☐☐☐☐☐

Because I was half way through my work, and I wanted to see if it was right
☐☐☐☐☐ ☐☐☐☐☐ ☐☐☐☐☐ ☐☐☐☐☐ ☐☐☐☐☐

To show my work because I was pleased with it
☐☐☐☐☐ ☐☐☐☐☐ ☐☐☐☐☐ ☐☐☐☐☐ ☐☐☐☐☐

Because I was completely stuck
☐☐☐☐☐ ☐☐☐☐☐ ☐☐☐☐☐ ☐☐☐☐☐ ☐☐☐☐☐

Because I was stuck on one question
☐☐☐☐☐ ☐☐☐☐☐ ☐☐☐☐☐ ☐☐☐☐☐ ☐☐☐☐☐

To sort out problems between children
☐☐☐☐☐ ☐☐☐☐☐ ☐☐☐☐☐ ☐☐☐☐☐ ☐☐☐☐☐

<u>I did not ask a teacher</u>

I did not ask because I did not need help

I did not ask although I was stuck

I did not ask because ....

Figure 2.2 Questionnaire called 'Asking the teachers'

The class discussion revealed that the children were learning about their own behaviour, and were interested by it. They were surprised how little time was spent fighting, and how much on joking. They remarked that only in some cases would they change their way of behaving as a result of the information: for instance, they said that time spent chatting to friends would not change – it was enjoyable, even if it did interfere with work.

Talking to friends:

Name:

Activity:

I spoke to my friends because

I wanted a spelling
☐☐☐☐☐ ☐☐☐☐☐ ☐☐☐☐☐ ☐☐☐☐☐ ☐☐☐☐☐

I wanted help with my work
☐☐☐☐☐ ☐☐☐☐☐ ☐☐☐☐☐ ☐☐☐☐☐ ☐☐☐☐☐

To find resources
☐☐☐☐☐ ☐☐☐☐☐ ☐☐☐☐☐ ☐☐☐☐☐ ☐☐☐☐☐

To find out what to do next
☐☐☐☐☐ ☐☐☐☐☐ ☐☐☐☐☐ ☐☐☐☐☐ ☐☐☐☐☐

For a long chat
☐☐☐☐☐ ☐☐☐☐☐ ☐☐☐☐☐ ☐☐☐☐☐ ☐☐☐☐☐

For a short chat
☐☐☐☐☐ ☐☐☐☐☐ ☐☐☐☐☐ ☐☐☐☐☐ ☐☐☐☐☐

For a joke
☐☐☐☐☐ ☐☐☐☐☐ ☐☐☐☐☐ ☐☐☐☐☐ ☐☐☐☐☐

To argue
☐☐☐☐☐ ☐☐☐☐☐ ☐☐☐☐☐ ☐☐☐☐☐ ☐☐☐☐☐

I did not talk to my friends much because..

Figure 2.3 Questionnaire called 'Talking to friends'

However they agreed that something could be done on problems related to asking the teacher and to sorting out resources. It was pointed out that, as things were, it was equally irritating to have remembered to bring a rubber or pencil sharpener as not to have done. If you had not brought one you had to borrow – but if you had, people kept on disturbing you to borrow it. The desirability of having a teacher at the table was also emphasised:

Getting on with work

Name:

Time: before play,
after play,
after lunch.

I did not talk too much

☺ ☐ ☐ ☐ ☐ ☐ ☹

I used my own ideas

☺ ☐ ☐ ☐ ☐ ☐ ☹

I did not copy and cheat

☺ ☐ ☐ ☐ ☐ ☐ ☹

I asked for help when I needed to

☺ ☐ ☐ ☐ ☐ ☐ ☹

I worked hard

☺ ☐ ☐ ☐ ☐ ☐ ☹

I did not boss other people about

☺ ☐ ☐ ☐ ☐ ☐ ☹

....

☐ ☐ ☐ ☐ ☐

Figure 2.4 Questionnaire called 'Getting on with work'

not only did her availability cut down on time spent asking questions about the work, but also it painlessly curtailed the pleasures of irrelevant conversation. Children thought they could work as individuals on the time they spent chatting. However they needed a group response to questions about resources. They then went back into tables – the groups they usually worked in – and came up with strategies to deal with the resourcing

Parveen, Kaneez and Tasneen, written by Parveen
I work all right with my group table but not as a group. I have got two friends, named Kaneez and Tasneen. I could work with them, but I can not work when we chat too much. If we do want to chat a lot, we will decide that we will talk a little while, and do our work a lot. So you know how I get on.

Diane, Suzie and Nazim
How to work better
If we could share rubbers and try to work together

If we shared getting the resources, e.g. one gets paper, one gets crayons

If we could help Nazim with spellings

Only talk quietly. For Peak we will be quiet, and we will talk quietly in other subjects such as topic work.

Only get out your chair when you need to.

Figure 2.5 Examples of table 'contracts'

question. Some of them can be seen in Figure 2.5.

The questionnaires themselves were criticised constructively. For instance, it was pointed out that 'having a chat' needed to be broken down into two categories of 'long chats' and 'short chats', because the former were far more disruptive to getting work done than were the latter. Rob, a classroom helper, made a suggestion that we design a new sheet on 'Wandering about'. This idea was taken up enthusiastically by the children. They helped design the sheet, which ended up as a single sentence, 'I got out of my seat because....', together with a list of words to help with spelling, like 'arguing', 'ask' and 'cupboard key'. Again, the children discussed what they had learnt about their own behaviour patterns, and what actions they might now take as a result.

Excerpts from Morwenna's Journal

> *What the children said about the sheets investigating 'wandering about':* They were easy to do; Qasim sent Manzar on errands, rather than fill in that he'd been wandering; Mosiah asked why we were doing them; answers from other children included the effect on yourself and the effect on others, of wandering about.
>
> *They said they had learnt:* that they wandered more than they expected; that they were distracted by things when they wandered; that they were talking a lot to each other; that whether they wandered about depended on the activity: 'Peak maths [the maths scheme] makes us get up and down a lot.' 'Menu writing [a recent writing activity] meant we stayed in our places more.' The children thought their behaviour only changed when they were actually doing the sheet. Carol and Rob both disagreed with this. They said they thought that the change was more long lasting. They had both been very impressed by the way the children were getting on with each other, especially during the work with clay [a recent craft activity].
>
> The children said they thought they had not met their goals, well, maybe a little bit. But they thought the strategies they had worked out to deal with problems of rubbers and sharpeners were working well.

As a result of the children's evaluation of what they had learnt, another self-assessment sheet was devised. This one was called 'Time', and was designed to help the children think about when they stopped work (Figure 2.6), so that they could carry on monitoring their own behaviour patterns.

The children were learning how to achieve their own ends by reflecting on them, both individually and in groups. They were also learning that they had valuable contributions to make to the teachers' practice. This process was to continue until the end of that academic year. We discuss the effects of the project that year and over the next couple of years in Chapter 5, where we consider learning and achievement.

We seemed to be moving closer to the first of the principles of fairness listed in Chapter 1: of empowering each child to voice their needs and wants, and to be able do something practical about it. The importance of this principle had only been dimly seen by us at the start of the project. Working practically with the children, and trying to be fair as we did so, had helped us make it explicit. We were still paying attention to the structural injustices which arise from differences of class, race or gender, but this concern never took centre stage. How far it should have done is an important issue. We come back to this towards the end of the next chapter.

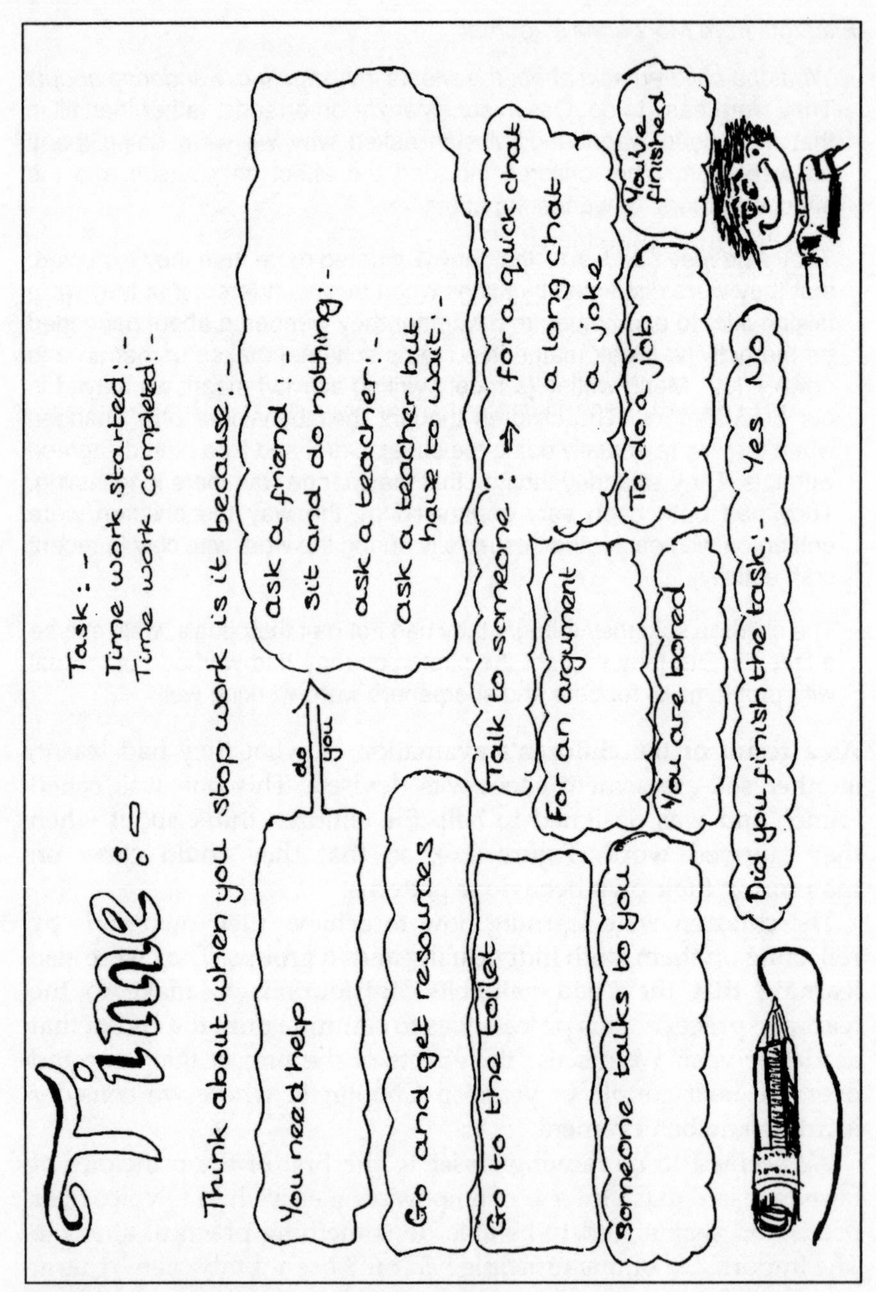

Figure 2.6 Observation sheet on 'Time'

We were also putting into practice the other two principles of fairness. The second is that the processes of putting fairness into operation are as important as the ends reached. We took the process of consultation very seriously, so the children saw that their views were really important. The third principle is that individuals should not be sacrificed to the needs of groups, but that the needs of the group is to be recognised as an important factor in the welfare of individuals. We were careful to attend to the children as individuals with particular needs and wants, at the same time as recognising the importance of factors like gender, race and class in making them the individuals they were.

The story continues: 'pressure'

The following year Carol was teaching a class of mixed Years 5 and 6 again. We had discussed what we were doing with a number of our colleagues in the school and university, and with members of the LEA advisory service, who had recently carried out an inspection of the school. As a result we wanted to build on our understanding of empowerment, but we also wanted to respond to some of these comments by colleagues. In particular, we wanted to explore the ideas of support and challenge, because these are so central to a teacher's role. Children have a sense of the direction they want to go in, and how to do it, but they still need the help of teachers to keep them going. They need both to be supported and also to be challenged. We had been very pleased with the children's participation in working out how to improve their own learning strategies and environments. We now hoped that we could work as a whole class on what support and challenge each one wanted.

We began with the words 'support' and 'challenge', because that is the kind of language that teachers use. We wanted the children to work with us in developing the right blend of each so that their learning and achievement improved, now and in the future. We thought the terms might be too difficult for the children, but the word we chose, 'help', turned out to be less useful than a word introduced by one of the children, 'pressure'. We think it is significant that 'pressure' is a word that has been important in African Caribbean masculine culture and that it was one of the two African Caribbean boys in the class who introduced the word. Again, we learnt from the children, and the project took a new turn, which would continue to influence us into the following year. Some of the results of this will be described in Chapter 5: what is relevant in the context of this chapter is the ways that we set about it and what we learnt from the children about the framework within which we were working.

One thing we learnt was something we thought we knew already. The social world and the academic world are not as separate for

1. What does helping mean?
   Or in what ways do you need helping?
   Or what sorts of help take place in the classroom?

2. What sorts of help do you need? (Can we make a definition?)

3. From the list can we decide which forms of help are 'support' (e.g. showing me your work) and 'challenge' (e.g. cause you to push yourself? improve yourself? 'think you've done it, but...)

....
...

4. Do you think you get enough help? What else could I do?

5. Who gets all the attention? What about children who don't get attention?

6. What do you feel about this? Is it fair?

Figure 2.7 Discussion questions on help

children as they are for adults. The same is true for the worlds of school, playground, neighbourhood and home. These, too, interconnect for children; by the time they are adults they will have learnt to see them as quite separate spheres with separate rules.

Of course we 'knew' this already. We both take PSE seriously. We had both expressed worries that the emphasis on subject knowledge in the National Curriculum would get in the way of children's learning. However, we were still surprised at our own preconceptions. (How well did we know what we claimed to know?) To our surprise, we both found that our own framing of experiences as either 'work' or 'play', 'school' or 'home', was so strong that it stifled this knowledge, at least in so far as everyday practice was concerned. Working with the children released the knowledge into the open, where it could not be ignored, and where we could use it in helping the children with the necessary support and challenge for learning.

Carol

It was important that the children were given a full explanation of the research project and why it was being carried out. They may not all have been able to gain an overview of the whole picture, and each would have taken it on board at their own level, but I felt it was important that the children were made aware that we (everyone participating in the project) were searching for a means to improve the situation in that particular classroom, and that their viewpoint was equally as valuable as anyone else's. They needed to know that they would be involved in all aspects of the research from being informants, to setting the questions and methods for data collection to using the results. This was important as it is more effective if the children are empowered to search for ways of improving a situation. It creates a feeling of ownership and makes the outcome more meaningful to them as individuals.

I decided to use a class discussion to introduce the study to the children and explain the reasons behind it. At this stage I felt the words 'support' and 'challenge' might be too difficult for them to be able to discuss, so I used the word 'help' instead. Prior to the discussion taking place I had set myself a plan of possible areas to discuss. Although I had outlined six questions I did not realistically think all would be discussed. I wanted to be flexible enough to let the children steer the discussion through areas that were important to them, or conversely to have enough questions to stimulate discussion if necessary. The plan can be seen in Figure 2.7. The dotted line represents the cut-off point, where I originally thought the discussion might end.

When it came to the questions of 'What does "helping" mean?' and 'What forms of help are useful?', the children were only concerned with issues such as 'Helping each other work; guiding; help with getting things; showing work; solving problems; if people are talking – stopping them; discussing with friends; talking helps; some noise is needed – that helps.' The type of help that the children were concerned with at this stage seemed to be in a social and pastoral sense and there were no specific problems mentioned. The discussion remained very general, and there was a sense that the children were simply giving answers that teachers would want to hear.

However the major concern for the children was the question of pressure. The term had a rousing effect on the children the first time it was mentioned. They were asked whether they felt pressure was a good thing, and they all chorused 'Baaaad!' and then they thought about it and chorused 'Goooood!', ending up with a clamour of competing shouts of 'Good!', 'Good!', 'Bad!', 'Good!', 'Bad!'. It naturally followed to discuss whether pressure was a help. Morwenna transcribed this section of the tape, so we could study it away from the situation. Some excerpts are given below. The sophistication the children show in discussing individual differences and the role of the teacher is impressive:

If you didn't have any pressure at all then you wouldn't do anything. You need a little bit of pressure just to make you get some work done.

But it can get on your nerves, because, like, it pressures you and you get in a worry about it.

I still work without any pressure.

You'd know what you had to do but you wouldn't have any pressure to do it.

If you have too much pressure you get so WORRIED and it's annoying 'cos [inaudible] little pressure [inaudible] if don't have any pressure at all you won't get any work done and you won't learn anything. That's the way life goes.

If you get too much pressure you can't work, and if you don't have enough pressure you don't work. So that's the reason you have to have pressure. In the middle, not too much but not too less.

Miss? Everybody has got different pressure because some people want more pressure and some people want less pressure. Some people want to work more harder. Some people don't want to work as hard.

Yeah, I work hard. Really, really hard.

If you get the work for the people who are better, then the people who aren't so good get loads of pressure that they don't want.

The people who are better at work and when that work comes for them, people who aren't so good at work, they get that work as well and they get loads of pressure that they don't want.

Paul's saying that some people can't work under pressure and some people can.

Some people want pressure because they want to work more hard and some people have difficulties and some people don't need much pressure because they know how to work.

If they want to work hard then they need pressure. If they don't want to work and they get pressure then they won't work. They'll just mess around, sit around.

You don't need loads of pressure to work though, you might just need, like, telling what you have to do, and then doing that, yeah.

I like pressure. I like a lot of pressure.

If you're ill, you come back and you, you've got too much work to do, yeah, that's too much PRESSURE, that is, if you've got too much work to do.

Paul's saying he wants to work hard, but he just doesn't understand some of the work so if he had easier work and then it got harder in stages he'd be able to work.

Fourth years [the children had not yet learnt the new ERA terminology] get more pressure. When you're fourth year and you know you can't work a lot, when you get to secondary school at least you have that type of work that helps you to work a lot, private work that helps you to work a lot.

Miss Davies, I'm just glad that we've had this discussion because some people might have WANTED this discussion to happen some time. ... Yeah, they would have been embarrassed to write it.

(Transcription of tape)

Taking the cue from this animated discussion, we went on to investigate the idea of pressure. I was very interested in what the children were saying about 'pressure'. However, I was not entirely satisfied that all the children had an understanding of what it meant, and I felt they needed time to consider what pressures were on them. After that we could go on to develop a wider awareness of what kinds of pressure were or were not useful to the children. The investigation of pressure which I describe next was used as a springboard the following year to investigate what kind of pressure and support helps advance academic work and achievement. Meanwhile the children had again succeeded in shifting the focus of the project.

A week after the first discussion with the children I presented them with my idea for a Pressure Picture. I had produced a basic outline to show the children. My picture suggested that pressure might be like a big weight pressing down on you, and I had drawn a picture of myself with a large weight on my head. In this weight, I told the children, I was going to write all the things that are a pressure for me, and together the children and I thought of some examples. I then suggested that there are things that help me with this pressure and support me. This I decided to draw as a keep fit kit and again we thought of suggestions for things that I might write in the picture. The children and I then went and produced our own pictures. They were asked to draw a picture representing what worries them and what helps them, and they were encouraged to write any comments they wished. These pictures could be shared with others, or remain confidential to myself and the child if they so wished. There were quite a variety of designs, from trees falling on a child's head, to a crane being used as a support. (Examples can be seen in Figures 2.8 and 2.9.) It became a very therapeutic exercise. For example in Figure 2.9 the child had previously been involved in an attempted abduction and so the worries are illustrated by the child being chased along a cliff and the helpful aspects are represented by the child reaching the safety of the sea.

These pictures were extremely valuable. They offered a view into the

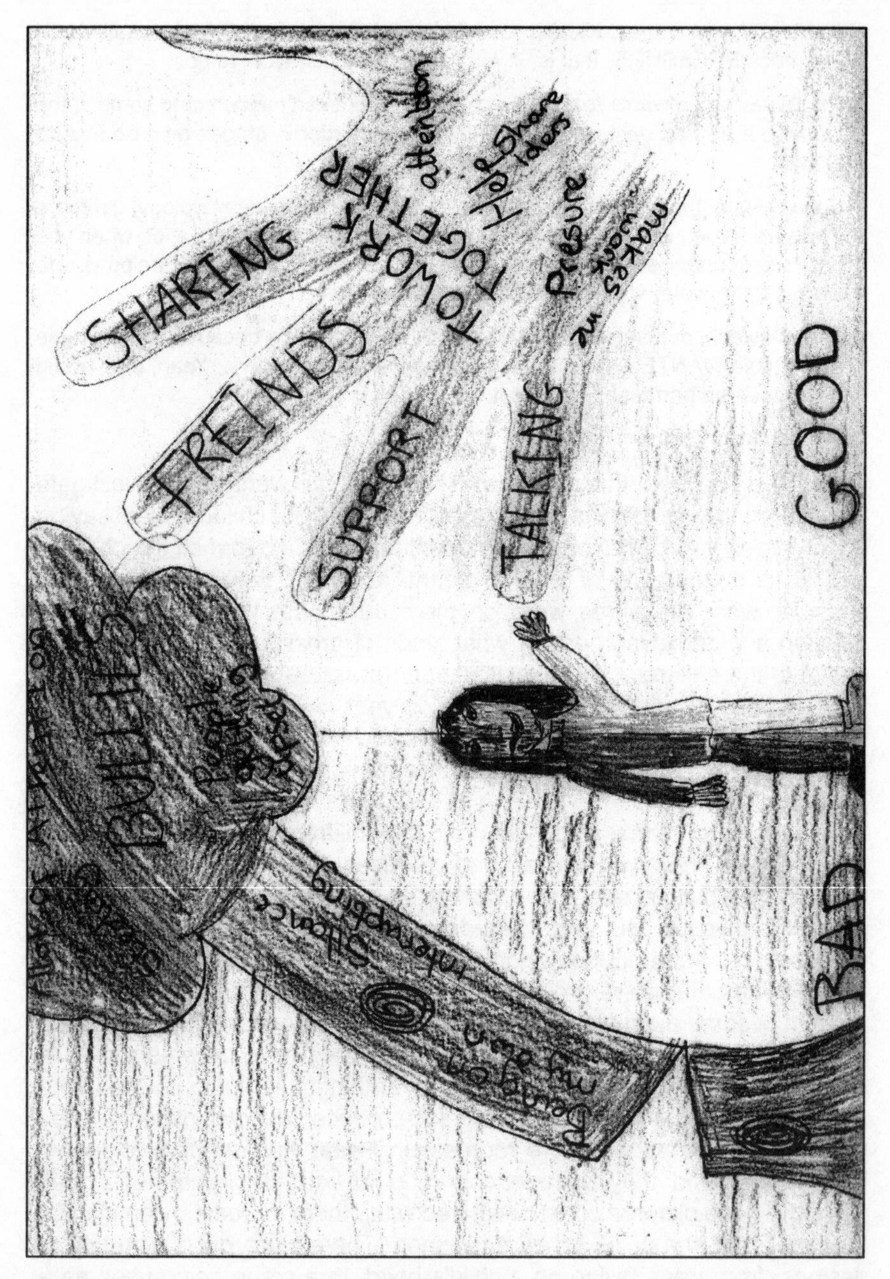

Figure 2.8 Pressure picture: falling tree

world of the child and I especially learnt a great deal through talking to the children about their picture. I collected all the pictures and analysed the comments written on them, putting them into three groups – those aspects seen as a pressure only; those seen as a support; and those that are both a support and a pressure. 'Pressure only' included: rules, being told off,

Figure 2.9 Pressure picture: child on cliff

jobs, Mel Evans (a swimming teacher), assembly, neighbours, stealing, weather, too much attention, dinner ladies, bullying, noise, choosing things. Areas seen as support included: getting help and comfort, sharing, working together, sport, computer, food, gerbils, television, homework, trips. Those that come into both categories were: time, playtime, Mum,

Dad, the family, friends, other children, school, work, sleep. The most interesting outcome was that the majority of the comments had little to do with academic subjects and most were related to home and other issues.

The issue of pressure is extremely important to the children. It is something felt by the children, and something which they feel ambiguous about; it can be both positive and negative, and varies with each individual. It is often felt in relation to the conditions of work, but can be social in nature, for example with friendships and problems such as bullying or stealing. Support, on the other hand, is more social. All this does not entirely map on to the question of support and challenge, but it does give a better picture of the class environment. Discovering these concerns helped me become more familiar with the children in the class. I not only knew them better as individuals, but through this work I became more aware of the children that were receiving insufficient support and challenge, and it helped me give more time to those less demanding children whom it is all too easy to overlook in a busy classroom.

I felt I knew the children a lot better, and the fact that I worked *with* them as opposed to *on* them increased their trust in me. Several children seemed to be offering more personal information or coming to me to discuss problems. Trust was probably aided by the fact that I took great care to keep my promises to the children. For example, one child was adamant that only I should see his work and I made it very clear that I would respect this wish. I was able to discuss with the children some of the issues they raised, such as bullying and stealing, and why teachers adopt particular approaches when dealing with these areas.

I have found it encouraging in view of the pressures and constraints of the National Curriculum that, although the children in my class do have some academic worries, they are in fact more concerned with personal and social areas of their school life. This is important to my teaching for it is easy to be fearful of using precious curriculum time to develop personal and social education work.

What did we learn about teaching and learning in fairness to children?

We were trying to do two things at once: (1) to improve teaching and learning and (2) to improve fairness in the classroom. We had assumed that the two went together, and we were proved right. We were pleased by the outcomes, and, as the next chapter shows, we took the Fairness project further the following year. Indeed, we have no doubt about the usefulness and importance of involving children in their own learning and their own learning to learn. We have demonstrated how well children respond when invited to reflect on their own learning – and how much they learn in the process, about themselves, about each other, and, most importantly, about their power to do something about it.

We have also shown that we should consider the viewpoint of the children we teach when seeking to develop and improve practice. It is not enough to listen to pundits and policy makers who rarely see the inside of a school and do not have to experience the difficulties and anxieties of having to learn and teach in the primary classroom. Surely to improve and raise standards effectively, teachers and educators should listen to all those involved in education? We found the children considered their education seriously. Most wanted to learn. They were able to discover and examine what helps them learn effectively and were able to work towards improving practice. Our work has not prevented there being difficult situations or areas of practice that are less effective, but it has improved the teaching and learning in the classroom and has helped prevent a lot of frustrations on both sides of the teaching and learning equation. It has also provided all of us in the classroom with strategies to deal with life's problems and so, together, we are now able to tackle many of the difficulties of our tangled up, untidy, real world.

It is important to us that all points of view are taken into account. Trying to do so has helped us frame some principles of fairness, which we introduced in the last chapter, and mentioned again earlier on in this one, where we said we were trying to put them into operation. How successful were we? How fair was it?

To recap, the three principles of fairness require us:

1 to pay attention both to the empowerment of individuals and to deal with sources of unfairness like race, class, gender, and special educational needs;
2 to value the process of creating fairness just as much as the conclusions reached about what to do in any particular school or classroom; and
3 to attend equally both to individuals and to those groups which have a strong effect on their identities, such as social class and gender, or cultural, religious, and racial affiliations.

Reflecting on the years that the Fairness project has been running, we are pleased with the steps that have been taken in the direction of empowerment. Each year we have taken some small steps, in one classroom, over that one year. Each year we start a little further forward.

Firstly, we think we are sowing the seed of future attitudes through helping the children experience and understand fair ways of acting towards others, and of the ways others should act towards them. Of course, we have no hard evidence that having their views listened to and acted upon will enable these children to make others listen to them and act on their views in future classrooms and in other areas of their life. (And a research project to investigate it would be a large and expensive one!) However, we are optimistic about this, especially since we are supported in our hope by some (large-scale and expensive) research that shows the strong effect of the quality of learning in the primary stage of education.[8] We believe that, for anyone, being taken seriously is heady stuff. Being treated with respect – and learning to treat others with respect – can only strengthen each child's belief that all people have a valuable contribution to make to the communities they live in.[9]

Secondly, we are increasingly clear that processes of fairness need to be emphasised. We were not doing something that can be squeezed into a busy schedule, perhaps on a wet Friday afternoon. As the project proceeded, it has become ever clearer to us that its value depended on the children believing that their perspectives and opinions mattered. Children are well able to recognise when there is merely a pretence of consultation. Typically, negotiations in a primary classroom about ground-rules of behaviour and work are based, if only implicitly, firstly on the teacher's ground-rules being tested out by their limits being pushed by the children, and then secondly, on the children's willingness to comply with the rules as negotiated. This willingness is based in part on the children's view of what is acceptable in a school, and in part on the degree of their respect for the teachers. Children of primary age are already adept at negotiations and understand that different rules govern different forms of them.[10] However, only rarely are rules negotiated more openly in the way that we have suggested. Such negotiations need time if they are to be seen by the children to be real, rather than cosmetic.

So far, we have not highlighted issues of social class, race, and gender in the discussion of this project. This may appear paradoxical in a project that is intended to highlight the importance of paying attention to the perspectives of all children. There is a tightrope to be walked here: on the one hand it is true, as we have pointed out earlier, that teaching styles which are good for disadvantaged groups are also good for all children. There is no need to point up particular social factors if they have not been relevant. On the other hand, their relevance can only be judged if attention is sometimes paid to them and the class 'viewed through the lens' of race, class or gender. We discuss this dilemma again, in some more detail, at the end of the next chapter.

Chapter 3

INCREASING TRUST IN THE CLASSROOM

We still had a lot to learn. Or so we discovered as the Fairness project continued into the following year. Again we were trying to improve teaching and learning and also to improve fairness in the classroom. Again the direction we took and the conclusions we reached were very much influenced by the views and perceptions of the children. As the year progressed, we came to see more and more clearly how crucial trust is, for establishing and improving fairness in the classroom.

Carol[1]

In September 1992 I was faced with the challenge of teaching a very mixed ability Year 4 and 5 class in an inner-city primary school. This was a new age group to me after those I had been accustomed to in previous years. The class was also made up from a set of children that had come from six different classes. I suspected that this might provide difficulties both for the children and for myself, but at this stage I did not know specifically what these might be.

The first problem I was faced with was where to begin.

A Review of What was Happening in the Classroom

I particularly felt it important to get to know the children and to explore what was happening in my class. I therefore decided to keep a diary over the first few weeks of the term to observe the class and review any problems that were occurring.

I also felt it important to be able to validate and verify my personal views and any information collected with those of others. I therefore discussed my feelings with the two other colleagues who were teaching the same age group and who formed with me our year group team. They had been interested in the progress of the project in the previous 2 years, and now wanted to be more closely involved. They agreed to participate in the study; they were more than willing to carry out similar work in their own classes, and to be involved with any observations and feedback of results. Both wanted to use the opportunity to examine ways of improving their own practice.

During the review period Morwenna and I both found the children to be very demanding of the teacher and not very independent; they appeared to lack 'social ground-rules', particularly in terms of communication skills, and they seemed to be very egocentric and unable to reflect about themselves. At this stage they especially found it difficult to suggest any changes they could make to improve themselves. An example of this can be seen in an activity which involved the children completing a worksheet entitled 'All About Me' in which they were asked to write down the things that they liked best about themselves and possible areas they would like to improve (Figure 3.1).

Most children could only write down comments such as 'I like swimming' and seemed unable to answer the question about what they liked best about themselves. They struggled to fill in the section relating to what they would like to change, and during the session I noted that they seemed unable to reflect about themselves with many voicing the opinion that they didn't want to change anything and were happy as they were. As a somewhat self-critical adult I found this amazing. However, when I reflected on this later I felt that the results may have been affected by the fact that the children did not know how to communicate their views and were still seeking guidance from the teacher, and indeed were probably trying to give me the answers they thought I wanted. I also thought that they may not really have had sufficient experience of the learning and teaching practices on offer to be able to express an opinion of what they would like to change or improve, and that it was highly likely that they felt unable to put themselves at risk and discuss any individual weaknesses because they did not yet trust me or feel secure in their environment.

Excerpt from Carol's Journal

3 October: Talk with Louise: whereas I thought my children aren't very reflective she reminded me that her infants were reflective – it wasn't difficult for them, just on a different level i.e. they could be told to think about why they'd be naughty etc. I suppose I'm thinking of something more independent which is at a higher level (I don't know) so perhaps that's why my class found it difficult – perhaps they are reflective but not in terms of themselves on a personal level and they need to be directed

Tuesday 22th September. A

WHAT I LIKE BEST ABOUT ME

WORKSHEET

I like neet writing.	I like playing with my Friends.	I like Skipping	I like swimming in the pool.
I like playing with Dolls.	I like hand writing.	I like playing games.	I Kke drowing.

What I like best about me

1 I like Swimming in the pool.
2 I like neet writing.
3 I like playing with my Friends.
4 I like playing with Dolls.
5 I like doing hand writing.
6 I like playing games.
7 I like drowing.
8 I like Skipping.

What I like least about me

I was surprised that I went to pakistan and I was sick and after a shew days I was feeling beter.

Things I would most like to change I chinge my hirestile and I will chinge my clothse

I will do this by going to the hiredresse and chinge my hire and I am going to say to my mum to make me other clothse.

Figure 3.1 'All about me'

still. (I expected them to be less directed.)

12 October: I did drama today – great – though some children couldn't cope or found it difficult. But oh my maths – most children actually achieved little – I was very disappointed. I've tried splitting the session (half spellings, half maths) so I can concentrate on maths – but still some are not working much – takes them so long to get settled. Also

M

WHAT I LIKE BEST ABOUT ME.

WORKSHEET.

I Do good drawing's.	I Like my Self.	Im frendly	I Like my math's.
I Like myself becase of my Swimming.	im half italyan and half Engcish	im Nice to peolple	im NOt raisist.

What I like best about me

1 I Do good Drawing's.
2 I Like myself.
3 Im fendly.
4 I like my math's.
5 I Like my self becase of my swimming.
6 Im half italyan and half ENgLish.
7 Im Nice to peolple.
8 Im NOt raisist.

What I like least about me

I was surprised that I BeAt somane in chess.

Things I would most like to change I would like to change my hight becase of my age.

I will do this by wishing.

Figure 3.1 'All about me'

noise still a problem. Mentioned to the children that it was difficult for us all. Asked them to think of a way of solving it. What a mixed day.

Thomas came and told me it was his birthday over the weekend.

When am I going to do all of this? I want the world to stand still so I can take stock and sort some these issues out – I have delayed too long.

> *3 November:* What about the children who don't seem able to work on their own but want to do pictures, talk about their grandmothers in Birmingham in the middle of class discussions about getting their maths done? But could it be they are using the teacher as a way of getting the answer, e.g. Maria who is brighter than she lets on but may get an easier life by concealing this and appearing as if she needs more help?

While I was keeping this journal, Morwenna was also keeping one of her own and thinking through these issues about the class and their ability to be reflective and speak about their own needs.

Excerpt from Morwenna's journal:

> It is very interesting writing this down. I find myself questioning things that I heard without a ghost of a question.
>
> *'Learning to sit on their bottoms':* I agreed with Carol as she said this that they had to learn this as 'total basics'. The ground-rules of each classroom are different, and have to be learnt. I would also teach children to do set work. However, we also talk about giving children power and responsibility to plan their own work. How are they supposed to tell the difference between doing this and choosing what to do? Learning the ground-rules is partly about learning what is expected and about which freedoms and responsibilities come within those expectations. This would need to be thought through in any discussion of empowerment.
>
> *Learning how to participate*: My thought when Carol told these stories [which were to do with inappropriate contributions during discussions] was that the behaviour is very like the behaviour of infants. They just haven't learnt the rules of discussion yet, and part of school learning is precisely to learn those rules. But when I added the comment about the joke [a child had recently interrupted Carol telling him off, to ask if he could tell a joke; we had interpreted this as need for more social ground-rules] I wondered if we had heard it that way in the context of a number of these irrelevant contributions. Maybe the child was trying to defuse the situation. The rule he had not learnt would be: 'If the teacher is angry, don't try and cheer her up with jokes and teasing (as you might a relative, as a teacher might do to a child). Take the anger seriously.' This is a matter of defining power and power relations. They are necessary and inescapable, but they need reflection, to see if they are the ones we would want.

I still felt very positive that the children would have more to offer and would be able to offer comments that would help improve my practice. I was sure that as the children felt more secure that they would begin to offer more and be able to discuss issues more openly.

So what could I do to help?

I did not want to pre-judge the situation, but, using the information from the review period I set down a plan of what I thought I needed to do and the children needed to know to help us to work together to search for ways to improve practice and help them work more effectively in the classroom. I decided that the children needed to:

1. Be able to operate as a class, and, that *we* needed to work together *as a class* to establish a number of ground-rules.
2. Be made aware of, and practise, certain skills such as listening and discussing. Without these I felt the children would be unable to participate in searching for ways to improve the learning and teaching processes taking place in the classroom.
3. Feel secure and trust me, especially if they were to discuss their true concerns, needs, and anxieties with me, and go beyond the stage of saying what they thought would please the teacher. They needed to know that they could volunteer information and that it would be listened to, valued and respected.

Once this stage was reached I felt it would then be possible for the children to identify what they genuinely perceived as their needs, and that together they and I could incorporate and balance their views of what helps them learn more effectively with those of my own.

Working Together: Developing Ground-Rules, Skills, Trust and Security

I introduced the idea of working collaboratively with the children to improve the teaching and learning experiences within the classroom in October. The reaction from the children was very positive. At the time the class were having difficulties with large class discussions so they and I together began by making a list of what helps when talking together as a class. This was then displayed in the classroom (*see* Figure 3.2).

I later analysed what the children had said, and decided that the children *did* know how to discuss, they just did not put this into practice. I wondered whether the children needed reminding of these things, and would they now try to put these into practice.

Next we all explored what we liked, as a class, about the class and what improvements we could make. I thought it would be easier at this stage for the children to discuss the class as a whole, rather than their individual

What helps a discussion take place

Being nice and kind
Paying attention
Listening
Being helpful to everybody
Putting your hand up
Co-operating
Being quiet - do not talk while other people are talking
Being good
Not talking when Miss is talking
Not fighting
Not hairdressing
Don't shout out
Don't argue
Don't fiddle about with things
Not being in trouble
Don't make a noise
Wait for the person to finish talking before you go away to work
Not to be stupid
Don't walk out.

Figure 3.2 A list of what helps when talking together as a class

needs, as it carried less of a personal risk, but still gave me the opportunity to value and listen to the children's comments and gain their trust. The list of improvements covered some 31 points and many areas reflected comments I had made in the first few weeks of term (Figure 3.3). For example, the mention of the need to take more care of displays is most likely to have appeared because I had recently told a child off for carelessly damaging a display.

I decided the list was far too long and several days later suggested to the children that they prioritise the areas they felt most important. The following five concerns were identified:

1 Take more care of displays.
2 Don't talk, don't interrupt when someone is talking.
3 Don't push in a queue.
4 Not talking so much when we are working.
5 Don't wait around to see the teacher if the reading flag is up.

I had to admit I was surprised by the choice of these five concerns, because although I saw points 2 and 4 as an area of concern I had no worries about the other three. Point 1, at least, seemed to reflect the children's beliefs about my priorities. What was interesting was that my two colleagues discovered a similar pattern, for although each class had

```
THINGS WE CAN IMPROVE

Everyone's writing and spelling
Handwriting
Everybody can improve their maths
Everybody can improve their writing
We could take more care
No accidents in school
Make the classroom nicer
Try and write our lines straighter like Miss
Take more care of our borders
Tidying up
Not being late
Improve our pictures
Keep work tidy together
Put your name on sheets
Take care of displays
Not working
Make sure everything is in your tray
Don't talk, don't interrupt when someone is
talking
Don't push in a queue
Not talking so much when we are working
Don't wait around if the flag is up
Don't play with lego when you are told not to
Take care of your books
Improve your reading
Don't interrupt when someone is reading to Miss
Take care of Bob, the fish
Don't swing on your chair
Don't forget to tidy up
Don't stab pencils into people
Look after your tray
```

Figure 3.3 The 31-point list of improvements to be made

identified different areas and priorities for improvement, each of the three of us could each identify the other two in their lists. For example, there was a 'No Running' improvement in one list which we thought reflected the fact that the teacher regularly has to stop children running through a corridor which is part of her room. This therefore supported the theory that the children were to some extent offering what they thought we wanted to hear and had probably prioritised according to how they read the messages that we, the teachers, were giving out. However, it was important that we explore the concerns of the children and listen to their opinions in order to begin to develop this notion of trust so I was happy to continue.

Both of us began to have a clearer view of the direction we should go in. We began to see the importance of trust, and of mutually agreeing ground-rules of behaviour which could both contribute to this trust and then build on it. We needed ways to increase trust. We saw that we should try and do this both directly and also by working on real issues: the children would see that we really do take note of what they say, that things really change and that we respect confidences. On the other hand it would be important to keep looking out for signs that they were not just trying to please us by what they said.

For the next month, while Morwenna was out of the country working on another project, Carol carried out a series of lessons in which the children were encouraged to work together – and which could not be done simply by *appearing* to work together! Every 2 or 3 days the children experienced lessons which were designed to send them all in the right direction: using working methods that depended on trust, and built on it. During this time, they were put into situations where they worked across friendship groups to think, puzzle, laugh and to create things by working collectively. Most importantly they were also encouraged to reflect on the processes they were going through.

Four examples of these lessons follow. As can be seen they cover a variety of curriculum areas and various National Curriculum Attainment Targets. They cover English AT1 on speaking and listening, and particularly build on levels 2 and 3. For instance, the activities involve the children in participating as speakers and listeners in a group involved in a task, talking with the teacher, and responding to a range of complex instructions. They also cover Attainment Targets in both PE (for instance, responding safely alone and with others to challenging tasks; recognising and rejecting anti-social responses including unfair play) and Art (for instance, communicating ideas and feelings in visual form based on what they observe, remember and imagine).

2nd November: Carol organised and taped a discussion on how to improve the problem of talking too much when working, using a Dictaphone. The children suggested that badges would help to remind them to listen and not interrupt when someone was talking. This idea was acted on straight away. It was important that they realised that they could work together to solve a real-life problem that was occurring in the class.

4th November: In PE the children learnt a number of co-operative games to help them form groups more easily. Among them were the 'Touch Blue', 'Bubbles' and 'Pretzel'. In 'Touch Blue', the children were asked to touch different colours or types of clothing to form groups. In 'Bubbles' they moved around forming groups of 4–6. When they were in a group, the bubble burst and the children had to go on to find another group. By this stage in the PE lesson they had been mixed up in a variety of groups and had contact with a large number of other children. They were ready to go on to a game where they had to solve a problem co-operatively. This game was called 'Pretzel'. Children formed groups of 6–8. One child in each group was nominated to be 'on' and turned their back. The other children in the group then joined hands in a long line and twisted themselves around like a pretzel. The child who was 'on' then had to untangle the line. The children thought this was great! For them it was just a game, though we noted with satisfaction how they were making real contacts with a variety of other children.

12th November: The children were shown the 'Rabbit Game', which always proves to be a real teaser – Carol has known it fox adults. She selected groups of about five, making sure they were mixed boys and girls. Each group was then given some mixed up jigsaw pieces. Each one had to make a rabbit. The difficulty for them was that to do so they had to swap pieces without talking and without snatching pieces from others. They had to think hard about other forms of communication, and about ways of co-operating with each other. An important part of the lesson was the feedback session on the game which included a discussion about the feelings it aroused. Children said how frustrating they had found it, but added that they had learnt a lot. Some felt good that they had achieved a completed jigsaw, and others said that they were surprised they could work with the people in their group.

17th November: By now it was time to see how far the children had become more open and reflective in class. They were asked to work individually designing personal flags. These had to show:

1 'One thing I am good at.'
2 'Something I'd like people to say about me.'
3 'Something I'd like to change about me.'
4 'What I would like to do in the future.'

The results of this exercise were most encouraging. The children seemed much more self-critical and open in what they were prepared to reveal about themselves than they had been at the beginning of the year.

By the time preparations for Christmas began the children had put into operation a number of improvements. They had made rules and signs to discourage people from damaging displays and to prevent people from waiting around the teacher when she was listening to someone read and had the flag up for privacy. They had designed badges which they wore to encourage people not to interrupt when someone was talking. They had invented a reward system they called a Push Chart to help themselves line up better (*see* Figure 3.4), and they introduced a system of 'Whisper Work' whereby when the noise in the class got too loud a gong was hit and everybody worked in near silence. (It was always a teacher who hit

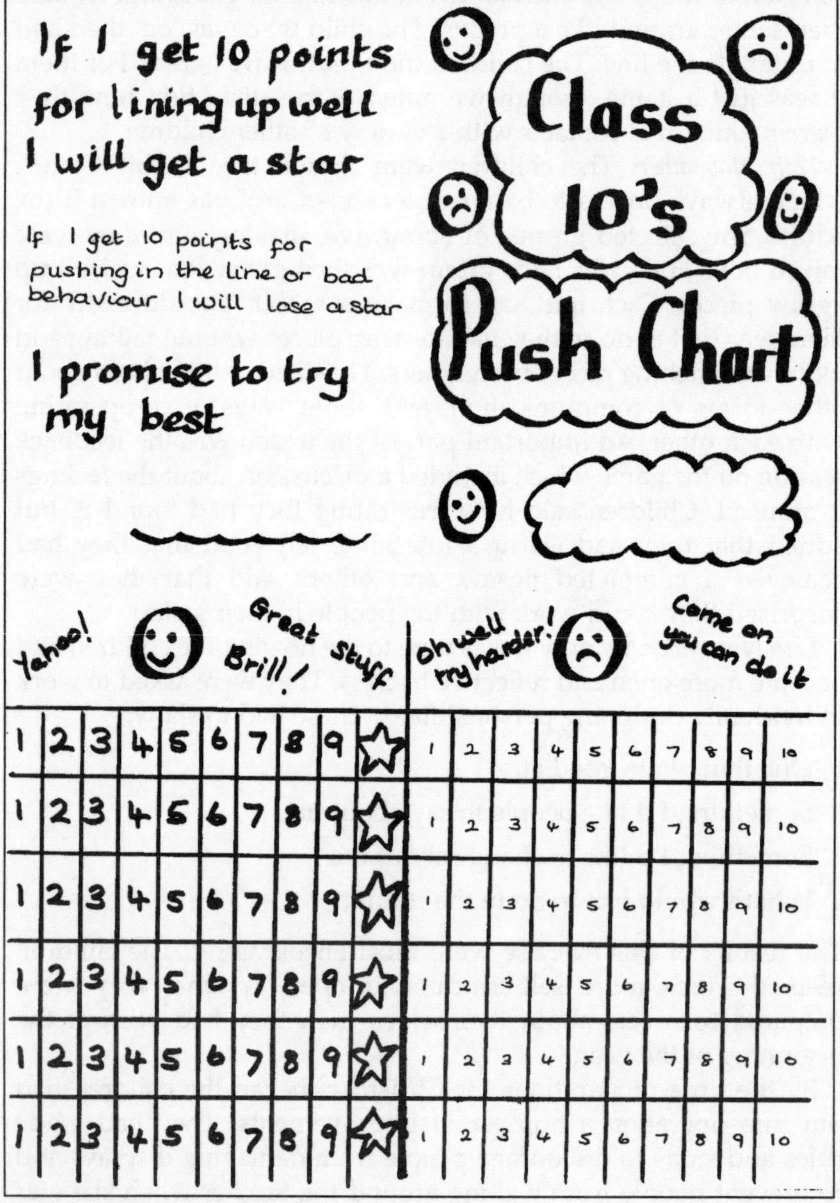

Figure 3.4 The Push Chart

the gong, but children could ask for it to be done.)

The children had therefore been able to find ways to try and improve the five areas they identified that needed to be improved in the class as a whole. It was often the case that the children were actually aware of certain skills that would help them work more effectively and they merely needed reminding about them and the opportunity to practise them. For example, the children actually knew what helped a discussion, but it was only after this area was given attention that there were signs of an improvement. As the study progressed we became increasingly aware of the benefit of actively highlighting appropriate skills and processes to the children to help them work more effectively. They did not always choose a method that Carol or Morwenna might have used but they were all successful, if to varying degrees. This highly satisfying success rate was probably a result of the children themselves owning the decisions made.

The next stage was to consider whether the children had developed enough trust to be able to discuss their own individual needs and enable them to move further forward to search for ways of making improvements.

So, how would we know the children were ready to identify their needs?

We noticed positive changes in the children. They were now able to listen and comment in class discussions, they were able to participate in small group situations with a variety of different children, and they had grown in confidence and were beginning to reflect and volunteer their own ideas and opinions. It was also particularly encouraging that the children were beginning to offer personal comments about themselves. This was shown in the personal flag activity of 17 November, where the children began to reflect and discuss changes they would like to make about themselves. This was a big step forward from the 'All About Me' activity where the children only told us what they liked doing. Carol was quite encouraged at this stage for although many of the changes the children discussed were to do with physical changes the children wanted to make about themselves, there were signs that the children were aware of other areas that they needed to develop (*see* Figure 3.5).

Morwenna was also able to report the degree of change in the children. When she came back from a month abroad, she recorded this in her Journal:

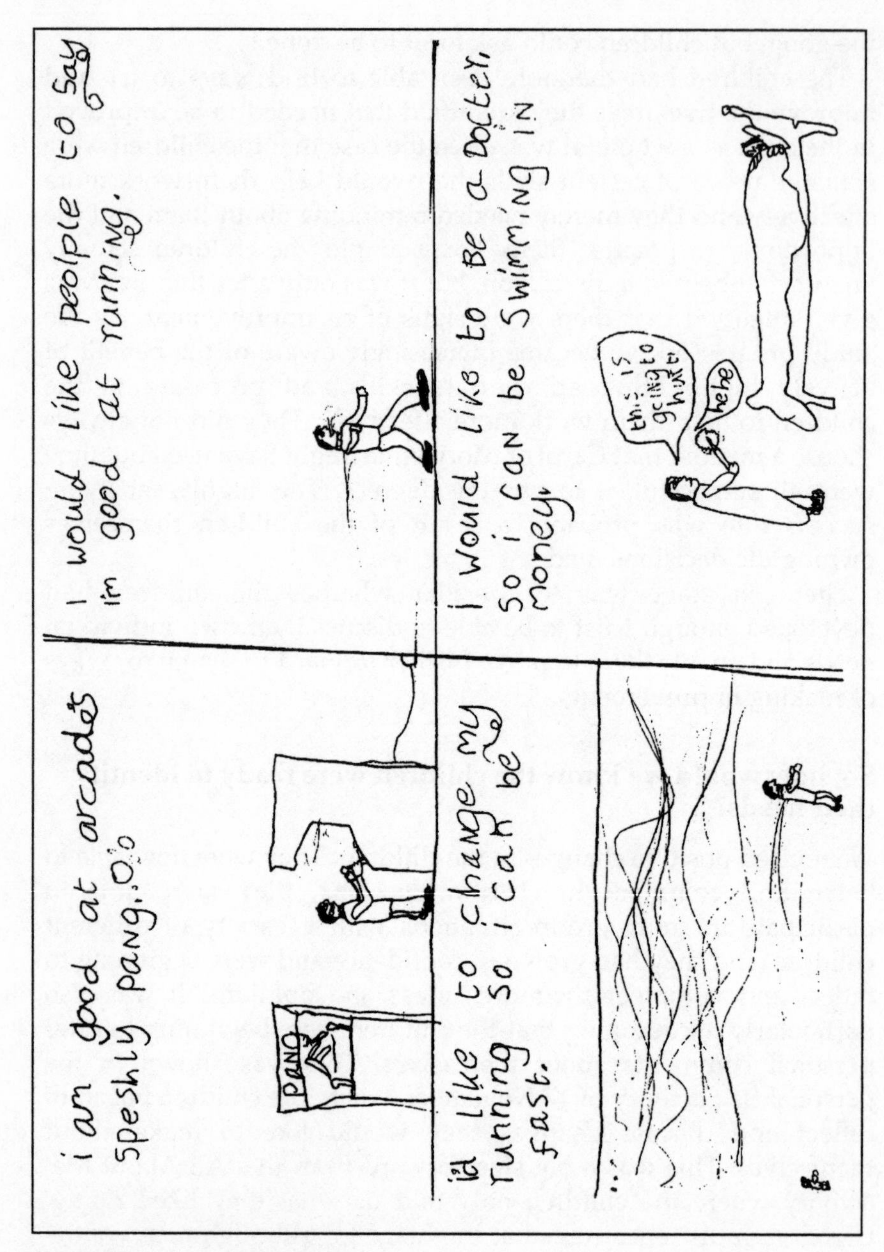

Figure 3.5 Personal flags

Excerpt from Morwenna's journal

> It seemed to be an entirely different class from the point of view of being able to take on such a project. I had been away since October, and the change felt very great. We need to pay more attention to what evidence such an impression is based on, exactly, if the observation of the class

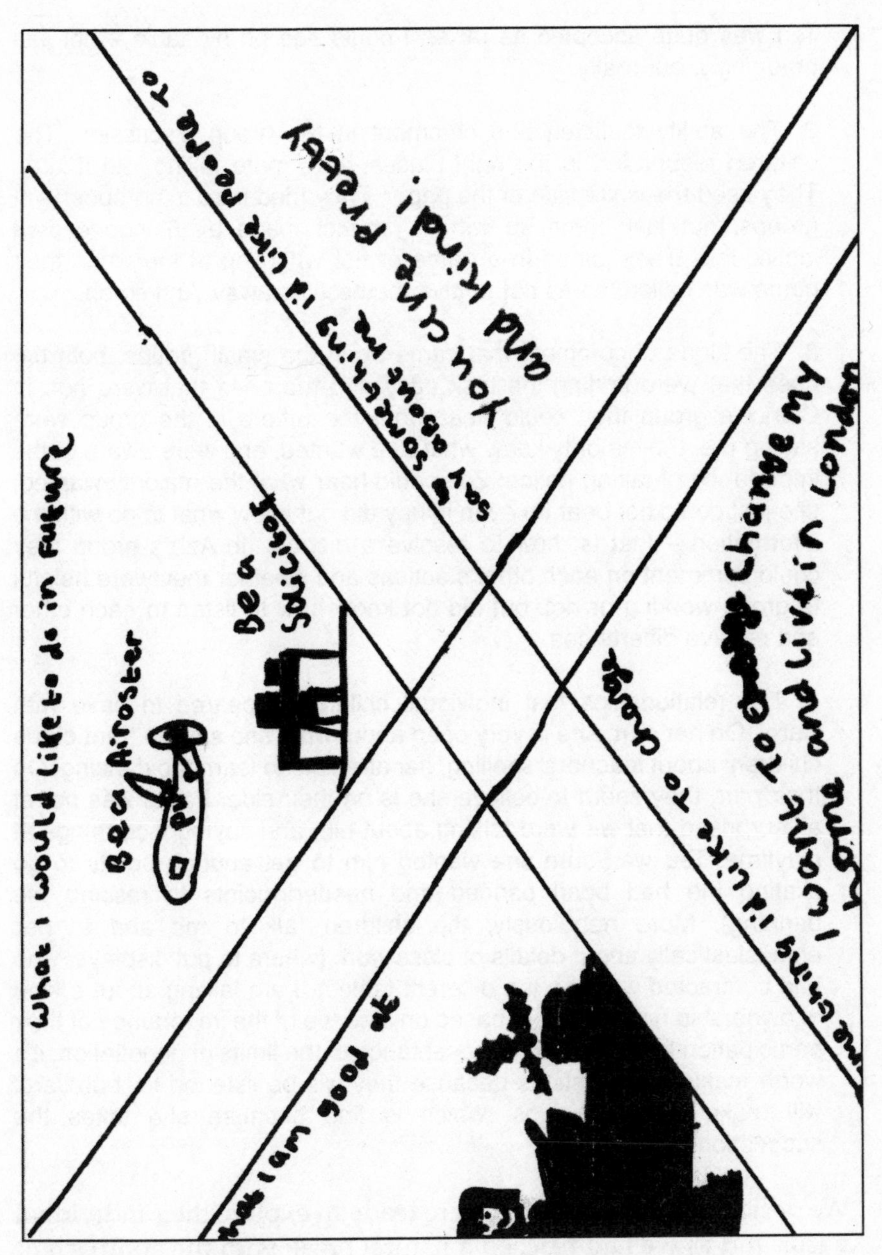

Figure 3.5 Personal flags

is to be rigorous. So what did I base my feeling on?

1. The groups in the class: how they seemed to be less rigid and fragmentary. The class is gelling. For instance, Uzma might not have liked working with Kalsoom but if I had not known this from Carol, I would not have known from the way they got on with the task in hand.

Ted was quite accepted as far as I could see on his table – not just grudgingly, but really.

2. The ability to listen and comment in the group discussion. The children responded in the right places, and, more telling, did it later. They used the white side of the paper. They tried hard to co-operate in groups, not just come up with a product made by 6 independent individuals. They joined in a game of not wriggling at me when their name was called, so as not to give themselves away. And so on.

3. The kinds of comment that came up in the small groups, both the ones that were finding the task easy and the ones that were not. In Clarice's group they could hear what the others in the group were saying (i.e. the majority knew what Zoe wanted, and were aware of the importance of taking notice: Zoe could hear what the majority wanted, she just could not bear it!) even if they did not know what to do with the information – that is, how to resolve a dispute. In Aziz's group they could comment on each other's actions and whether they were helpful to group working or not, but did not know how to listen to each other and resolve differences.

4. The relationships that individual children appeared to have with Carol. On her part, she is very open about what she says in front of the children: about teachers' spelling, her attempts to learn tap dancing. On their part, they seem to believe she is on their side. Faisal was not at all surprised that we were talking about him and saying nice things at playtime. Ted was sure she wanted him to get enough points to go skating [he had been banned and needed points to rescind the banning]. More nebulously, the children talk to me and to her enthusiastically about details of class work (where to put displays; who had contracted what on the different tables). I am talking about a kind of ownership here, which is based on a sense of the importance of their participation together with an acceptance of the limits of negotiation: it's worth making suggestions because they will be listened to, but Carol will make final decisions, which is fine because she takes the suggestions into account.

We decided that the children were ready to explore their individual needs and as we had reached a natural break with the approach of the Christmas holidays we decided that we would commence the next stage of the work in the Spring term.

Carol

Identifying needs

We began on the first day of the new term by asking the children what they would like to improve about themselves, both at school and in their personal life. It seemed appropriate to use New Year Resolutions as a vehicle for the children to identify the areas that they would personally like to improve on (*see* Figure 3.6).

Figure 3.6 New Year resolutions

I consolidated what the children said by recording the different comments and the number of times these were repeated. The results were very wide and varied. Ninety-one resolutions in relation to being at school were obtained from 23 out of a possible 28 returns:

Improve reading	13
Improve work in general	12
Do not mess about	7
Do not talk when teacher is	7

Do not swear or fight	6
Improve handwriting	4
Improve spelling	4
Improve language	4
Co-operate and share	4
Get to school on time	4
Improve topic work	3
Improve maths	3
Be better at listening	3
Be more confident	3
Be tidy	3
Be kind and nice	2
Improve drawing	1
Use a ruler	1
Use a rubber	1
Line up on time	1
Don't sulk when told off	1
Tell the truth	1
Do what I am told	1
Be patient with the teacher	1
Concentrate	1

In relation to their personal lives, the most popular goal was to stop eating sweets, but in relation to being at school there was a spread between wanting to improve school work and wanting to work on more social aspects, such as being kind. Probably the most interesting aspect was that children were beginning to move from identifying areas for improvement and were thinking about *how* they would carry out these improvements.

Over half the children who wanted to improve their reading went on to suggest how they would go about this. This may have been because of a heavy emphasis on reading in the previous term. However, three out of the four children who mentioned handwriting indicated how they might improve it, and all the children who mentioned maths went on to say how they could make improvements and there had been no similar focus in these areas.

I was extremely interested by the variety of comments and wondered if there would be a similar spread of ideas if I asked the children to focus on the most important area they needed to improve. I also wondered if some children were still writing down comments they thought I wanted to hear, particularly areas such as listening, as this was something we had discussed in detail in the previous term.

I therefore felt it would be valuable to repeat the activity so I re-thought the activity and re-designed the 'My Goal' worksheet used in the previous year. I introduced it to the children explaining that sometimes the teacher did not know what they really thought and that I wanted to know what was important to them and what they felt they should try to improve. The children were delighted and one commented 'It's no good not telling the truth because we are only spiting ourselves, it means we won't get what we need'.

Despite a few initial difficulties, the children completed the sheets and the results were collated to view the spread of replies and the number of times each one appeared. Again the comments were very varied, and although academic areas did cause some common concerns, the personal and social areas of school life were far more individual to each child. Many issues discussed were only mentioned by one or two children. For example, 'I will try to smile' was a highly personal comment by a rather withdrawn child and it became the start of her discussing her problems openly with her parents and me. The most encouraging signs came from two boys in the class. One told me how happy he felt that I was listening to the children. The other has severe special needs with poor concentration, but he managed to sit for a whole session and wrote down what he wanted me to know. Indeed, I gained a lot of valuable information about the children. Several discussed their anxieties such as getting behind with their work, not having enough confidence, and being frightened of certain activities.

A similar picture also arose in the two other year group classes who were carrying out similar projects. We three class teachers were all highly interested in the personal comments of the children. These were impossible to quantify but had been extremely beneficial in getting to know the children. By becoming aware of some of the anxieties we had all been able to give some children more support and this was valuable. For example, the child who was withdrawn began to participate in large class and team games; her parents even bought her a book about increasing her confidence. I therefore felt it would be valuable to ask all the children about what worried them and what helped them. This could also throw light upon any needs that had been missed in earlier research.

I decided to adopt the same pictorial technique I had used the year before with the 'Pressure Pictures'. As before, these were extremely valuable. They offered a view into the world of the child and I learnt a great deal through talking to the children about their picture. Indeed on a personal level this activity was the most rewarding and enlightening for me, not just in terms of what the children told me but also in their confidence and trust in sharing their fears and feelings with me. One particular example was the child who told me about the bullying he receives at home.

It was noticeable that the teacher was seen as being an important help. Nearly a third of the children mentioned me by name and a further third mentioned 'the teacher' or other teachers by name.

I began to think we as a class were ready to move on the support and challenge issue Morwenna and I had begun to tackle the previous year. I wondered if I could now ask the children in what ways the teacher helped the children and did she always help. I was conscious that all the work so far had looked at the children and I did not know whether the children had any specific needs from the teacher. I was also aware that the children had given me their trust and put themselves in a vulnerable position in order to improve practice. It was now my turn to take a risk and ask the children what they thought about me. I felt this to be an important step as it took trust on both sides and would not have been possible at the beginning of the academic year.

With the help of my colleagues a basic worksheet was designed to help the children think about what I do. From this I initiated a discussion with the children based around the following informal questions:

- What things do I do that are helpful for you?
- Is there anything I do that does not help you?
- Are there times when the teacher cannot help you?
- How do you feel when the teacher cannot help you?
- Are there times when the teacher does not listen to you?

The discussion was taped and a transcript made. From this it was apparent that the children had a positive view of me as their teacher. They liked my sense of humour and they recognised that sometimes the teacher had to do things, such as tell them off, in order to help them. However, they did have some frustrations and this revolved around getting help from me. A major problem was seen to be the queue. If there was a long queue they might ask their friends for help, or they might feel uncomfortable about seeking help in front of others, or they might become distracted and not complete their work.

This was something that I had not been aware of and it caused me to reflect on what I was doing in the class and whether it was what I thought I was doing. I began to ask myself what aspects of practice in the classroom prevented the children from working on their individual needs and goals and I thought it would be useful for both the children and myself to observe ourselves in action.

At this point I discussed this with the children and suggested that they and I might make a video so we could see what really takes place in the classroom. The children were keen so I enlisted Morwenna's help to make the video. It was decided to video a maths activity where the children had to work individually at their own ability level.

However, the children were concerned about the difficulties of making the video; they thought it might affect their behaviour and not really reflect what takes place. They decided they would try hard to ignore the camera and on the day of the video we allowed 20 minutes to pull faces for the camera and overcome any shyness before the session began. Morwenna thought that this willingness to play was an indication of trust and openness.

Excerpt from Morwenna's journal

> I have taken videos of children in class so often, for students in their initial training, that I thought I knew what to expect about the children's reactions. But I was wrong! Usually the children seem oblivious to the video after a few minutes or so embarrassment. These children who knew me well, and who had themselves decided to be videoed, seemed acutely aware of it all the time. Nor have children in other classes so obviously wanted to come and ham it up as television personalities before the session started. During the session Paul was always glancing across at it. Amina and Kalsoom kept their backs slightly turned all the time, too, in a way that must have been deliberate, since I was moving about. My thought is that the children are not just being 'good' children acting realistically for the camera, as they would be in any class where I was videoing a student. They are able to be open about their feelings of self-consciousness.

Later, I and the children viewed the video with a mixture of embarrassment and fascination. However, possibly because of all the previous work on trust and security, the children were able to volunteer some very honest comments. They were quick to point out who was not working. They noticed that 'everybody is moving around' but went on to say 'sometimes we need to walk around and sometimes we don't'. They told me they moved around for resources or for help or 'to get away from work rather like a break'. The children suggested four areas that they felt were preventing them from achieving the individual goals they identified on their 'My Goal Worksheet', these were: talking; being distracted; wandering about; and, the queue to see the teacher.

I agreed. I believe I had always been aware of the first three, but it was only when I viewed the video and was away from the queue situation that I was able to see the problems the children had raised in the earlier discussion. The children on their part said that until they saw the video they had never been aware of how much wandering about they do.

The results of all this work are discussed in Chapter 5. In this chapter we have been focusing on the importance of increasing trust as kind of 'pre-wash cycle' necessary before any effective work on improving teaching and learning can take place – but which itself improves teaching and learning, just as the pre-wash cycle begins to clean the clothes.

What's new?

The Fairness project builds on and supports other work and other research, but it also introduces new processes and new strategies. We have been influenced by work of researchers who have found that the children often hold different views and have different agendas to their teachers.[11] We have also been influenced by research which shows that children spend a lot of their time trying to please the teacher, and, indeed that learning how to do so is part of learning how to be a pupil. Thus we felt that the results may have been affected by the fact that the children did not know how to communicate their views and were still seeking guidance from the teacher, and indeed were probably trying to give us the answers they thought we wanted.[12]

We have also, of course, given the focus of our study, been influenced by all the work done in the 1960s and 1970s on the educational significance of social class, and on equal opportunities in terms of race and gender, in the 1970s and 1980s.[13] The authors of this body of work emphasise the diversity of perspectives and attitudes that individual children and teachers bring to the classroom, and the importance of developing classroom practices which take account of them. Some of this work starts from the perspective of the individual, while taking account of social factors.[14] Other work starts from the perspective of society and its divisions, while taking account of individuals.[15] In either case all these authors agree with Alexander, Rose and Woodhead (1992) that teachers should be involved with the development of the whole child. They agree that if successful cognitive development is to take place teachers must satisfy social and emotional needs and thus 'take account of how children learn'.

In short, our project builds on the rationale that although teachers have a wealth of expertise and knowledge valuable to the development of a child, children equally have valuable experiences and knowledge to offer to benefit the teacher. It is essential for teachers to find ways of tapping that experience and knowledge. Moreover, teachers need to make sure that they are not simply assuming that all the children are individuals, but that they also realise how much that individuality springs from the social background of the society as a whole and the many varied communities within it.

It is also important to emphasise that we are doing something new. We build on an established body of work, but, at the same time we point out that its full implications for teaching and learning –

that principles of fairness are needed to ensure that all children are able to benefit from school – are not always appreciated. There are still only a few other teachers and researchers working in this way. Firstly, it is unusual for researchers to work *with* children rather than *on* them, even in work directed at improving equality of opportunities.[16] Secondly, it is often thought that juniors are rather young to be reflecting on learning processes and study skills. Indeed at the end of the first year of the project, some local inspectors expressed surprise at the work we were doing, for just this reason. However, a group of infant school teachers were immediately enthusiastic about doing something similar with their own classes, when Carol went to speak to them about our work. Those working in the midst of the everyday, practical world can often see possibilities that might appear to be surprising to those more removed from it.

Some dilemmas

It is time to return to the questions first raised at the end of Chapter 2. How fair was the project? Again we were pleased with the steps taken in the direction of individual empowerment. We also went even further in the attention paid to the process of fairness; the need for time for ownership and trust to develop. It took nearly a full term before the children were beginning to offer more personal opinions and put themselves at risk. This was very worthwhile when viewed over the year but it does suggest that to negotiate effectively with their pupils a teacher has to be prepared to invest time to develop trust. In the account of the project we were careful to describe just how much time was needed to build up the process – and at the same time to show that this was not time 'stolen' from the curriculum, but, in fact, was achieved within the normal curriculum, by giving lessons designed to further the aims of increasing trust and empowerment for the children.

We now turn to the question of including the perspectives of all groups and all individuals. In the relatively small-scale world of primary schools it is hard to judge how far individual children are influenced by their social background, gender, affiliations of ethnicity or religion, or their experience of racism. Such judgements are always about trends, not about individual members of the group. They are, therefore, relatively easy to make on a larger scale, such as within an LEA. These facts about the large scale are important in alerting small-scale institutions of the power of social factors, but remain difficult to apply in the case of individual children. If we return to Mosiah who was introduced in Chapter 1, we can see that children like him are not under-achieving when judged by national averages. They may, however, be having problems of various kinds at school, including, as is the case with Mosiah, not fulfilling their academic potential. Moreover, individual children are unlikely to be average members of their groups, because averages are made up of a large number of non-average cases: as Mosiah also shows, since he was not from an 'average' African Caribbean background. None the less, just as he was not typical, neither was he particularly atypical, either.

It is important not to fall into the trap of simply viewing children as individuals, and forgetting that their individuality is rooted in the various groups from which they come. Gender differences are real – however alike some individual girls and boys may be. Similarly, working-class children from poverty-stricken areas are not the same as the children of well-off middle class parents – however alike some individual working-class or middle-class children may be. The undoubted effects of social factors has to be taken into account in ways that do not rely on the use of large-scale methods.

We dealt with this problem in two ways. First, throughout the project we continued to make observations about the children viewed as, say, girls or boys; Asians, African Caribbeans or whites; and as working or middle class. For instance we counted how many contributions to class discussions were made by various groups, and interaction patterns among the children were noted. We used these observations to reflect on race, gender and social class dimensions of children's experiences in the classroom. Secondly, we took care to reflect on events in the classroom, using the 'lens' of gender, race or social class, in order to view them differently. It was clear to us that children did not fit neatly into some of these categories. Where should we put the one half-Chinese boy, for instance? What social class were some of the Asian children whose families did not fit our understanding of English social class? But the lack of fit did not matter because we were using the categories to question our understanding and interpretation of events rather than as hard and fast categories from which to judge them.

This was not an entirely satisfactory solution. Reflections on any observations were shared between the two adults, and only sometimes were they fed back to the children. It was more usual for us to share reflections on mixing sexes – or on working with children with special needs – than to share reflections on mixing race or class. This secrecy, at odds with the openness of the rest of the project, raises serious issues.

Is it really possible to involve the children in formulating issues related to group interactions or to the content of the curriculum in relation to race, social class and gender? They hardly ever raised them for themselves explicitly, though a glance at friendship or working groups in the classrooms shows that all of these factors implicitly play a part in children's actual practices.

Riverside school has a policy to deal with racism. As we show in the next chapter, it is well understood by both children and adults, and is used when necessary. Similarly, sexism is understood by children and adults, and it is not tolerated. On the other hand, it is likely that children hardly have a language to discuss social class, nor does social class appear in the school curriculum in the same way as race or gender.

While children are used to identifying themselves and others as boys or girls, they are less ready to mention ethnic background, though they will do so. Further, while nobody has doubts about who are boys and who are girls, ethnic identifications, and ethnic self-identifications are more problematic. Therefore while we had discussions with the children about whether working groups should be mixed in terms of boys and girls, we did not have equivalent discussions about mixing children by race. Social class is more difficult again, though it plays its part just as obviously as the other factors. Similarly, while it is clear that both teachers and children often agree in their judgements about who is 'clever' or 'trouble', these were never factors we discussed openly in relation to choosing groups. Thus our observations about race, social class, special needs and, to a lesser extent, gender, were not shared with the children. Perhaps such topics may require a methodology which does not involve all the participants. However, this is to go against the spirit of equal opportunities as identified in this book.

The ethical issue is a difficult one. Teachers who make attempts to be fair find themselves caught in a difficult dilemma. On the one hand attention to individual empowerment can collapse into an individualism which makes gender, race and social class invisible without reducing their power to affect the lives of children. On the other there is the dangers of using categories like 'race' and 'gender' to stereotype children, when in fact they are busy trying to deal flexibly with the multiple and changing identities available to them.

If pupils became used to voicing their perceptions and reflecting on solutions to their own problems with learning, then it would be easier to make schools appropriate for all children, in all their individual and social variety. Safety and trust are preconditions, of course. Teachers would not have to rely on their own hunches, or on quickly dated research about what makes teaching 'girl-friendly', 'multicultural', or 'antiracist'. The pupils could tell them.

Indeed, paradoxically perhaps, the very smallness of the project is its strength. In large-scale surveys individuals and their perceptions can too easily get lost. The educational world of the children we teach refuses to stay still. For instance, what was true about girls or Asians 20 years ago is not likely to be true today. Both white and Asian communities have responded to issues of gender and racism, and individuals have changed accordingly. If the educational world is to move in the direction of equality and justice, rather than in another direction, then it has to allow children to develop their own perspectives, express them and then get used to relying on them, in the sure knowledge that they will receive serious attention from teachers.

Chapter 4

LEARNING IN SAFETY: MAKING SCHOOL SAFE

Feeling safe or learning in fear

Morwenna

It was a sunny afternoon in the summer term, during the first year of our Fairness project. When I arrived in the class it was to find that the children were spending the afternoon filling in the 'All About Me' forms for their school records. Some of the questions related to Personal and Social Education as my Journal entry shows.

Excerpts from Morwenna's journal

> The question about friends, together with 'what makes me sad' was very interesting for me, because it allowed me to ask questions of the kind that would usually be difficult to approach: e.g. about bullying. One set of children I asked were Zafar, Michael and Nat, all of whom seem to be rather on the fringe of groups at the moment, 'Everyone gets bullied' was their thought (expressed by Michael with agreement). They were unable to say whether everyone was a bully or whether it was just a small group of people. They immediately volunteered the names of bullies though, including Qasim and Manzar (with the evidence that Manzar was in his socks for kicking). I also spoke to David and Scott [who are best friends], because David said he didn't like being called names. On being asked 'why' (a difficult question for anyone to answer!) he said he didn't like being called a Welsh rabbit. He's proud of being Welsh, but clearly thought he was being 'racialized' (to use Elinor Kelly's term[17]). Scott was indignant when David suggested he used the term, agreeing that he said 'rabbit' but not 'Welsh rabbit'.

Another issue about the 'friends' question was raised for me by Kaneez. Carol and I agreed that she is friendless at the moment because she has been too aggressive with her two erstwhile best friends, Tasneem and Parveen. And I am glad that they are not putting up with the aggression, and colluding in it. But I did wonder about the gender issues here: the aggressive boys in the class are allowed (are they?) more outlet for their aggression – not in class, but generally. And their friends react differently when they do turn the aggression onto their class mates. Again it would be interesting to follow this up: the suggestion is that friendships and bullying interact differently for boys and girls. David Lane says, 'Bullying among boys is more likely to be part of power-based social relationships; for girls affiliation activities are more frequently the source of bullying activities' (Casdagli and Gobey, 1990, p.9). It would partly be a question about ethos of this school, and partly about the attitudes of the community at large.

Bullying / harassment is something that is central to any kind of Equal Ops work, since the evidence is that it is closely linked to sexism, racism, etc. Equal Ops issues are: (1) bullying / harassment interferes with the learning environment, and therefore with attainment (compare the title of the book published by the Commission for Racial Equality (1987), called *Learning in Terror*) and (2) it is likely to be a way of learning racism, sexism, class and disability prejudice.

This Journal entry was written in the first year of the Fairness project. So, early on in the project, it was already clear to us that bullying and harassment were important areas of concern in any work to do with equal opportunities. At that time it was harder to raise the issue of bullying: schools were still in the business of denying that they had a problem. Moreover, we were still learning the importance of trust and openness if we were to learn from the children what most concerned them in their school lives, and what affected their ability to learn. However, even very early on, we saw the importance of at least keeping our ears open and improving our own awareness of both bullying and harassment – even if we were not then very sure what to make of it. Since then, we have become clearer about both issues (bullying and harassment) and we have also become clearer about what teachers and schools need to take into account in their responses to ill-treatment of children in school.

Even if the school at that time did not admit to bullying and other forms of harassment, it did have a policy on racist name-calling and attacks. This was, in itself, valuable as a way of dealing with some forms of harassment and bullying. The experiences of Shaibu and Yusuf demonstrate why.

Eight-year-old Shaibu became very upset when he heard Clara

and Zara talking together while they played with the gerbils in a corner of the classroom. There were two gerbils, a black one and a brown one, and all the children were very fond of them. Their names were Dandelion and Burdock. Clara, an outgoing and cheerful African Caribbean girl and Zara, a quiet, reserved but confident Asian girl were picking them up, stroking them and talking about them. The problem arose because Zara found it hard to remember Burdock's name and was referring to the animal as 'Blackie'. Clara had no problem with this. She probably did not even notice. Shaibu, however, became very upset when he heard the word 'Blackie'. Shaibu is sweet natured but easily upset. He has a quick, hot temper, which constantly gets him into trouble. He is proud of his African Caribbean background, and he feels racial abuse particularly deeply: unfortunately, other children know that calling him racial names will upset him more quickly than anything else – although they also know it is wrong to use them. So it was not surprising that he thought Zara was being insulting. Carol talked it through with the children. Zara tearfully explained what she had done. The children involved were asked if they thought Zara had meant to upset anybody. They thought not, and since it was also clear that she understood that the word could be upsetting, the incident was resolved for everybody involved.

This incident shows the significance and power of a policy, if used flexibly, to both uphold the school's attitude to racist comments, and to defuse incidents before they reach explosion point. Imagine what might have happened if Shaibu had thought he had to deal with being called Blackie on his own? Or what might have happened if he had gone home and reported his perception at home? As it is his deep upset at racial abuse is validated by the structures of the school at every level from classroom to headteacher.

Harassment and bullying are not only what children do to each other. It is important that staff know they have to conform to policies, too. In Riverside this happens as the next incident shows. Yusuf was a child who tended to react with aggression to taunts. However, he was learning, slowly but steadily, that he ought to go to the teacher, rather than react violently. One day he came to his class teacher, very upset, saying that another teacher, Graham, had been racist. A boy had been calling Yusuf racist names in the playground, but when he had gone to Graham, he had not been given a chance to explain properly. Instead Graham had reacted angrily to both boys, punishing them both equally. The class teacher checked the story, and then went straight to Graham and told him that what he had done was unacceptable. This was very important for Yusuf who felt he had been supported by the school policy on racism. Graham admitted he had handled the problem wrongly, and Yusuf was allowed to stay in at the next playtime to help his teacher sell crisps with his teacher, which was a coveted privilege at Riverside, that year![18]

Having a school policy on racial name-calling and racial incidents is a start, but it is only a start. It is important to get clear about what makes children feel safe in school, so that they are not learning in fear, and they are acting in ways that will diminish sexism, racism, class and disability prejudice.

A good place to start, as the years of the project has shown us, is by asking children. Here are some of the things some Year 3 and Year 4 children said about safety, as part of a general discussion on what makes school a fair place.

Morwenna It's difficult to feel school's a fair place if people are nasty to each other and call each other names. So what do you feel about that? Mala said right back at the beginning that she thinks school would be better, well, she used the word, 'bullying'. It could be more like name calling, or just being nasty. It could be any of those things. So what do you think about them, and how could we make school a fairer place?

Shakir When somebody says something horrible to you, people just come… you're walking back off, they just come and hit them again.

Rose I think school's not that safe, because when we're playing outside, like in the little yard, teachers don't always look up that end where you come out, right, and if they don't and its open – sometimes it's open – so people can just walk through it and like strangers can go right in the yard and take you out.

Philip Miss, I think the school should have a burglar alarm because there's so many rooms and you can break in and climb over walls and stuff like that.

Carol We have actually got a burglar alarm.

Leku I think there are too many people calling people like Asian people 'Paki' and all that and black people. Some people call me the swear words like b…[19] and all that.

Poppy People always say swear words and they don't get told off at all.

Nasreen No more swearing in the yards, or bullying.

Poppy Well I think there should be cameras in the little yard because everybody's like, little, right, and everyone's falling OVER. Yeah! Banging HEADS and stuff, and falling OVER.

Carol When you have a problem and it's to do with somebody being nasty or somebody calling you a name or anything like that, do you feel safe that you can tell a teacher and it will be dealt with?

Rose No, because, the dinner ladies, they don't sort things out, right. When you tell the dinner ladies you need a problem sorting out, right, and there's no other dinner lady outside to tell, right, sometimes they say, 'Go inside and tell somebody'. They just go and tell another dinner lady.

Aidan There was one thing I want to say. A boy was bullying me and I told the lady and she kept on saying 'I'll watch him.' But she doesn't.

Tundi You know, when you could make the slide – sometimes, children could fall off the side of the slide, like some of the little ones. You should make one of them tube thingies so when you go down it would be even more exciting, and you won't fall off and get injured and have to go to hospital or have to go back to your mother's or father's house. So it would be more fair.

Leku Me and my brother, Kofi, he punches someone, and gets in trouble; then Kofi runs off; because I'm playing with Kofi, Kofi runs off; I get in trouble; that's the thing. I get in trouble, because I'm next to him. I get in trouble. Because me and Kofi look alike, the person who got kicked by Kofi they go, 'Him!' and point at me.

We have not reported the whole of this discussion. We have only included examples of each idea, but we have kept the comments in the order they were made. A feature of the original discussion was the way there was this mixing up of different kinds of things that affect how safe the children feel. These children do not distinguish between different kinds of things that make them feel unsafe. Children have not learnt to compartmentalise and categorise their lives, as we first observed in Chapter 3. (As we observed there, too, we already 'knew' this, but we seem to need to be reminded. We obviously don't know it as well as all that.)

The children mention worries about getting hit, getting bullied, getting sworn at, and racial harassment, but they are also concerned about strangers – outsiders – coming into the school to get them, the failure of adults to deal with their quarrels and problems, and the physical environment. Some of the worries stem from their imagination. Surely, the worry about the safety of a slide is related to the thrill of the moment sitting at the top of a slide just before you start (just as adults enjoy the thrill of danger on rides in the fairground, screaming with a combination of fear and pleasure).

It would not be particularly helpful to these children to distinguish the various reasons for their feelings of safety, although it is useful for us teachers to be reminded yet again what the school looks like from the perspective of its pupils; to whom the distinctions between home and school, classroom and playground, everyday trouble and imagined terrors are more blurred than they are to adults.

However, we are adults, and it is useful for us to draw up some categories of responses to children's fears that help in making school a safer, fairer place. The three principles of fairness (introduced in Chapter 1) help us do so. These categories of responses depend on noticing, firstly that fears, and their consequences for children, may arise because of individual circumstances or because the child is a member of a group defined by race, gender, class or abilities. Secondly, responses to children's fears can, in themselves, be the results of fair processes. Thirdly, when dealing with these kinds of problems, responses to children's fears need to take into account both the interests of individuals and the interests of the various communities from which they come.

Harassment and bullying: seeing the differences

The main categories which it is helpful to distinguish are harassment and bullying. These are categories which are helpful for adults dealing with children's needs for safety. They are not so useful for children. We explain more, later on in this chapter. The distinction we are making matches the distinction made in the first principle of fairness between the individual and group, and emphasises the importance of the third principle, that all individuals find their identity in the communities in which they belong. A word of warning is needed. We are using the word 'harassed' in a narrower sense than it is used in everyday talk. When we say 'harassed', we refer only to the kind of harassment in which an attack on an individual is implicitly or explicitly an attack on a whole group which is 'seen as different': be it for reasons of race, sex, disability, or social class.

Adrian Mitchell expresses how difference is used as a basis for attack, in part of his poem called 'Back in the Playground Blues' (1984):

Well you get it for being Jewish
And you get it for being black
Get it for being chicken
And you get it for fighting back
You get it for being big and fat
Get it for being small
Oh those who get it get it and get it
For any damn thing at all

Only some of these differences are purely personal (like 'chicken' or 'fighting back'), and others take their significance from the structures of injustice in the society (like being Jewish or black). It is these last ones where an attack on an individual is also an attack on a whole group which is 'seen as different'. It is these which give rise to harassment, in the narrow sense we are using here.

Our way of using 'harassment' is like the sense in which it is used in phrases like 'sexual and racial harassment'. This is not quite the same as the everyday use of the word. Using *ordinary* ways of talking, Parminder was harassed. She was a popular Year 6 girl, but she began to get a series of horrible letters. She found letters shoved into her tray in the classroom or left in her coat pocket in the cloakroom. The school tried hard to find who was writing them, but all that happened was that the letters began to say things like 'You've told the teachers, but you'll never find me'. For the purposes of this discussion we would prefer to call this form of bullying 'persecution' or 'continual bullying', rather than 'harassment', because there was no mention of anything to do with sex, race or religion in the letters. They were simply nasty about her in a personal way. If they had contained allusions to her being Asian, a Sikh, or a girl, then, in our terms, that would have been harassment as well as persecution and bullying. Since they did not, this problem may have been entirely individual; there is no evidence about the reasons for it because the culprit was not caught.

Ahmed Ullah was murdered in a playground in a Manchester secondary school because of harassment. He himself was a strong popular boy, who was not a victim of bullying. He was certainly much more of a high image child than was his attacker, Darren

Coulson. The writers of the report on the affair, the Macdonald Report, *Murder in the Playground*, describe him as (Macdonald, 1989, p.12):

> a big, strong lad, bright, intelligent and good at running. He also had a strong sense of justice and did not easily tolerate injustice.

They speculate that the reason Darren Coulson made a habit of tormenting the small Pakistani children was just because he was a child troubled by his own low image. They think that he drew comfort from being able to draw on his own whiteness in his attacks on Asians, especially, of course, when they were smaller, younger children who could not retaliate. Ahmed, confident in his own strength and popularity, took responsibility for the younger boys because they were of the same ethnic group as himself. Darren's racial insults affected him in the way that more personal bullying, of the kind that Parminder suffered, would not. His sister, Selina, is quoted as saying (Macdonald, 1989, p.12):

> Ahmed was a tall youth, and I believe that because of this he was singled out by the English boys as a 'leader' of the Asian boys in the school. They seemed to want to provoke trouble with him because he was in a sense representing a challenge to them.

Indeed, when Darren Coulson put the fatal knife into Ahmed Ullah, he was heard to say, 'Do you want another one, you stupid Paki?' Hannah Arendt, a philosopher writing after the Second World War, said: 'When I am attacked as a Jew, I must defend myself as a Jew'. This seems to describe the dilemma that Ahmed Ullah found himself in. It is also the dilemma faced by David who was attacked as a 'Welsh rabbit' and also by Shaibu, by Yusuf and by Leku (in the discussion on safety), who all had to deal with racism. It is a different problem from that faced by Zafar, Michael and Nat (in the Journal entry), or Parminder, who are bullied, hit and kicked, but not for being a particular race or gender.

In our terms, David was *harassed*, because he has to defend himself as Welsh, as well as against name calling; Parminder does not have to defend herself as Sikh, although she does have to deal with the awfulness of being *bullied*. It sounds as if Leku is being *harassed* by his school mates, and *bullied* by his big brother, Kofi. All of these children feel distressed and got at, of course. In no way do the distinctions between harassment or bullying imply that either of them feels worse to the victim.

All these examples of harassment have focused on racial harassment, but we could have chosen other areas of focus.

Sexuality is one that is often missed and ignored by teachers – though not by children!

Carol

'Lesbian' is used as a nasty insult. For instance, there might be two girls walking around the playground holding hands. It's not that common, but very occasionally I have heard someone say, 'Oh, you're lesbians!' The girls have come in really upset. Sometimes they have known what it is, or if they haven't, they have known that it is meant as an insult, or as a swear word. In fact, they have said, 'They've called us lesbians; what does it mean?' While this is bad for them, they can usually cope, with a bit of support.

The use of the word as an insult causes problems for a child whose mother is in a lesbian relationship. This happened to Tom. He was actually very open about his 'two Mums' – and he had no contact at all with his Dad. Other children used his openness as a way of irritating and upsetting him. He would come in really upset because the word 'lesbian' is recognised to be an insult, even though he was not, actually, ashamed of his mother or of her sexuality. In the end, it was Martin, another child in the same class who put a stop to it. Martin, unlike Tom, was a high image child: really bright, really able at school work, always in the school play, good at football, well in with the other children, liked by the teachers, in fact, good at everything. His mother, too, was in a lesbian relationship. Unlike Tom, he never talked about it, either to the other children or to the teachers.

One day, Tom had come in, again, really upset. I discussed it with the children, saying the usual things: we are all individuals; it was wrong to attack Tom; they knew that they were deliberately trying to irritate him when they knew they shouldn't. A short while after this conversation when I was working with some children on a nearby table, I heard Martin saying 'I don't know what you are going on about. I think everyone's an individual. Anyway, there's nothing wrong with being a lesbian. My Mum's a lesbian.' After that, Tom did not have very many problems, because he had a kind of protective umbrella. It was lucky for him of course, that Martin spoke up when he did.

Children need to discuss their home circumstances sometimes. The difficulty comes for children whose home circumstances are factually described in words that are insults. Marie, for instance, who had lived with her aunt most of her life since both her parents died, wanted to talk about her 'Mum', as she called her aunt, and her 'real Mum'. In a way she was very similar to Tom, and she could have faced problems if other children had played on her sensitivity about her situation by using it as a reason to irritate her. But even if that had been the case, she would have faced fewer problems because 'orphan' is not a term of insult as 'lesbian' is.

The use of the term 'lesbian' as an insult causes problems to those children who hear it used this way, who have not themselves been on the receiving end – yet. We wonder about 7-year-old Mary and 6-year-old Paul whose mother is in a lesbian relationship, but who haven't had any problems with other children about it, or least not that their teachers are aware of. But as soon as they learn that having 'two Mums' is the same as having a lesbian mother (and we do not know whether they know this yet) they will learn that there is something that can be used against them, insultingly. They will also learn, like Ahmed Ullah and like Martin, that there is a moral pressure on them to go to the aid of other children in similar circumstances, even if they are not, themselves, directly having problems.

These children will also have to face the dilemma of whether to pretend to be like so-called 'normal' children, or whether to face the consequences of being open about their mothers' sexuality. Any child who feels that their ordinary home life is abnormal – who feels marginalised – will have this problem. Naz, an Asian girl who is now a University undergraduate, remembers vividly how when she was at primary school, she used to lie when asked to write about 'What I did in the holidays' or 'What I did at the weekend', in order not to have to face the consequences of describing her thoroughly respectable and normal Asian home life to her white teacher, and to the largely white class.

Tom and Martin both suffer from harassment, although only Tom was directly tormented. Mary, Paul and Naz are also subject to harassment, and are pressured to lie about themselves. Bullying is always tormenting to the victim, and it occurs for a bewildering number of reasons: witness Tom, coping with unkind peers; Parminder, coping with her unknown persecutor; Leku coping with his big brother.

Harassment is not the only kind of bullying which has implications for fairness and justice. There is another kind of bullying which needs to be addressed for reasons of improving the fairness of the classroom and the school, as well as for simple moral reasons of stopping cruelty.

The problem between Bartholomew and his cousin Leroy seemed to be more the result of a macho sub-culture, than of any particular nastiness or psychological disturbance in the perpetrators. Bartholomew seemed to be a classic case of a 'victim' – a child likely to be bullied. When he was in Year 1 and Year 2 he was already having trouble with other children bothering him. He would be tearful at the thought of coming to school at all. The problems continued into the Juniors, at least at first. He and his friend Stevie were both being bullied, and complained about it to their teachers. The teachers took a long time getting to the bottom of what was going on. It was true that the two little boys were getting bullied by older boys, and one in particular, called Leroy, a relative of Bartholomew's. The older boys were duly called to account. However the case did not stop there. Leroy and Bartholomew continued to get into fights: it turned out that Bartholomew was following Leroy about, rather than avoiding him. It seemed that he was both wanting and not wanting to play with Leroy – and similarly the older boy both wanted and did not want to play with his young cousin.

The problem for the two boys, when the teachers finally got to the bottom of it, was that they had no model for two boys playing that did not include fighting. As Bartholomew's teacher said, 'Both thought that playing together meant hitting seven bells out of each other.' With her help, the two boys got together one lunch time and had a long discussion on the subject of what it was that got them into trouble, and what stopped them from playing nicely with each other. The result was a contract, drawn up using the boys' words and written out by the teacher: 'Leroy and Bartholomew's guide to playing nicely' (Figure 4.1).

The importance of reducing a macho sub-culture was also recognised by the following two headteachers: the first is the head of a school described further in Chapter 6, which has such problems with vandalism that Rottweiler dogs patrol the playground at night. She is talking about the effect on the school of the sub-culture of the environment:

> It's about changing attitudes towards masculinity and the vandalism. I think that's symptomatic of the macho-ness of the whole culture that the youths, the young boys in the community…that's how they express themselves within their own community.
>
> The macho thing, we've had it in on the playground, parents and youths threatening one another and hitting one another. They tend not to come into school, but the level of aggression is quite high, I would say. You wonder what's going on when they get home.
>
> It is worrying that these children are being nurtured in an environment that seems to say that there's no hope for you anyway, no prospect of employment for a start, and you get what you want by means of violent and aggressive behaviour.

Leroy and Bartholomew's guide to playing nicely

1. *We've got to talk to each other about the rules of the games and also about the things we've done.*

2. *Be nice, friendly and good.*

3. *Keeping out of trouble by playing sensible games such as dobby and tig.*

Signed: *Date: 12 Dec 1994*

Teacher ....

Leroy ....

Bartholomew ....

We will start on January 3rd 1995. After the first week Miss will talk to us. We have to make it work otherwise we won't be able to play together.

Figure 4.1 Leroy and Bartholomew's guide to playing nicely

Another head, from a well-off area, describes another way in which macho culture affects how children behave to each other in school.

> We've talked about the culture that these children come from. It is a reasonably affluent, fairly middle-class culture. And every culture has a sub-culture. And the staff and myself, we do feel that the sub-culture here is a sort of Thatcherist sub-culture: Me! Me! I am important, I! I am the only one that matters. What I want must be right. Go for it and push everyone else out the way. And there's no such thing as society. That's absolute anathema to me, and I think it is to most of the staff as well.

> We've talked about it as a staff. No matter what the values are in the home, the school is entitled to its own value system. Hopefully there is a match and not a mismatch. You don't so often these days hear the children say, 'Well, my Dad says I've got to hit so-and-so back.'

Most of the work on bullying, including the work on which the

Department for Education has drawn in its useful guide, *Don't Suffer in Silence*, is very individual in its approach (DFE, 1994). The problem of bullying is seen as a problem of certain individuals – whether they are bullies or victims. The solution is seen as drawing on peer pressure, and establishing an anti-bullying ethos in the school, backed up by clear guidelines for action. We endorse such solutions, but we also want to point out that some cases of bullying arise out of the same social structures in the society at large which support sexism, racism, class prejudice, and the rest. Bartholomew looked like a classic 'victim'. A purely psychological approach would have suggested he needed help with this attitude. However his problems with Leroy were more the result of the sexist, macho culture in which he was learning how to play, than of his individual attitudes to others and himself.

Our conclusions draw on, but go beyond, most recent research on bullying, which we argue is too narrow in its perspective.[20] For instance, Besag's work, useful and thorough though it is, is based on a definition composed of four facets, none of which use categories such as gender, race or social class. The facets are as follows. Bullying:

1 may be verbal, physical, or psychological;
2 may be in the form of socially acceptable behaviour;
3 is necessarily repetitive, causing distress by threat of future attacks;
4 is characterised by the dominance of the powerful over the powerless.

She goes on to categories of victim and bully, on the basis of their personal characteristics and family backgrounds. She also summarises research that shows that reasons for bullying vary with gender, and that children from ethnic minorities are more likely to be bullied. This last fact is accounted for in terms of labelling, which she points out, itself draws on stereotypes of scapegoated groups and on visible marks of difference, 'such as red hair, glasses, a stammer or other noticeable feature' (Besag, 1989, p.45).

Besag sympathetically describes the effect of racist bullying including the hurtful power of name-calling, but fails to discuss the effects of such bullying on other members of the same social group. Therefore she does not see what is special about name-calling that draws on racism, sexism or class prejudices. She herself remarks on the hurtfulness of name-calling. Unfortunately some other researchers are less careful. In *Don't Suffer in Silence* (DFE, 1994), for instance, the reasons given for challenging bullying are all to do with the effects on pupils as individuals (p.8) though there is a brief mention of racial harassment later (p.26). Worse, name-calling is apparently not considered to be very serious (DFE, 1994, p.18):

> *Dealing with minor incidents:* Mild sanctions can be useful in responding to one-off incidents of bullying which do not result in physical harm. A reprimand may be sufficient to deter a pupil from name calling or mild teasing.

Harassment and bullying: making connections

Elinor Kelly is a researcher who was commissioned by the Macdonald committee investigating the context of the murder of Ahmed Ullah for Manchester Education Committee, to look into bullying and harassment. She has developed the ideas that we are discussing here about the differences between harassment and bullying. She has also developed the idea of 'racialising or sexualising discourse', which was referred to in the Journal entry that began this chapter.[21] In using this phrase, she is drawing attention to the power of language. Children regularly use language to exert power, whether aggressively or in self-defence. Thus they use the words that they know will hurt, often regardless of their views about the literal meaning of the word. (For instance, we described the way children in the playground use the word 'lesbian' without understanding it.) When any child calls another child names, using factors related to sex, race, religion or social class, an attempt is being made to define both of them in sexual, racial, religious or class terms. The same is true for special needs, too – either related to physical differences or being called 'stupid' which is particularly powerful in school contexts where slow learners stand little chance of hiding their slowness.[22]

Particular incidents of either harassment and bullying can be minor or major, but both need to be dealt with for rather different reasons. From the point of view of fairness, both are wrong but for different, if overlapping, reasons. Bullying may have no trace of harassment in it. On the other hand, harassment often sounds like bullying and often feels like bullying. What is being suggested here is that the two need to be distinguished by the teachers, because although they feel the same to the child, pretty much, their effects are different, and need to be understood and dealt with differently. However, since they feel similar to children, an integrated approach is needed, lest it is thought that one is enough.

We began by saying Riverside had a racial incidents policy but not a bullying one. All schools now are required to produce evidence of 'the views of pupils, parents and teachers on the incidence of bullying and the school's response' under the Framework for Inspection by OFSTED. Many schools are already producing a bullying policy. It is a rare school that has a comprehensive harassment policy too, let alone one that has an awareness among staff of the different significance of different kinds of bullying; individualised and connected to issues of general fairness and justice.

What we have learnt about dealing with fear

It is increasingly obvious to us that fairness in school can only be achieved if children do not feel afraid while they are there. Unfortunately, it is just as obvious that bullying, harassment and, therefore, fear lie in wait in every school. However, there is a great deal that can be done. It is possible for fear and its causes to be dealt with, with the result that while bullying or harassment are not eradicated, they are at least minimised, contained and those who suffer from them feel supported. It is important that schools respond to these issues as a whole – parents, children, teachers, governors, and all the support staff.

The children themselves are in no doubt about the importance of safety, judging by Carol's present class. When we invited them to express their views about fair schools, the responses were overwhelmingly related to the significance of feeling safe and valued. One black child's drawing emphasised the hurt of name-calling, and others expressed a desire for kindly attitudes to spread among children and adults (Figure 4.2).

Figure 4.2(a) Picture about fairness

Figure 4.2(b) Picture about fairness

Chapter 5

VERY FAIR WORK: ACHIEVEMENT IN SCHOOLS

Judging achievements

In Chapters 1 and 2, we described Mosiah, an intelligent boy, who was dismayed at his own inability to settle to work. His standard of work was average, so he would not show up on any set of statistics as 'underachieving', but actually he was achieving well below his potential, in terms of the academic work that he should be capable of. He was, in our view, achieving well in the area of self-reflection, but not so well in the area of creating social relationships which would help rather than hinder his own ends, which were *both* being top dog and *also* being good at school work. Suzie, who we also introduced at the beginning of Chapter 2 would show up as 'underachieving' because her academic test scores were well below average for her age group. Her social skills of coping with outsiders and lame dogs do not appear on any standardised tests – and indeed, how could they be measured? We were unable to say whether she really was 'underachieving' academically. It seems probable that she could do more: working class white girls – and this describes her – do not, as a group, achieve high scores at school. But maybe Suzie was already doing the best she is capable of? How could we tell? John appeared a little later on in Chapter 1, counting straws with his Special teacher, who was working one-to-one with him containing his frustration, as well as teaching him maths. He is also of a group that is likely, statistically, to 'underachieve' – a white working-class boy. We are fairly certain that no matter how hard he tries he will achieve less in relation to other children of his age.

Achievement in relation to the average for all children can obviously be only the first point of reference, and not the last, for any given child. If 'underachieving' refers to achievement in relation to the particular child's capabilities, which it must do in the end, then it is hard to see how anyone could ever tell if any particular child is underachieving. How *could* we know what Mosiah, or Suzie, or John, was really capable of? The concept of 'underachievement in relation to the average' only really becomes very useful in relation to large numbers of children. We explain this further, and discuss it some more at the beginning of the next chapter, in the section called 'the numbers game'.

Learning to learn: getting support and challenge

In Chapters 2 and 3 we described the process of our Fairness project which aimed at improving teaching and learning in the classroom at the same time as making the classroom a fairer place. In this section we focus on what was achieved as a result of those projects in relation to improving teaching and learning. As we pointed out right at the beginning of Chapter 1, only if all children achieve well, can a school or classroom be judged a fair one. Whether we are thinking of various ethnic minorities, of gender or of social class, one of the touchstones of a fair system is that all of these groups are able to benefit from their education and to achieve well as a result of it.

At the end of the first year of the Fairness project, described in the first half of Chapter 2, we observed improvements in two areas. We thought the children had learnt a lot about working together in such a way that they were able to spend more time concentrating and learning from each other. We also thought that they were showing considerable improvement in being able to reflect on their own individual learning and on what strategies they might each individually develop about how to help themselves learn.

There were several indications that group work was improving. A large part of this was the result of the children having become conscious of the way resources could become a problem. An afternoon doing clay work, as a class, was organised by the children, with no problems. 'Can I borrow the rolling pin?' was heard, in contrast to the snatching and quarrelling the children had commented on in their first discussion about the problems of group work. The children and the adults all agreed that the strategies that had been worked out to deal with problems of access to rubbers and sharpeners were working out well.

Carol also noticed that individuals were reflecting on their own needs. For instance, Sohel said that he had decided to ask three and only three questions of her, and had obviously thought hard about which ones they were to be. Beth was able to reflect on the reasons she needed to see the teacher so much. As pointed out in Chapter 2, the children themselves said that they had learnt about the ways their actions could affect their own learning: that they wandered more than they expected, that wandering led to distraction as they passed other children, and that they were spending a lot of time chatting to each other and cracking jokes.

In that first year, further evidence that individuals were better at reflecting on their own needs was provided when we asked children how they were achieving their individual goals, and what their new goals might be. They used a similar form to the one they had filled in during the first month of the project. The forms were private – confidential to Carol and me.[23] In the event one child did not want us to see what he had written and neither of us made any attempt to make him change his mind. Two months and a holiday had intervened between the writing of the first set of goals and the second set. It is not surprising that the details of what they had put had changed (Figure 5.1).

	First set of goals: "I need to improve on... My goal is.... I can achieve it by / help I need..."	**Second set of goals:**
Manzar (Asian boy, working class)	*Improve:* my behaviour and I need to improve on my attitude. *My goal:* to improve my spelling and reading. I *Achieve by*: my concentration	I think I waste time chatting. I am less confident at maths. I waste my time finding rubbers. I have arguments. I have improved on my work.
Sybil (White girl, middle class)	*Improve:* I tend to go along with other people's ideas instead of coming out in the open with my own ideas. When working on my own I don't get as much done because I don't enjoy it so much as I would with others. *My goal:* to try and enjoy work when on my own. *Achieve by*: Ask my dad (a school teacher) to give	1. We (Sybil and Reva) think that we don't go to see the teacher or ask the teacher enough 2. We found that we spend a lot of time getting resources

	me some homework and then lock myself in my bedroom with nobody else in there.	
Suzie (White girl, working class)	*Improve*: Reading, swimming, maths, concentrate and not talking when I talk I don't get any work done. Listening, behave, do my work in neat, to finish my work. *My goal:* Concentrate. Swimming *Achieve by:* I can improve on swimming by going in the holidays. I can improve on concentrating by not talking and trying to work hard.	1. I learnt a lot. When I talk a lot I never get any work done. 2. When I work on my own I can get more work done, but when I work with some one I don't do any work. 3. When I sit on a table they are always talking to me.
Karl (White boy, working class)	*Improve*: Writing reading, maths, being quick at work, no arguing, messing about, getting better at games and PE, not getting my book messy, no copying, no cheating. *My goal*: Got to fill every page. *Achieve by:* Writing with a pencil.	1. If I talk to people I don't get on with my work. 2. If other people mess about so do I.
Kamaljeet (Asian girl, working class)	*Improve:* I don't like group work, it makes me feel funny. I've got to work on my spellings and maths. *My goal*: I will try my best to work on my spellings. *Achieve by:* I get help from my friends and teachers.	I think I talk too much because me and Tamsin talk too much about going to our houses. I learnt that I can do my maths.
Juliet	*Improve:* Talking or	I think I learnt that I

(White girl, middle class)	chatting because sometimes I spend more time talking than doing my work. Being bossy because sometimes when we go into a group without even thinking I take on the role of the leader and I organize everything. And sometimes other people are like that too so I get annoyed from them doing it even though I do it. *My goal:* not being bossy *Achieve by*: I think to achieve this when I go in a group I must try to not be the boss and let someone else organize it. But I'm not really sure what help I'll need.	talked quite a lot but not enough to stop me doing my work. Also I spent a lot of my time helping people with their work with things like spellings. But I don't really mind that. I think I spent quite a lot of my time asking for rulers, rubbers, etc because some of mine have gone missing or I've lost them. I've also learnt that I made a lot of jokes which may have slowed me down in my work but I'm not really sure. I learnt that I had to ask Miss Davies quite a lot of question in subjects like Peak maths or working in the practical area on the castle but I didn't have to ask many questions when I was doing language work and I think that's because language is my stronger point. Also I've learnt by doing the sheets is that a lot of the things which I would have asked I have been able to answer myself rather than wasting time. Sometimes even when Miss Davies says 'Use a dictionary for spellings' I prefer to ask for some reason. I don't really know what else to write so I'm going to finish now.
Craig (White boy,	*Improve:* Writing, maths and messing about in the	1. I learnt a lot when I talk to other people

working class)	class room. Reading, getting better at things, and trying harder at things. *My goal:* Writing. I want to improve because I will be able to write better. *Achieve by:* I will need help with my maths. I might need a calculator, it is easier.	2. When I sit on my own table I get more work done. 3. When I take my topic work in there are nothing to show.

Figure 5.1 Changes in some children's self-reflections about learning

What was interesting to us was the way the quality of the comments had changed. The children seemed much more able to focus on the process of learning rather than on the content of what was being learnt. For instance, one child now showed that he understood the importance of 'concentrating', over and above identifying particular areas for improvement, such as the areas of 'swimming' and 'reading' he had mentioned in the first form he had filled in.

The children also seemed much more able to think of particular processes they needed to work on rather than global ones. For instance, one child had moved from saying 'Writing. I want to improve because I will be able to write better' to 'I learnt a lot when I talk to other people and when I sit on my own table I get more work done.' Of the 20 children who were present on both occasions (and let us see their work) only one had not moved in these directions (Sybil): on both occasions she had insight into her learning processes, but little idea how to correct them, other than by exercising will and determination. Of the others, nine had become explicitly conscious of learning processes, aside from content, while ten had become more aware of details of the processes.

In the following year, Year 2 of the Fairness project, we focused on pressure (*see* the second half of Chapter 2), and in Year 3, the one after that, the aim was to improve support and challenge (*see* Chapter 3). In both of Years 2 and 3 we had had similar results with respect to teaching and learning, but the evaluation was more detailed in the final year, so we focus on that one here in order to explain how achievement was enhanced as part of the Fairness project. In Chapter 3 the story was left at the point at which the class as a whole had discussed the video of them working.

Carol

After watching the video, the children and I went on together to make improvements. The video gave us an opportunity to view the situation from the outside and it gave us the determination to make improvements. I had actually thought we should all continue to observe action through the use of self-observation sheets but the children were keen to make immediate improvements. They suggested that a basket of resources on each table (pencils, rubbers, sharpeners, etc.) would help prevent some of the wandering, distraction and talking. They also proposed a card system, similar to those seen at supermarket delicatessen counters, where each child has a card with their name on which they give to the teacher when they need help. The children then continue with some appropriate work until their name is called from the pile of cards. They also decided to continue with the Push Chart, a reward system to help themselves line up better.

I was prepared to try it so as a class we decided to trial the suggestions for a 2-week period. After an evaluation 2 weeks later, the children found that various situations were improving. The queue was getting better, though talking was still a problem for some children. They suggested a talking chart, on the lines of the push chart. It was already June, and the various strategies devised by the children carried on successfully until the end of the summer term.

By the end of the academic year we – the children, my colleagues and I – all felt we had been able to make huge improvements in practice over the year. The growth of trust in the classroom led to the children developing in confidence and becoming secure that I really did want to work with them to improve our practice, thus further allowing us to establish a good working relationship. Over the year, the class and I had become a stronger unit, able to discuss problems openly and able to search for ways to improve the situation. Decisions made, such as the use of the Push Chart, the baskets and the cards, were in use right up to the start of the summer holidays. The children felt they were producing more work, were on task for a greater percentage of time and found it easier to work on their individual goals. This was also commented on by the nursery nurse support, a visiting LEA inspector and a parent. As a result of gaining the children's trust through working together I was able to gain a greater knowledge of the children and this gave me the opportunity to offer them more appropriate support, according to their needs.

The opinions and perceptions of the children helped me reflect on my own practice and gave me a different and valuable viewpoint on my actions. The children within this study had a distinct and worthwhile perception of the educational situation in which they operate and their views were a useful element in improving practice and in providing a better environment for learning to take place. Without them I might never have been aware of the problems of the queue or that personal and social areas of school life perhaps caused more concern for this particular class than academic worries.

Increasing trust and involving the children in negotiating improvements actually helped those improvements succeed. The children had taken a full part in the progress of the project, so they owned the decisions made and they therefore had a full understanding of the purpose of the action, and probably a stronger desire for its success.

Looking back over the third year of the project, we wondered if some of the improvements noted in the first year were perhaps just evidence of an improvement of trust. Perhaps the children had become more open, more willing to risk what they could say? To answer such questions, further work would be needed. Meanwhile, although there are many unanswered questions, we – as well as the children – have learnt a lot about improving teaching and learning. At the end of Chapter 3, we said we were pleased with the steps taken in the direction of individual empowerment, and in our understanding of the processes of fairness. We are also pleased with the increase in the children's ability to reflect on their own strategies to improve their own learning – and in many cases with improvement of their work too. (It is, of course, impossible to say with any certainty how much this improvement would have occurred anyway. In work like this, there can be no 'control' groups or 'double-blind tests' of the kind found in medical research, for instance.)

We were paying attention to teaching and learning strategies, to openness, and to critical self-reflection, rather than directly to race, social class and gender. However, we continued to view the class through these lenses, checking on interaction patterns, raising issues of mixing the sexes in discussions of groupings, and employing strategies which sometimes mixed up races and social classes, and sometimes allowed children to choose their own kind of people (however, they themselves implicitly defined this).

We were working with the view that each individual needs to improve their own learning processes and outcomes, regardless of how well they are doing compared to how other, similar children are doing. On the other hand we acknowledge that it is also important to pay attention to gender, race, and social class, since each of these factors seem to have an effect on learning processes and outcomes. In the Fairness project we chose not to put as much emphasis on working with groups of children defined by social factors as on individual empowerment. In another context we might have made a different choice about where to put the emphasis.

There are other good ways of resolving the dilemmas about how much emphasis to put on individuals and how much to put on race, social class and gender. Any or all of these ways might be used by the same teachers at different times in their professional lives. Three approaches are described next which choose a different emphasis. They all start with a focus on gender or race – but at the same time they keep sight of children as individuals, never stereotyping them by viewing them as simply representative of any particular social grouping.

Learning to read to look for a job: gender and literacy

A project on gender and literacy has been going on for 2 years in Green Park School, though it had its beginnings a year earlier than that. It began as a result of an OFSTED inspection – in fact, among the first few carried out.

The inspection report pulled no punches. It said:

> The standards of reading and writing are poor. Inspection of the pupils' reading skills and the results of standardised reading tests in Year 3 indicate that approximately 75% of the children achieve below average levels.

It went on to relate low levels of literacy to poor achievement in other areas of the curriculum.

Not surprisingly, after they had read this report the staff as a whole – and particularly the management – made literacy standards and the implementation of various strategies to raise them a high priority within the school.

Green Park school is set in a large area of flat green municipal grass. It takes children from Green Park Estate, which consists of 1940s local authority housing. It is no leafy suburb to the industrial city where it is located. Unemployment is high. Half the children are entitled to free school meals. The sections of concrete pipe donated to add variety to the play area were stolen within 24 hours. The sturdy brick walls separating the school from the road are regularly pushed over. The building materials, brought by the Council workmen sent to mend it, are as regularly stolen or scattered. This school for small children – there are 400 Nursery, Infant and Junior children – now has Rottweilers patrolling the grounds at night.

The surrounding area has none of the buzz and energy of the inner city. Nor does it have the variety of the countryside with its mixture of commuters, agricultural workers and landowners. By contrast to the inner city and to the countryside, Green Park Estate is remarkably mono-cultural. It is largely white: there are only 8 black children in the school. There are no areas of private housing to bring in the middle classes.

Perhaps in the circumstances it is not surprising that the children have difficulties with literacy. On the other hand, without high standards of literacy, what hope do these white working-class children have, growing up on the margin of an industrial city which is steadily losing its traditional manufacturing base?

Helen, the deputy head of the Juniors, had responsibility for language within the school. She decided to analyse the results of a standardised reading test carried out a year after the inspection, to see if there had been any improvement in Year 3. There was none. However, she noticed a gender difference. There was hardly any difference in the scores of boys and girls across the whole school – but within the 'below average' grouping, significantly more boys achieved very low scores.

It seemed to her that these working class boys seemed to be particularly vulnerable. This view was strengthened by some large-scale survey research which showed that at age 10+, boys were already much less likely than girls to read books. Whitehead and her colleagues found with regard to non-book reading that the group most at risk:

> will consist of boys in low 'ability and attainment' groupings with manual fathers, and it is certainly the case that this group is one which schools need to watch (and often do watch) with special concern. (Whitehead *et al.*, 1977, p.273)

In order to gain a clearer insight into gender-related issues in reading, and thereby consider and develop strategies which would encourage success for all children, Helen felt she needed to explore three key areas.

The first of these was how boys and girls viewed themselves as readers. The second was whether there was a link between these views of themselves and role models at home. Although there is an increasing emphasis on home–school reading links, all the material presently available seems largely to ignore, or to accept as given, gender divisions of labour in the home, including gender divisions of labour with respect to reading and writing.[24] Indeed, in a lot of the work on home–school links it can be seen that there is a tacit assumption which overrides the apparently gender-neutral word, 'parent', that the 'parent' in question is, in fact, the mother. A third area to explore was linked to the question of children's views of themselves as readers, in terms of to what they attributed their own success or failure. Research suggests that individuals habitually attribute their own success to luck, to effort or to innate ability, and that the two genders tend to adopt different patterns of attribution. This is important if only because such attributions strongly influence the possibilities for change: put simply, if success is attributed to effort rather than luck, then it is worth trying hard.[25]

Helen decided to interview some of the children. She felt that complex and delicate questions about self-perceptions were not going to be answered using a questionnaire. Finding time in the busy life of a deputy head was not easy. We are intentionally describing something that took place in the busy every-day of a real school, without extra resources, and during the upheavals following the introduction of the Education Reform Act. Interviewing a large number of children was not a possibility.

In the end only six Year 3 children were interviewed – but twice and in some depth – with a view to gaining insights rather than establishing facts about the perspectives of the children. There was also an explicit intention of following up issues arising from the study. Therefore the children selected were all from the class that Helen would be teaching the following September – she would be able to follow up the issues more easily if she was working closely with the children as their class teacher. While no child can be said to be 'typical', the children selected were chosen to be not untypical. None of them were at the extremes of ability, and all of them had both male and female role models at home.

The six children – three boys and three girls – took part in two group interviews. The interview questions were carefully designed to focus on an issue of fairness – gender and social class – and to shed light on how children might view themselves and their schools and their homes. They were designed to help the school develop new ways of approaching literacy: fairer processes which lead to greater fairness of outcome.

In the first interview Helen questioned all six children together. The first question was 'Why do we learn to read?'. This was intended to probe the children's understanding of the purpose of reading and, indirectly, the perceived status of reading in the curriculum. The second question was 'What kinds of things do you read?' which checked the levels and types of interest in reading. The final question was 'How good do you think you are at reading and how do you feel about it?' This question was meant to compare children's views of their achievements with the 'facts' of their test scores, and identify whether achievement and attitude seemed to be linked in any way. The boys tended to dominate the discussion. Although this had been anticipated, and a turn-taking system built in, Charlie and George (though not Jason) were inclined to interrupt the others.

The second interview was carried out with the same children in single sex groups, partly to avoid domination of the discussion by the boys and partly to see whether the effects of a different group dynamic affected the responses to the questions. In the second interview the questions were: 'Who reads what at home? ... Which of them reads the most?', 'What do girls/ boys like to be best at in school?' and 'What are girls/ boys best at in school and why?' In order to avoid either 'leading' the children, or risking hurting their feelings about family relationships, there was no mention of 'Mum' or 'Dad'.

Thus over the two sets of interviews answers had been given to questions: 'Why do we learn to read? Who reads what and how much? How good are you at reading and why? What gender differences are there in achievement at school and why?'. The questions asked, and indeed, the whole process of interviewing, look deceptively simple – like a friendly chat with a few children. In fact, the process and the questions were designed and carried out so carefully that they have begun to make a difference to literacy teaching throughout the school – and to the policies about home–school relations.

The response to the question, 'Why do we learn to read?', was unanimous. All the children agreed that they had to learn to read in order to get jobs when they left school. However Helen observed that if the children perceived reading as being more important in some jobs than others, this would be significant when related to their own aspirations, so she went on to explore their ideas about jobs. She asked for examples of jobs and what part reading played in the given examples. The boys cited traditionally male occupations. The girls' responses focused on the utilitarian functions of reading as related to everyday activities, usually of a domestic nature. The girls seemed to find it oddly difficult to come up with 'jobs', though Lucy said, 'You'd need to be able to read to look for a job in the paper'. There seems in these responses to be a gender-based notion of how labour is divided in society and, embedded within that, views about the function and importance of reading and literacy (*see* Figure 5.2).

To the two questions about who reads what and how much, for both children and adults there was a common thread. Females appear to read more than males, and their reading tends not to be

BOYS	*GIRLS*
POLICEMAN (has to read reports and letters); LORRY DRIVER, TAXI DRIVER, DRIVER (has to read maps and things to know where you are going); SHOP WORKER (read the back of stuff, and prices); CAR MECHANIC (doesn't have to read).	TEACHER, FIREMAN, You need to be able to read to look for a job in the paper; You need to be able to read for shopping (food, tapes, a car); Visiting the library, Visiting the clinic, Travelling (by car and plane).

Figure 5.2 What part reading plays in jobs, according to the children

linked to employment, though it may be to domesticity. For instance, Jason said that his mother reads things that she writes herself and she borrows books from her friend; that his sister reads her reading book. Dad, on the other hand, reads the instructions to his building set. Charlie's mother reads her mail order catalogue, while his father reads 'letters from his work and off the computer'. Sharon stated that she reads most in her family, and her mother reads magazines. Her brother reads 'learning books' and computer books. Her father was not mentioned. Melissa's mother is the most avid reader in her family. Both parents read newspapers, whereas Melissa, herself, reads books. Her brothers sometimes read their reading books or games.

The reading preferences of adults (as perceived by the children) were, to a large extent, reflected in those of their same-sex children. During the first interview, the boys stated a preference for 'learning books', computers, word searches, and Lego instructions, whereas the girls like stories, comics and magazines. The gender-based division between fiction and non-fiction was rigid. The girls like fairy tales (with sad endings) and short stories, whereas the boys specified 'books that show you something' and 'books with armies and soldiers.' When pressed, the boys admitted to enjoying adventure stories or 'stories where someone gets killed or in jail' but the girls could not be shifted from their view that non-fiction was 'boring', in spite of being reminded of books catering to their interests (animals, pets, other countries) in the school library.

When asked how good they were at reading the three girls all said 'quite good'. The boys' responses were more varied. Charlie clearly saw reading performance in relation to the hierarchy in the classroom since he felt he was 'in the middle'. George stated that he was 'a little bit good', and Jason, whose test score indicates that he was the poorest reader in the group said he was 'good'. In fact, the girls were all higher scoring in the reading test than the boys, in spite of the fact that they all qualified their apparently good ability with a 'quite'. The children were asked how they knew their level of achievement. The boys seemed to depend on external, visible tokens of success, such as the number of stickers, or the reading scheme level, or what the teacher says. George said, 'You feel embarrassed if you don't get on the levels'. The girls did not mention levels, but seemed more inclined to measure success by what 'people' (i.e. teachers and other adults) say.

The children had clear views about gender differences in achievement at school and the reasons for them. When asked what boys and girls like to be best at and what they are best at, responses were strongly influenced by gender and gender stereotypes. The boys felt that the girls liked to be best at writing and 'finding out stuff in class'. They also liked to be best at handwriting. The boys, on the other hand, like to be best at drawing. The girls' perceptions of what they themselves like to be good at were similar, namely writing and reading. However, they seemed to hold more stereotypical views of the boys than did the boys themselves. The girls felt that the boys just wanted to be good at football and PE. Sharon added 'drawing' to this list as an afterthought. The boys believed they were best at drawing and the girls were best at reading and writing. They were all most emphatic that girls were better at reading than boys. The girls echoed this view, but with much less assurance and conviction than the boys.

Charlie and George attributed girls' success to effort and conformity: 'They read at home' and 'they get more practice because they're sensibler'. Jason suggested that girls might have 'better brains' but George and Charlie disagreed with this statement. When asked if they thought boys would be better readers if they practised more, they agreed, but could not account for why girls read more at home, nor how boys spent that time. The girls, on the other hand, attributed their perceived success to the boys' failure to succeed. Melissa said, 'Girls are best because boys keep being stupid and bragging round class', and Sharon supported her, adding, 'When there's something funny in the book they laugh and show everybody.' Girls in the same situation 'laugh to themselves'. They attributed the boys' failure to choice: 'They probably don't like it' and they 'might think it's boring and football's better.' When they were pushed on why girls were successful, Sharon tentatively suggested 'Maybe girls are cleverer than boys sometimes.'

As a result of this small-scale study, nothing definitive can be said about girls and boys in general, or even about girls and boys on Green Park Estate. However there is plenty here which is thought provoking about possible directions to probe further, and strategies to try – in this particular school and also in others.

How well children read is bound up with their understanding of the purposes etc of reading, as Gordon Wells' studies first showed (Wells, 1985). Helen's observations are supported by research. A large-scale study in the West of England investigated the relationship between writing, gender and class. The results show that working-class white families are far more likely than their middle-class counterparts to perceive writing as women's work. In both working-class and middle-class white families it is the women who do the writing related to emotional work, for instance letter writing and sending cards (Griffiths and Wells, 1983). In middle-class homes, unlike in working-class homes, males do far more writing than females. Nearly all of it was work related: report writing, letter writing, note taking. The responses of the children fit well into the view that literacy is inexorably bound to 'social status and identity', as Judith Solsken says, reflecting on her study of 13 children in their first 2 years of school. She points out the many ways in which early literacy learning is linked to children's negotiation of their social identity especially in relation to gender and work. Other studies show the links children make between literacy and their ethnic identity, which is itself marked by both gender and class.[26]

Children come to see certain kinds of reading as appropriate for them in gender or class or race terms. They are actively engaged in identifying themselves in these terms, as they understand them. One factor that comes out strongly from these six children is the gendering of reason and emotion as masculine and feminine. Sad stories for the girls and factual, useful books for the boys is one way of expressing this gender division. That it is a construct for the children is seen by the way that the three boys would admit to liking stories but only if pushed. The three girls remained adamant that they do not like facts. It is as if the facts related to reading that they will admit to as suitable for females are the ones that go with domesticity: shopping, or visiting the clinic.

Helen drew a number of conclusions about what the school might try to improve literacy for all in the school, based on the premise that gender-typing adversely affects all children (and indeed adults) and that there is a will to remedy the situation in terms of a whole-school approach. She was careful not to create new stereotypes. The conclusions she drew about new approaches that might be tried started not from any view about 'how girls respond to literacy'. Rather, she started from the view that some children reacted in ways which depended on their own understanding of gender – and new approaches which take this into account are worth trying. She states that:

> An awareness of our own stereotypes is essential if we are to effect change. As teachers we must empower all children to achieve success; they must be allowed to develop as individuals with choices not restricted by stereotyped notions of class, race or gender appropriateness.

The conclusions that Helen drew were tentative suggestions about ways to go forward. They are only tentative suggestions, but she felt – and we agree – that her hard-pressed colleagues would welcome *not only* clearly worded practical ideas *but also* the opportunity to treat them as revisable and open to change. That is, she was working towards developing a team within the school who would work together and take the project further. In her words, she had to 'sell it to the language co-ordinators, who are the ones who actually determine the policy for the school,' and also bring in some other, energetic, new members of staff who were, she felt, more aware of gender and equal opportunity issues.

She expected that her colleagues would consider the conclusions in the light of their own knowledge and experience, undertake their own observations related to them, and try out – and rigorously evaluate – strategies based on them. In this spirit, she drew up a clear list of conclusions, and presented them to her colleagues. They are as follows:

1. There is a need for a whole-school approach to 'equal opportunities'.

2. The school needs to sensitise the parents to their significant contribution to children's views of themselves as readers. At a practical level, there is a need to consider approaches to the task of establishing and developing home–school reading schemes. Traditionally the mother figure is assigned responsibility for early literacy development, thereby helping to establish reading as a 'female' activity. The increased involvement of male role models could begin to deconstruct this notion.

3. Within school, the content of the established reading scheme needs to be examined, not only terms of the gender and other stereotypes it portrays but to ensure that the materials provide appeal to all children. Non-fiction is undoubtedly under-represented in established reading schemes. These need to be supplemented in order to cater for the interests of specific groups and individuals and to widen young children's understanding of the broad canvas that constitutes 'reading'. Whilst boys appear to be disadvantaged by their apparent reluctance to engage with fiction, girls too are disadvantaged, particularly at secondary level, by their apparent aversion to non-narrative texts. Appropriate materials and role models should help to cater for *all* interests and needs.
4. Teachers need to clarify the varied purposes and functions of reading for children. If children relate 'reading' only to 'getting jobs', and if they aspire to jobs or domestic lives where reading is of minimal importance, they will have little incentive to learn to read.
5. Teachers need to engage with those issues surrounding 'attribution'; that is the ways in which children seek to discover and explain their own success and failure. Teachers need to reconsider how much attention and verbal feedback children are given, how extrinsic, tangible rewards are allocated, and the reasons they themselves give for children's successes.

The conclusions were indeed tentative – as is clear from what actually happened next.

The world of primary schools is never the smooth-running rational world that planners take it to be. There is a need for any processes which are meant to change situations in school, to be rooted firmly in the practicalities of schools and classrooms, where there are a large number of continual unpredicted alterations, ranging from staff changes, to fluctuating government pronouncements, to illnesses, to unexpected reductions (and occasional windfalls) of resources.

In this particular school the head became ill, so Helen found herself Acting Head for, as it turned out, the whole of the next school year. Not surprisingly, her ideas for action took an unexpected turn. She was no longer able to work directly with the children she had interviewed – or indeed with a class of children. On the other hand she had more influence over policies in the school, including the use of resources and the writing of the development plan.

Looking back, and reflecting on the gender and literacy project, a year later, at first she felt disappointed that she had not been able to follow it through in the way she had originally hoped. On further reflection she realised that the school was in fact moving steadily forward in ways which were influenced by the earlier stage of the project, but the paths and destinations were not quite the ones she had originally expected.

One path forward took in issues of ownership and language policy in relation to gender and literacy. She began by picking up on a remark made by Avril, one of the newer teachers, about a book about weapons of war in the school library. She described the incident:

> Avril said to the other people in the library (who were all fairly entrenched in their attitudes) 'What do you think of this?' There was a lot of, 'Oh well, the boys like to read it', followed by 'Well, should we be letting them read it?' There was a lively discussion about it. It went back on the shelf in the end, but at least we had had the discussion, and it wasn't just 'Oh well, if you want to throw it away while you are Acting Head, then you know you can.' It was a lot more profitable.

In her position as Acting Head, she was able to draw on this incident, support Avril, and raise the issue in other meetings. The result is that the school as a whole were all a bit more aware of what the children were reading, and were more prepared to question its value not only with other staff, but also with the children. Moreover, the issue of the connections between gender and literacy were being made explicitly, in a way that seemed to have been influenced by her earlier presentation on the subject. Another path went in the direction of improving home–school links. Helen's work had sensitised her to the importance of working with the parents on literacy. In her position as Acting Head she was in a good position to work on what had been rather weak links between the school and its community. She started with reading. A booklet was produced, explaining how parents could help with their children's reading. Parents took it away, but it was hard to say how effective it was, because few of them came into school to discuss it with the teachers, no doubt just because of the existing weakness of home–school partnership. It was decided that a new start could be made with the new intake of Year 3 children. Helen reported:

> We had a much better response from them than from the parents who are established. So I think we've got to think longer term. In the meeting we touched briefly on the issue of gender, and it was interesting that there were two men in the parents' meeting, which was unusual.

Other initiatives were also started: a home–school liaison scheme was set up for a few weeks, focused on reading; coffee mornings were organised by a parent governor. The gender and literacy project has gone well beyond the initial classroom and school-focused ideas of its beginning. The new developments are almost all long-term ones, which will take time to grow and have results. Meanwhile, the interest in the issues that is being established among the staff should mean that while the growth may be rather slow, it is well rooted and strong.

The gender and literacy project is an example of how a teacher can resolve the issue of how to ensure that all social groups achieve well in school, keeping hold both of the importance of dealing with how structural injustice affects achievement and of individual empowerment. Helen's work focused on gender, but also paid attention to individuals and their empowerment. It is an example of a project undertaken by an experienced and senior teacher which focused on achievement in relation to fairness. We now turn to another carried out by a teacher near the beginning of her career.

The chocolate machine: gender and technology in the reception class

Robin has been teaching for 3 years, in a socially mixed, inner-city school. For the last two of them she has been following up a concern first raised when she was a student. She tells the story herself:

> Three years ago when I was a student I did some research. I noticed when I was watching some groups of children in school doing Design Technology that it was very much a case of the boys going 'We can do this' and the girls stood back. It was not a case of the girls saying, 'It's not for me'. In fact some of them were very keen to do it. It was not that the boys thought DT was not for the girls, more a case of just pushiness, more a case of 'I can do that, get out of the way.' So when I started in this school, I decided that I would segregate for science and DT. I found that if I gave them free choice the girls wouldn't go anywhere near the construction kits.
>
> What I did was this. Some mornings I said, 'Well, I'm sorry, but the boys just don't go near it. This table's for the girls.' I explained the girls didn't get time on the construction otherwise, that the boys tended to take over. The boys weren't that happy. It was, 'Miss, why?' and 'Oh, no, we don't!' They're not aware that they do that. They weren't very happy but they accepted it in the end. Some of the girls were keen; but for some of the girls it was, 'Well, I don't want to do this,' or they would do it for 10 minutes and then it was, 'Can we do something else?'. It depended

very much on the construction kits. If they had the one where they could build houses, those sort of things, they loved it. Things that were a bit more abstract, they weren't that keen. The boys would play with almost all the things, quite happily.

I persisted that year with giving the girls their own time. I persisted with it again this year. What I found was, when I'd done it once with the girls, they were much keener to join in and they were much keener to go to it first. It seems like they've got the ideas – they've now worked on it on their own, without somebody else barging in – they now know what to do with the construction kits. What I tend to do is still get them out for Choosing Time, and see what happens. In those times, after my input with the girls only, the girls would go to the construction kits out of free choice. After a while they'd stop again so they'd obviously need a new input.

I had an interesting one where the girls made themselves a machine for making chocolates, and I asked them to draw it on paper for me and put their names on it. The boys were really keen when they saw that, and they made their own machine and they drew their own machine. Now, if I'd set the boys that task before, they wouldn't have done it. So, because they'd seen the girls do it, and I made a lot of fuss of *them*, they were dead keen. For a while I had lots of odd machines for different things, and they were coming up to me and showing me.

Robin's description of what happened with the chocolate machine shows how both boys and girls gained from there being 'girls only' times with the construction kits. The girls gained a chance to experiment with the kits, to learn the associated language, and to experience success in the area of 'Design Technology'. The boys gained a new perspective on what could be done at the construction kit table – and they learnt new ways of recording and explaining what they were doing. Both girls and boys learnt about their own gender roles; that girls could not only enjoy playing with unfamiliar equipment, but also could be inventive and innovative in what they did with it.

Of course, everyone, adults as well as children, tends to shy away from things when they do not understand how they work or why they are doing something. Robin's strategy answers the need for this information. But what she did goes further than this, because it also addresses the problem that boys who need more information could get it from working along with a table of more experienced boys, without being too uncomfortable. The girls, on the other hand, found it hard to get time on the construction table, even if they were confident and wanted it. Robin remarked that she sometimes felt uncomfortable segregating the children by gender – and only kept it up as long as is necessary, but remained convinced it was worthwhile overall.

In her book, *Changing Classroom Cultures*, Debbie Epstein describes a similar experience, when she was Head of Infants in Bankhead school, 'a large junior and infants school serving a large, newish Council estate in a shire county' (Epstein, 1993, p.58). Some of the girls in her class complained to her that the boys would not let them play with the big bricks. The boys, for their part, insisted that 'girls don't play bricks'. After some discussion, the class agreed to the suggestion 'that there should be "girls only time" with the bricks each day' (p.114). After a few weeks the girls were producing buildings which were much admired by the boys. At this point the 'girls only' times were stopped for a while, but they had to re-establish them three more times during that year. Some boys remained resentful. Six-year-old Brian wrote: 'I think its not fair to hav girls times. bricks is for boys.' But other boys changed their minds. Six-year-old Michael wrote: 'I used to think girls don't do bricks. Now I like to play with Clare in the bricks. We make lots of good buildings.' Meanwhile the girls were able to learn from the experience of building with big bricks. They also learnt the important lesson that it was possible for them to experience success in an arena which was unfamiliar at first.

Section 11 teachers speak: raising black achievement

We have been looking at initiatives by individual teachers. We now look at another approach to improving achievement in schools and classrooms which comes from government and LEA initiatives. Section 11 projects focus on race. These projects are concerned with the achievements of black children. Thus they place an emphasis on individual empowerment, but within the context of dealing with the way that learning for black children is affected by both racism and cultural background.

Section 11 funding has been available to schools for the last 30 years. (The words 'Section 11' refer to section 11 of the Local Government Act of 1966, which was the beginning of Home Office funding towards black children's education.) Section 11 teachers are familiar figures in inner-city schools, although their jobs remain precarious. Since 1990, Local Authorities have had to bid competitively for Section 11 funding, specifying ways in which projects meet specific criteria including language skills and home–school links, though not for the maintenance of cultural traditions among ethnic minority communities. This process has been time-consuming and uncertain.

Since April 1994, funding for Section 11 projects has been further threatened by new financial arrangements. It was decided that money available for education would no longer be ring-fenced by the Home Office. Resources were transferred to the Single Regeneration Budget for promoting urban renewal, so that education projects had to bid competitively against projects which might include housing, safety, rubbish collection and large construction projects. An outcry about the effects of Section 11 cuts during 1994 led to a climb-down by the Home Office in November 1994: the Home Secretary doubled the amount that had previously been allocated, to £30 million, restoring the status quo. The money is supposed to remain available until 1996–97, but the future of the funding arrangements remains uncertain.[27] Meanwhile, Section 11 teachers in schools all over the country continue with their day-to-day work of supporting learning and achievement of black children.

Teachers employed under Section 11 described their work to us. Ray, Alex and Viv work in a number of different schools in more than one LEA. They describe what raising achievement means to them, and how they set about it. Ray said:

> I think that black culture is another part of improving achievement, and it's something we've probably neglected in these schools a bit, in the past. It means that those children do feel a sense of identity, that they need. I think we've got some way to go with that, actually, although we've done quite a lot this year, that we've not done before. We celebrated Haile Selassie's birthday, and had exhibitions round the school of black achievements and history.

For Viv, on the other hand, achievement is measured by a needs analysis carried against nationally defined levels of literacy and oracy:

> The main focus of work in this school would be on those children we felt were most in need as a result of needs analysis and the audit of language levels.

Section 11 projects are set up for children picked out by their ethnic background: for instance, Ray works on a project on African Caribbean achievement, while Viv works with Asian children. Clearly, these projects were set up to help put right structural injustices due to race relations in Britain. However, all these Section 11 teachers also place an emphasis on methods of working which enhance individual empowerment. Viv described a method of working with children, on the basis of the needs analysis, which relies on the kinds of self-reflection about learning that we used in the Fairness project:

> I've talked with those children and I've asked them, 'If I'm coming into your class – we think there's a need – how would you best want to use me? How could I best support you?'

Similarly, Alex shows a clear concern for particular individuals and how they see their education:

> When I'm on a course and people are talking about African Caribbean achievements, what I have to do is think about individual children, like Vic, or Michael. And I'm going to know the family quite well, too and the sort of backgrounds. But the interesting thing for Michael is, well he's very bright. Intellectually he's very sussed. He knows what's going on. He understands the system: how black kids fit into that system. He's still not doing very well.

Dilemmas abound for these three teachers. These dilemmas are related to what we said earlier in the chapter about, firstly, how to recognise and assess achievement and whether individual children are doing the best they can and, secondly, about dealing with strands of both 'race' and 'empowerment', without losing sight of either.

All of these teachers said that achievement was something that could not be described simply, and that it was hard to be sure when children were doing their best. Ray said:

> We have very few black children who underachieve in this school. In this school – as in this part of the country as a whole – it tends to be the Pakistani Moslem children who are lower achieving. I think it's a lot to do with class. Perhaps I'm making sweeping statements but I *feel* that a lot of the Indian children are perhaps from more middle class homes, and fewer of the Pakistani children. Obviously it's hard to categorise by social class when it's not your culture.

Alex explains another difficulty:

> The issue for teachers and Section 11 teachers in particular, as well as any mainstream teacher, is why aren't children achieving to the level they should be, looking at, well exam results, statistics, but also in terms of positive self-image and identity and all those issues.

Even Viv, who focused so closely on language levels and national standards, said that there were two ways of looking at it:

> I suppose I look at 'achieved' as having moved on, but, in project terms, you have achieved if you have met your goal, if you are working at, say,

level 5 of the National Curriculum.

One of the most difficult problems for these teachers, at least in terms of not simply viewing children as members of a social group, is explaining to children. Ray expressed it like this:

> Sometimes they say, 'Why do you only work with the brown children?' then I really try and explain what my job is. I haven't really explained it with black children, I must say. It's easier when they are bilingual kids, because you can say, 'At home they don't speak English, so they have to have extra help in school.' You feel very unfair when you're working with a particular group of children and you're working with them every week. They seem really privileged especially when they are doing craft or science or art. In some classrooms, the teachers have perhaps not got that confidence, and they don't do it unless there's somebody there to help them.

Alex echoes this:

> I would shy away from saying, 'I've come to work with Michael, because he's black and he needs help.' I can't think of a good way of explaining that to that group of children. Robina [a white girl] mentions it a lot. It's very difficult to say, 'I'm not going to work with you, but I'm going to be in the room'.

Raising achievement and improving learning

In this chapter we have been exploring what it might mean to find fair ways to raise achievement and improve learning for all the children. We explained how we teachers are all working in the dark about the real potential of individual children in our classes, even though we all make judgements about it. Equally it is not possible to be sure about how children see themselves, as members of various social groups. As a result, teachers are faced with the difficulty of finding ways of doing the best they can for all the children, but never being sure if they have managed it.

We began our Fairness project with only a foggy understanding of what the issues were. We now see more clearly that it is important to retain a double emphasis, on individual empowerment and on looking at children as members of a number of different social groups. We described four different ways of resolving the difficulties of retaining this double emphasis, ranging from learning, in our own project, to individual empowerment, to learning, in Section 11 projects, to working with children as members of particular social groups. The fog has cleared enough for us to see these beacons, but there is a lot more work to be done before the issues are quite clear. We go on to discuss issues of achievement some more, in the next chapter.

Chapter 6

SELF-IDENTITY, SELF-ESTEEM AND ACHIEVEMENT

Improving achievement: improving self-esteem

In the last chapter we looked at a number of ways of improving achievement for children, which stemmed from a concern for social justice. This has been a continuing theme of the book: in Chapter 1 we said that fairness is made up of two strands, one of which dealt with the empowerment of individuals and the other with the righting of structural injustice due to race, social class, gender, and special educational needs. Firstly, fairness in education means that each individual child grows up empowered to work out their own wants and needs in life – and to have the skills, attitudes, and knowledge to reach for them. Obviously, both the achievements of children and also their self-esteem are essential. No one can set about finding their own path through life without sufficient self-esteem to do so, and equally, they need to have the skills, attitudes and knowledge to put their plans into action.

Secondly, a fair educational system will be one in which all children achieve to the best of their potential. If one group of children – marked by gender, race, or social class – are not doing as well as an equivalent group, there is cause for concern that the system is not fair. Equally, if one group of children, marked by gender, race, or social class, have much less self-esteem than an equivalent group, there is cause for concern that the system is not fair.

Research has been directed at finding out how well children are doing, in different social groups, and how good they feel about themselves. The trouble with this research is that it does not necessarily tell individual teachers or heads what to do next, to improve things in their own classrooms and schools. The numbers and statistics that research produces are like a thermometer used by a doctor to assess the health of the patient. The differences and inequalities in achievement and self-esteem are a symptom of something wrong somewhere in the system – in the classroom, the school or the nation. We will begin by looking at the symptom, but will go on to say what can be done about the cure. As with any disease it is possible to treat the symptoms rather than look for a cure, like taking painkillers to stop a headache. But treating the symptoms will not cure the root cause (the reasons behind a chronic headache need attending to), and there is a danger of making the health of the patient worse in the long run (too many painkillers can be bad for you).

Symptoms get in the way of the patient living a normal life. (It is hard to go about your everyday life with a throbbing head.) Achievement and self-esteem are important in themselves as well as being indicators of other problems. Both are essential to children if they are to lead worthwhile lives, as we said at the start of this section. So the symptoms of underachievement and low self-esteem need to be attended to, one way or another.

Achievement: the numbers game

The National Curriculum Council document on *Equal Opportunities for All* (1990) asserts the need for schools to monitor the performance of 'constituent groups such as boys and girls and members of ethnic minorities'. We agree with them. So do a lot of other people: there is always intense interest from all sectors about the achievement of children. Rising or falling standards, the numbers of children above and below the average for their age group, the relative performance of boys and girls: all these figures are the stuff of newspaper headlines.

Behind the newspaper headlines are reports of careful research into the achievement and progress of groups of children. They show the existence of trends, and, just as importantly, the ways that individual schools make a difference to the children they teach, within those trends. MacGilchrist has written a useful short overview of this research, drawing mainly on London schools, showing that both there is a powerful link between socio-economic inequality and achievement, and also that despite background factors (1992, p.7):

> Recent studies demonstrate how schools can not only 'jack-up' achievement for all, but override disadvantage by narrowing the gap between the lowest and highest achieving groups.

Girls still tend to outperform boys across the board, at primary level, and different ethnic groups perform differently. The particular pattern of ethnic group performance tends to vary depending on which part of Britain is surveyed. In the studies carried out in London, children of Bangladeshi background performed worse than most other groups, but in studies carried out in Nottingham they did not.[28]

The situation is complicated. This is hardly surprising, since factors of gender, race and social class have all to be taken into account as well as differences of region, of LEA, and of city and countryside. Like all figures they need to be approached with particular questions, and only when they are can a great deal can be gleaned from them.[29]

So far, the studies we have referred to have all been of large numbers of schools, rather than of a single school or classroom. There is a good reason for this. A school can carry out such monitoring but, as we said in Chapter 3, statistical monitoring can show up trends, but it can say nothing about individual children. And the statistics of a single school need to be treated carefully and used tentatively, with caution. In Chapter 5 we described Helen's use of the data available to her school about reading levels. Other schools could do similar useful exercises, but the more diverse a school's catchment area, the harder it gets. Also in Chapter 5 we quoted Ray, a Section 11 teacher, explaining how hard it is to make sense of figures about achievement, when both ethnicity and social class need to be taken into consideration.

In a single classroom, there are too few children to monitor performance statistically. Statistical monitoring can only take into account the variables of social class, race and gender (to say nothing of different ethnic minority groups) by using far larger groups than are found in a single classroom. Therefore, a single class of 30 children can produce very little of use statistically, unless there is an unusual degree of uniformity of background among the children. For instance, in the first year of our project, a high proportion of the white girls were middle class, but there was only one middle-class white boy. Moreover there were very few white working-class girls – so few that it would have been foolish to make any generalisations about them as a group. Comparisons based either on gender or social class among the white children would have been statistically unsound, and therefore liable to be misleading.

Monitoring can mean something more tentative and provisional than getting and using hard statistical evidence. It can be very useful to gather numerical data in the classroom, as we have already shown. To continue with the same example of one of the classes from our Fairness project, it was easy for Morwenna to monitor the number of interactions between Carol and different groups of children (categorised by race and gender). This was done regularly, with a variety of results. In one class discussion, it was found that there was no discrepancy related to social groups. In another, it seemed that the Asian boys were quieter than all other groups.

Monitoring performance was much more problematic than monitoring interaction. For instance, it seemed that gender was a factor in determining who found it easy to work in groups. It may well have been that race, gender, social class and learning abilities were all factors: in that particular classroom, it appeared to be the white middle-class girls that found it easiest to work effectively in groups – but only with other children like themselves. The working-class white girls, on the other hand, found it easiest to accommodate difficult members in their groups without conflict, but did not always produce their best academic work as a result. Alternatively, it may have been that the particular patterns of friendship which each of the groups demonstrated affected how well they were able to deal with other group situations. This may have had nothing to do with social factors, rather depending on the individual personalities involved. Helen was equally tentative and provisional in her use of the figures related to literacy in her school.

Sorting and grading children

Over the last few years primary teachers have been embroiled in a debate about one method of gathering statistics about achievement, SATs. Debate has raged about whether to administer them, whether they are useful as they stand, what use they will be put to, and, indeed, whether any kind of national testing of 7 year olds is a good idea. Underlying the debate are a number of questions about the reasons for assessing children. On the one hand, assessment can be all the processes by which teachers learn about the educational development and progress of children. On the other hand, assessment can be a means of sorting, grading and managing children (*see* Drummond, 1994; Gipps, 1995; Gipps *et al.*, 1993).

The debate is one about values. The opposition to SATs has a principled basis. Here are some comments by Jacqui, one headteacher who is bitterly opposed to SATs, one of the current national systems of testing, not because of extra work, but because she feels they go against everything she believes in, educationally.

> We put achievements into the Merit Book. There is a certain lean to recognising academic success, but the staff have been trying to reward small acceptable acts of behaviour. It's recognised on the basis of the individual child: so we could recognise the first 50 words for spellings or finishing a story. You get some who only ever start a story – never, ever, finish a story. We also have a friendship book for the children so that they can recognise acts of kindness and things like that from among their friends.
>
> We feel that the SATs are very narrow. We feel that they're just a quick snapshot portrait of how a child is on the day, and that they give no credit at all for – or recognition to – the way the child has worked in the past, and any progress that has been made. I know it's early days yet, and obviously over a period of time they could be analysed on the basis of the progress a child has made, but because of the way they're organised we feel that some children could stay at particular levels for an inordinantly long period of time, particularly at Key Stage 2. We feel that we have worked so hard, so very, very hard, for so many years now to give children a feeling of success; and that all that these tests are bringing to us is the opportunity to give children a feeling of failure. I think that is our biggest complaint about them. You have to go on testing the children until they fail. You cannot test them until they have success and then let it be. You have to keep testing them to the next level and then they fail. I find that obscene. In the face of everything that we've done over these last 10 years, that is really the most bitter reproach I can make for them. It's an underlying ethos of failure.

Underlying Jacqui's comments about testing is a view that assessment should not be used to sort and grade children along a single, narrow line of achievement. On the other hand, Jacqui certainly approves of some forms of assessment. She says:

> I'm absolutely 100% behind moderated teacher assessment. We don't mind being moderated at all, either self-moderated or cross-school moderated, or moderated across a family of schools. We need guidance with all of that, because its all new stuff. Yes, fair enough! But we don't need this hammer on the head business with SATS.

Jacqui also uses other systems of assessment. In the earlier quotation she refers to the use of a Merit Book. She is arguing for recognition of achievements across a broad spectrum, and for the assessment of those achievements to be used to help children's progress right across that broad spectrum, rather than to grade them against standardised national tests in a few areas. In effect, she fundamentally disagrees with the view of achievement that is implicit in the SATs.

Achievement is such a slippery word that it is not surprising that its assessment leads to such difficulty. The important questions for us all – as teachers, parents, children, governors, employers, workers and citizens – are: what is achievement defined as? And, if there is a difference of opinion about this, whose definition wins out?

Achievement can be defined in terms of basic skills, of a range of academic skills or as something much broader. Even here, there is room for disagreement, for instance about what counts as a basic skill: people vary as to whether they are thinking of literacy and numeracy, or if they include IT skills, or whether they include being able to behave properly in class. Out of this disagreement comes much of the debate around the government's systems of assessment that have increasingly been part of the Education scene since the 1988 Reform Act, and around alternative systems like Records of Achievement. Again it can be seen that this kind of question is at the heart of the quotation above from Jacqui, the head bitterly opposed to SATs. Her alternative systems stem from a much broader approach to what counts as achievement.

Jacqui's approach also allows a range of people within the school – the head, teachers *and* pupils – to have a say in who has achieved well, and in what area. Chapter 5 mentioned Helen at Green Park school. Her study showed that the pupils she spoke to saw achievement as largely directed to things that would help in getting a job. She herself saw the importance of reading as something much wider, and wanted to improve achievement across the range of reading, including both imaginative and informative books. The OFSTED inspectors had looked to the results of standardised tests in reading and writing as their benchmark, and the children must have picked up their own teachers' benchmarks in their emphasis on 'levels' as an indication of success. The inspectors would necessarily be relying on the implicit views of reading to be found in standardised tests, and the children, like their teachers, were relying on implicit views of reading to be found in the reading scheme.

At national level, achievement is assessed through tests. These tests become increasingly important as a means of sorting and classifying children and schools. Inevitably they are used to identify the winners and losers in the system. While overall standards can rise for all children, the differences between the best and the worst remain important in deciding who wins out in the long run. We can't all win, so who should lose?

The truth is that tests tend to be set, chosen and given by people who are already in winning positions. Whether they realise it or not, they tend to value people who have achievements like their own. This is only natural, because their own achievements are part of their own sense of value and self-worth. It is much harder to see the value of other kinds of achievement – or ways of expressing them. Somebody who loves rugby football and Renaissance painting may fail to recognise the worth of aerobics or of the tradition of Arabic calligraphy.

People who have valued their own childhood experiences, including books, games and hobbies will want to pass those on to the next generation. Other kinds of childhood experiences may be equally valuable. People brought up with a lively sense of local history may find it hard to value the perspectives of children whose home life is rooted in the experience of international migration. There are plenty of prejudices, rooted in gender, about the value of activities stereotypically found in the opposite sex. As long as there are sections of society who are 'marginal', who do not create the resources, write the books and set the tests, then their children will find it harder to match their own sense of values and self-worth to the achievements expected of them in school. This situation gives a clue to the relationship between achievement and self-esteem.

Feeling good and doing well

How children feel about themselves – their self-esteem – has a close relationship to how children perform in school – to their achievements. We, like other teachers, can tell plenty of stories about children who have, apparently, suddenly improved on how well they are doing, as a result of an increase in their general feelings of self-esteem. And, again, we know of other children who suddenly increase in self-esteem as a result of a particular achievement. How does this knowledge of individuals fit the wider picture given by educational research into self-esteem and achievement?

There has been an enormous amount of interest in playing the numbers game about self-esteem and achievement. Much of the research has concentrated on investigating the relationship between self-esteem, achievement and other factors.[30] A puzzling pattern emerges from this research. Why is it that so-called 'marginal' groups, like girls, black people, disabled people, and members of the working class have less self-esteem in comparison with boys, white people, able-bodied people and those who come from the middle class – at least in relation to educational factors? And why is it that these 'marginal' groups are the low achievers on the whole? (We use the term 'marginal' here, rather than, say, minority, because females, for instance, are marginalised even though they make up half the population.)

We are talking about trends here. There are plenty of individuals who go against trends. Philip, a white middle-class boy, has low self-esteem: here is his teacher talking about him:

> Philip's poem was super. He was a child that was underachieving. He's the middle one and the other two are really, really superb. And often, when he's praised he doesn't take it in at all. Pauline, his Mum, and I both know this. I praise him a lot, but at first she wasn't sure I was. I'm going, 'Look, I've given it a star!' and she'd go, 'But he doesn't come and tell me!'
>
> This year he's blossomed. The older one left this school, and that's helping him. Also he's one of the top dogs in my class, academically – he's one of the oldest – and it's probably the first time in his life he's been in that position.

Philip does not fit into the trends that research identifies. As a white, middle-class boy, he 'should' have a high self-esteem, as well as being a high achiever in relation to other children. Clara, and Luther her brother, do not fit the trend either. Neither of them have any problems with self-esteem, and both of them are achieving well for their age, even though they are African Caribbean and the trends suggest that it should be otherwise. And you don't get more self-confident than Karen, a white working-class girl, who is not very good at school work. She is proud of her school work when she knows she has done her best. She speaks up to give her own views, and woe betide anyone who tries to give her a verbal put-down. She can guard her own sense of her own self-worth, and defend her friends too. However, the perplexing trends remain, as the research shows, despite individuals like Philip, Luther, Clara and Karen who do not fit the patterns shown by large-scale research.

There are two standard answers to this puzzle. One answer is that the low self-esteem of 'marginal' groups is caused by low achievement, which in turn is caused by their 'marginal' position in society. (For instance, the argument goes, working-class children achieve worse than they might in reading because of lack of books at home; girls achieve worse than they might in technology, having fewer mechanical toys.) If this answer is right, it is necessary to work on the achievements. The second answer reverses the argument. It says that 'marginal' groups in society are likely to have low self-esteem. (For instance, the argument goes, girls have learned helplessness; black children suffer from racism.) The low self-esteem causes low achievement, so it is necessary to work directly on self-esteem.

We think neither of these answers are satisfactory. We think the patterns are best understood as a symptom of the state of fairness in the country and its education system. We argue that achievement and self-esteem are both by-products, so to speak, of other factors, themselves related to social justice. These other factors include race, gender and social class. As we show in the next section, all of these factors contribute to the creation of an individual's self-identity. So they also contribute to their particular self-esteem and their particular set of achievements. The reasons for the puzzling pattern of low self-esteem and achievement in the those who are 'marginal' are best found by approaching the issue of self-esteem through understanding what produces self-identity, including how it is rooted in the communities in which children grow up.

Issues of self-esteem cannot be raised in isolation from questions of social justice in society at large, and the fairness to be found in school. In emphasising this we are returning to the third principle of fairness we stated in Chapter 1: individuals are always rooted in the groups and communities they come from. It is in social groups that children find themselves (in both senses of 'find themselves'). If particular groups experience unfairness of particular kinds, then it is not surprising that those unfairnesses contribute to their sense of self-identity.

Self-identity

Human beings each have a sense of who they are, where they are coming from, when they are most themselves: this sense is a sense of self-identity. Human beings get most of their self-identity from other people – from all the personal and social relationships they have, or don't have. Some of these are found in the family, in the way individuals relate to parents, brothers, sisters, cousins, aunts and uncles. As we said earlier, Philip is affected by his position as middle child – or so his teacher believes. Some of a person's sense of identity comes from the kind of love received from others: whether it is conditional on 'being good'. Some of it comes from the reactions of family and friends to their particular set of personal characteristics, talents and interests. Some of it comes from reactions of others to a person's physical self; to whether they are big or small, girl or boy, Chinese, African Caribbean or Asian, white or black, able-bodied or in some way disabled. All these characteristics become social because of other people's reactions to them. Other people also react to dialects and accents, to clothes and hair styles, to a person's religion (or lack of it), to the kinds of films they like to watch, and whether they are good at sport. So all these personal characteristics, too, are social, although they seem to be – and feel – so individual.

Within these relationships human beings react to other people by liking or disliking them; by including them in their set, or by rejecting them from it. They ask themselves 'Do I belong here?' 'Does he belong here?' 'Does anyone like me?' 'Do I like her?' These questions face children as soon as they go into a new class; and they continue to affect everyone, children and adults, all their lives, in all their many personal and social relationships.

Sometimes, looking for a place to belong can be painful. Foday found it very difficult negotiating where he belonged, where he wanted to belong, and where others would place him. His difficulties stemmed from his feelings about race. He was a very intelligent child whose parents came from Freetown in Sierra Leone (like many Africans from Freetown, they spoke English as their first language). His mother was, in the words of his teacher, 'a lovely lady', but had had to put her child into care when he was a toddler, while she sorted out her own problems with her violent husband. The child had been passed from one carer to another, and by the time he came back to his mother, his behaviour was really difficult for both her and his teachers to handle. In the end, at the age of 9, he was sent for play therapy by an Educational Psychologist, and it all came out that he did not want to be black. All his friends were white – and since he was so intelligent, he found himself gravitating to high-achieving children in his class, who were mostly white and middle class. He felt that being black was a big problem, and a disadvantage to him, because, he remained convinced, people would not be able to accept him for himself, but would always regard him as different, as black.

This complex problem arose from the particular set of circumstances in which he found himself: the procession of (mostly white) carers when he was young; the small proportion of African or African Caribbean children in his school; and the differences between his own home life and that of the middle-class children who were his friends. This set of reasons for his difficulties only make sense because, as we all know, they occur against the background of our racist and class-ridden society which sees colour and social class as significant and reacts to individuals accordingly.

Echoes of the difficulties that Foday faced are to be found in the experiences of Mosiah who we discussed before, in Chapters 1 and 3. They are also to be found in the experiences of Shaibu and of David, who were first mentioned in Chapter 4. All of these children had to find ways of negotiating their own sense of who they were (whether or not they were glad to accept their own ethnicity, as most of them were) and how others would react to that perception.

Ways of dealing with feelings of belonging or not relate to gender and social class as much as to race. Morwenna's journal entry at the beginning of Chapter 4 mentions Kaneez, and her desire to keep within her friendship group, made up of Asian girls, and her simultaneous desire to express herself aggressively (as boys in her class, of all ethnic groups, were able to do.) She needed to negotiate a group – or set of groups – for herself where she felt at home, even though she did not fit 100% into any one of them.

Teachers can help. An example is provided by Springfield school where Jacqui is head. In Springfield, children who had always played games in rigidly gender-demarcated groups, were enabled to express their individuality by playing games with the opposite sex if they wanted to, without risking being ostracised for it. When Jacqui took over as head, the school had previously only taught football and netball. Both sports were supposedly for both sexes, but no boy dared choose netball, any more than any girl would choose football. The staff introduced a series of new sports including basketball and skipping. From the beginning it was pointed out to the children that basketball, though apparently so much like netball, is played by very fit men; moreover, skipping – which up to then had been considered to be a girls' game for the playground – was used by boxers, runners, and footballers as a stamina training activity. Soon the children could be observed skipping in mixed groups in the playground. The basketball team was made up of both boys and girls. The football and the netball continued to be single sex, as before. Meanwhile, more new mixed games, including athletics and orienteering games, have been introduced, and are steadily gaining in popularity with all the children.

We have talked about race and gender as reasons for belonging (or not) in groups. Let us look at this process more closely. People can think of themselves as individuals, as members of small groups where everyone knows everyone else, and as members of large groups where no one could know all the other members personally. Some of these groups, whether they are small or large, are those defined by structures of a society – gender, race, social class, and age. There is no choice about being a member of such a group.

There are other sorts of groups which are those defined by membership, where individuals choose to belong, or feel that they belong: 'our sort of people'. 'Our sort of people' is defined by family and friendship, shared interests and shared ways of seeing the world. It may be also be defined by gender, race, social class, sexuality and age, in so far as an individual identifies as a member. Foday plainly wanted to opt out of being 'black'. He did not think of this group as being 'our sort of people', whatever anyone else thought. Kaneez, on the other hand, demonstrated by her choices of friend that both gender and race were important to whom she thought of as 'our sort of people'.

Children may be able to identify 'our sort of people' with quite a high level of sophistication. Carol remembers reading *Bill's New Frock* to a group of Year 6 children. It is about a boy who wakes up to find himself a girl. When the children discussed the book they began by saying that it was sexist. When they were asked to consider why it had been written, especially in view of the fact that it is a modern book, the girls (though not the boys) were able to dig deeper. While the boys just decided that they did not want to be girls, some of the girls were able to explain quite a complex position. They said that they wanted to be respected, that there wasn't anything stopping them from doing boys' things, but, they went on, they wanted to be girls and they were proud of being girls, and at times they wanted to do girls' things.

Social groups begin to affect us from the day of our birth. Consider two babies, born this year, in a single city in Britain, in the same month. One is the first child, a boy, called Neil. Another, Sean, also a boy, has an elder sister. Each one is growing up with adults and other children – with whom he is developing close relationships.

It cannot be overestimated how much it matters to the sense of self, whether a baby is loved and accepted in the family. So it matters that both these babies were welcome. It also matters how Sean's sister reacts to him – and that Neil is, so far, an only child. But how important are gender, social class, disability and race for Neil and Sean? These factors appear from the first. Within the family the implications of belonging to wider groupings such as gender soon make themselves felt to any child. The importance placed on gender is shown by the fact that the first question about a baby tends to be 'Is it a boy or a girl?'. It is hard to imagine a mother or father who does not place any importance on the sex of their children. Moreover, the rest of the world certainly does attach importance to it.

Similarly, race is significant to these small babies born in Britain. Neil is white. He will not learn this for some time. Sean is of mixed race. His mother is African Caribbean, his father is white. He will learn the significance of this quickly, both from his parents, and from others. In her autobiographical series of articles, a successful New York lawyer, Patricia Williams, describes the bitterness of discovering as a small child that she was 'coloured' (insultingly, from her white friends) as well as Negro (as her family had told her she should be proud to be). She says that she has spent her life 'recovering from the degradation of being divided against myself' (Williams, 1993, p.120). We imagine that a similar unhappiness affects some of the children we teach, like Foday, or Mosiah.

Social class is another thing for Neil and Sean to discover. In fact both their parents are middle-class professionals. It would be a different world for them if their parents were shop workers or cleaners. Neil and Sean cannot escape learning this. Nobody in Britain can escape it, in the end. Carolyn Steedman, now a successful historian of education, describes, with lasting anger, learning her social class membership from a middle-class health visitor. She was 4 years old. It was just after her sister was born. The health visitor had looked at the bare floorboards and curtainless windows and said, 'This house isn't fit for a baby' (Steedman, 1986, p.2).

Children vary in how much importance they attach to the fact that they are boys or girls, or to their race, religion and social class. However, all children will learn, very quickly indeed, that they are seen as sexed and gendered beings. Many of them will learn as quickly about the significance of their race, religion or social class. In most cases, they also actively try to belong, working out what membership means – what it is to be 'our sort of people'. This means negotiating the different messages that come from parents, siblings, television, friends, grandparents, neighbours, books, videos, and the general public. Children's gender, race and social class memberships depends on how they receive these messages.

Soon enough, Neil and Sean will be grown up enough to go to school. Even if their gender was not thought particularly significant at home, it will be important at school. Social class, race, disability and sexuality (though only dimly understood at first, through jokes and insults, as we explained in Chapter 4) all make their presence felt. Black children, for instance, are likely to encounter racial remarks early on. In Debbie Epstein's (1993) case study of Badminton Middle school, a turning point for the staff was the evidence provided by the deputy head's interviews with black children. In this predominantly white school, the children told him how they hated multicultural assemblies, or pictures of Zulus in books. He was told by the children (Epstein, 1993, p.68):

> about the prevalence of racist jokes and one of the girls remembered vividly 'the first coloured joke when she was 4. It was made by another 4 year old.'

Increasingly, each child has to make more decisions about belonging – about where to find their sort of people. When Alice first went to school, she suddenly lost her previous ambition to be a doctor. She told her mother that girls were nurses. Her mother was rather upset at this and pointed out that girls could be doctors, they needn't be nurses, and that the child's Aunt Mary was herself a doctor. To her mother's consternation, the child replied that if she couldn't be a nurse, then she wanted to be a farmer's wife. She had learnt her lessons about belonging, not from her mother, and not from the teacher, but rather from all the other sources of information in school about who her kind of people were. (This child has now become a young woman studying medicine: early lessons can be re-learnt.)

In any group, there are those who are only just accepted into it by the other members. The rest of the group may be uncertain about how far to include those on the edges. This means that those on the edges know that their acceptance may be conditional on their conforming to group norms. That is, they are likely to have to pretend to be exactly like the rest, at the cost of hiding their real feelings and lying about themselves. Think of Naz, the university student first described in Chapter 4, lying about what she did at the weekend. Think of the boys at Jacqui's school who can only now admit to liking skipping with the girls.

Sometimes, the things that lead to someone being accepted or rejected had not previously been taken as being of any particular significance by the individual concerned – or at least, they had not seemed significant until they made a difference to group membership. For instance, small children may not have realised the importance of race or religion to their self-identities, but they suddenly realise this at school (even if they can not explain it in words). Listen to this infant teacher who was describing how children form groups in her class. She is a teacher who mixes her approach to seating the children so that sometimes they sit with friends and sometimes they have to mix with all the other children:

> If you get one Asian girl on her own, which I've been given a couple of times, unless they were a strong personality they find it very hard. They

> feel not part of everything. One girl actually retreated into herself quite a lot, until two other girls came up together from the nursery. Then I saw a different child.

If race and gender become the reason for acceptance or rejection it becomes increasingly crucial to the child's sense of self – even if it had not seemed important before.

Acceptance in a group strengthens the bonds. It is often thought that this is only true for minority groups – like the Asian girls in the infant school. This is not so. Consider the boy choosing to act masculine (as he understands 'masculine'). He has chosen a group where he belongs. He then works to maintain this group membership, by distancing himself from all girls and not very masculine boys. He needs to do this particularly vigorously if he is insecure about how masculine he himself appears. Notice, for instance, how often the jokes and insults which groups of boys enjoy depend on gender. Ten-year-old Luther had a problem with this culture of masculinity. He liked Kim, but the only way he could express this was by calling her nasty names, and being really horrible to her. Kim, for her part, quite liked Luther but she disliked being called names. The situation got so difficult that the school had to intervene. However, finally, in Kim's words, they 'worked out how to be nice to each other'. Apparently the compromise included the two of them undertaking various activities together – but only when there were none of his male friends around to embarrass him. The culture of masculinity which caused the problem in the first place has been barely challenged. Luther will continue to be hampered in his social relationships by his gender.

Problems arise for children who do not fit into groups where they want to belong. One strategy is trying to 'pass' – to use the American term. Girls can try to become 'honorary males'. They risk being ostracised as not properly feminine, and facing all the insults that go along with this judgement. Black children can try to become 'honorary whites' – what other black people call 'coconuts' or 'Bounty Bars', insulting terms which are supposed to indicate that the person is white on the inside, although black on the outside. Foday was all set to become an 'honorary white', and he risked facing these insults from other black people. Naz had taken this step in primary school, and was trying to undo it, years later, at university, after she had discovered that it was never going to be a complete resolution to the dilemmas of race and racism in which she found herself.

Another strategy is to abandon the attempt to join the group. The result of this is that whatever it was that caused the rejection in the first place – be it race, social class, gender or disability – is made that much more powerful in the developing sense of self-identity. Shaibu's experience is relevant here. At 8 years old, he has learnt that being proud of being black goes along with being deeply hurt by racial insults. He is unable simply to be black, without defending himself, without it being a continual issue. Protestant or Catholic children have the same sort of problem as Shaibu, if they live in Northern Ireland, though their cousins on the mainland are likely to avoid facing it.

In effect, people in a position where they have either to 'pass' or to be rejected are asked to make decisions about how far to be their own real selves. They choose which goals to aim for, depending on who they think they are. If the goal requires them to leave part of themselves behind, then in choosing it they choose falseness. If they choose not to try and achieve that goal, they abandon that part of the self that wanted it, and again they choose falseness. The choices children make at primary school will affect the kinds of choices they make at secondary school. The Macdonald Report describes the way that Ahmed Ullah, the boy murdered in the playground, was trying to negotiate the difficulties of identifying as both Asian and good at school (Macdonald, *et al.*, 1989). Tony Sewell describes similar difficulties facing African Caribbean boys in a secondary school, and the way that many of them find that they achieve little at school, despite having a positive attitude to education (Sewell, 1995).

This has been a long section and it will be helpful to summarise it. Very briefly indeed: we have said that self-identity is the result of a continuing process of negotiation over finding 'our sort of people'. This can lead to feelings of confidently 'being myself' or unhappily having to pretend.

Self-identity, self-esteem and achievement

Only a few of the judgements about 'our sort of people' are related to achievement. Acceptance comes from being one of a family, a class, or a community, being the 'right' sex, social class, or colour, and sharing both fun and work. Only a few of these are affected by achievements. All of them affect the child's self-esteem. Being loved or rejected, or being in a position to love or reject others, affects how lovable children seem to themselves. Thus the social relationships an individual makes are *both* the source of self-identity, and *also* the source of self-esteem.

Children who believe themselves to be lovable regardless of any particular achievements, will be able to value whatever it is that they can do. The logic goes: 'I am loved and valued, therefore what I do is good,' rather than 'What I do is good, therefore I am loved and valued.'

If children feel that a part of themselves is left outside the circle when they join a group, then to that extent they will feel that part of themselves has been de-valued by the group. This has bad effects on both their self-esteem and on their ability to perform wholeheartedly to a high standard in school. It also means that some of their experiences (and achievements which depend on drawing on those experiences) are left out from what counts as an achievement at all.

Raising both achievement and self-esteem

We began the chapter by remarking on research into the numbers of children in different social groups achieving well, and feeling good about themselves: the image we used was of a thermometer, assessing the health of the education system. We have shown, in the course of this chapter, that the symptoms of underachievement and low self-esteem among some social groups are in fact symptoms of the same disease: too little fairness both in the school system and in the social system of which schools are a part.

The disease produces more than one symptom – like a virus causing both a headache and a stomach upset. A cure lies elsewhere than in reducing symptoms by working on them directly.

We have already discussed some ways of improving fairness in the school. In the rest of the book we go on to look at some other areas, including management of the whole school, curriculum planning and work forming links with the homes and the wider community. The theme of the importance of self-identity underlies all of this.[31] Evaluating such work can go on in the individual schools and classrooms where it happens. However, it is equally important that, at local authority level and at national level, statistics are collected: to return to the original image, the temperature needs to be taken to check on the health of the patient.

Chapter 7

CHANGING SCHOOLS

Management, change and fairness

So far we have been focusing on the classroom. There is another aspect of making schools fairer places, for children and also for staff. This is at the level of the whole school – and the way it is managed.

The management of a school is a very important part of getting fairer schools. This can get overlooked. Sometimes, in the hurly burly of simply getting things done in a busy school, the relationship of management to fairness can get forgotten. As the pace of change has increased over the last decade, considerations of deeper issues of social justice have sometimes lost out in comparison to surviving the next crisis or responding to the next initiative. Schools are living in what Mike Wallace and Agnes McMahon have called 'Turbulent Times' (1994). But, overlooked or not, fairness and management are inextricably linked.

In the book so far, we have focused on the way that fairness is brought about by attention to individuals and groups, in an atmosphere of trust and respect, valuing each other for who they are. This atmosphere is just as important for the teachers as it is for the children. They too need to be treated – and to treat each other – with trust and respect. Teachers need to value each other, both as individuals and as members of the various social groups to which they belong. Such an atmosphere comes about from the way the school is managed.

There are two other reasons for the inextricable linking of fairness and management in schools. Firstly, teachers in a badly managed school have not got the space to be fair to children or to each other. They are too busy dealing with chaos, and with the feelings of crossness, frustration and mutual suspicion that go along with bad management. Secondly, the way a school is managed affects anyone wanting to make moves towards greater fairness, in the classroom or in the school as a whole. Some schools easily make changes, and the staff feel excited and energised in the process. Other schools get stuck, and the overall sameness that results makes the staff feel more dull and tired than they would in a moving, changing school.[32]

Management is not just about headteachers and their deputies. To emphasise this, the next section starts with a story where the main characters are neither headteachers nor deputies. It is fiction – but it is fiction which is based on a true story. The person who wrote it preferred it to be in this form, for a number of reasons that seemed good to her and good to us.[33]

The diary of a middle manager (head of Keystage 2 – 'B' allowance). Aged 44¾

The swimming saga

MONDAY SEPTEMBER 5th – Our systems manager came to see me and said there was a problem with swimming for this year. Basically we've got 5 swimming sessions for our 8 junior classes. The senior management and head have suggested that we should concentrate on sending the lower juniors so that we attempt to get all children swimming the magical National Curriculum 25 metres. Can I sort it out with the Keystage 2 staff? (Well this is really an instruction, not a question, so suppose I'd better call a meeting.)

TUESDAY SEPTEMBER 6th – Working lunch to discuss the start of the year. I raised the problem of swimming and mentioned the message I'd had from the senior management, carefully remembering that the systems manager is part of the Keystage 2 team and asked for comments and suggestions. Not much was said. The lower junior staff were happy to take the four Friday sessions so they could swim every week, and they said they'd go away and make a timetable and contact parents to come and observe, and the upper juniors said they would take the one Thursday session and develop a programme to take the children who were struggling at swimming. Well that seemed easy enough. Perhaps I can get on with sorting the Assembly timetable.

WEDNESDAY SEPTEMBER 7th – Isobelle came to see me, complete with swimming timetable for the lower juniors and a list of parent helpers who had been pressurised, sorry nicely persuaded, to be our observers. Great! We're all set for next week.

THURSDAY SEPTEMBER 15th – Tony caught me on the way home. He'd just come back from the first upper junior swimming session. He said that he and the upper junior staff weren't happy with the swimming allocation and they wanted more time. I gritted my teeth and smiled while thinking, 'Why didn't you think about this back at the meeting?'

FRIDAY SEPTEMBER 16th – I called a quick junior meeting to discuss the swimming problem. The lower juniors said that they had already arranged the parents and children for the term but would it help if they took three sessions on a Friday and organised a rota so the classes swam every three out of four sessions? This was acceptable. Isobelle said she had been going to sort out the maths scheme books – but she'd do a new timetable and see if she could re-organise the parents instead.

WEDNESDAY SEPTEMBER 21st – Isobelle came with the new swimming timetable and arrangements so perhaps now we can get on with some of the other jobs.

FRIDAY SEPTEMBER 30th – Swimming seems to have gone without a hitch this week. Thank goodness.

MONDAY OCTOBER 3rd – Well I spoke too soon! Our systems manager came to see me. There's been some kind of problem. We've lost our Thursday afternoon swimming time, even though we put in a bid for more time. So swimming will have to alter again. And this time the head has decided that all children will go swimming so the upper and lower junior classes will have to take two swimming sessions each and swim every other week. All this over swimming! What a waste of time! What am I going to say to Isobelle?

This diary is fiction, a small amount of poetic licence with reference to a rather more famous fictional diary. The story it discusses, though, is true, and is probably one which is being played out in a variety of forms in educational institutions up and down the country. It's one of those small, niggly management situations that seems to grow all out of proportion, causing stress to staff and often upset to the children; it is often the result of the lack of management skills within our schools and inability to see how apparently small management decisions and changes have wide reaching consequences and affect a whole variety of people. Isobelle was fed up of having to go over old ground and re-do jobs she'd already done rather than work on new, important tasks. The head of Keystage 2 was similarly fed up with people changing their minds both at senior management level and from the classroom floor. The children and parents were probably equally fed up not knowing when they were actually going swimming; more parents contacted school or came in school over this one issue than any other during the month when the saga was being played out.

Managing fairly and managing well

But what has this story to do with fairness? How decisions are made is a central issue of fairness. When people decide to do something – or fail to make any decisions at all – their reasons involve principles. The diary writer's actions were all done for reasons. It is no accident that she gritted her teeth and smiled at Tony. It is no accident that she called a meeting the next day to discuss the problem. The principles underlying the reasons that she did these things involve issues of fairness: respect for others, recognition of the need for democratic decisions, a wish not to upset anyone, a desire to have the problem resolved with as little hassle as possible. Some of these principles are fair ones. Others are unfair. It is entirely likely that the diary writer would not easily be able to explain her reasons, let alone the underlying principles. People are only rarely able to explain their reasons and even more rarely the principles on which they are based. However, they still act for reasons, and on principles, whether those reasons and principles are fair ones or not.[34]

Principles then are also involved in the way changes are made. The following issues are all related to how fair a school is: who makes the decisions; why the decisions are made; how decisions are communicated; how the effects are felt; how the effects are communicated back to those who made the decision; and the results of that communication. Management theorists talk about making decisions and communicating them, but hardly ever do they tackle the problem of holding onto values in the midst of upheaval, which is the normal situation for primary schools.

Management theorists used to talk as if making changes was a matter of making rational judgements about well understood situations. In their investigation of *Planning for Change in Turbulent Times*, Mike Wallace and Agnes McMahon (1994) usefully review a number of management models, showing how the emphasis on rationality is now giving way to models which acknowledge the speed of external changes in schools, but which still do not recognise the number of constraints, combined with lack of information about the future, that primary schools have to deal with. Values, where they are included at all, come in at the stage of agreeing a mission: they appear as part of agreeing and clarifying goals. However, the aim is really for management to be 'more effective'. But this is an oversimplification on the part of the theorists. The three principles of fairness that we introduced in Chapter 1 are as important for management as they are for classroom interactions. They appear at all stages of management.

The first principle of fairness emphasises the two strands of fairness; the empowerment of individuals and the need to deal with the existence of structural injustice due to race, class and gender. The second principle emphasises that the processes of interaction are as important as the results. The third recognises both the value of each individual and the way that each individual is rooted in their community. Obviously, if individuals do not feel recognised and valued, or if they feel that they are systematically excluded they will not work well in any system that has been devised, however sensible and rational it is. So fairness is, in fact, more effective, as a way of management. But it is also important for its own sake. As one teacher said, when writing her personal priorities for the next year, in relation to her input to her School Development Plan: 'Standing firm on what I believe in: I must remember this.' Another teacher put that she must focus on 'having a voice': both of these teachers are reminding themselves that getting through the business efficiently is *an* important, but not the *most* important, aspect of their jobs.

It is a pity that the many books on educational management and change that have hit the bookshelves in recent years barely recognise what these two teachers see so clearly. Their authors persist in writing as if management is divorced from principles like fairness, justice or equality, even though they cannot avoid using words like 'empowerment' or 'ownership'. This chapter aims to redress the balance a little.

Over the last few years, the management side of schools has grown beyond recognition. Indeed it is quite rare to find a headteacher nowadays who has the time and energy to get down to some 'real' teaching and takes a class. More and more they are becoming the business person in an office, who with a bit of luck may be available to take the odd assembly just to show the children that they really do exist. This isn't necessarily their own choice, but has been a side effect of schools being asked to take over more of their own management.[35]

This growth in the awareness of the need to develop management issues is further reflected in the changing nature of teachers' additional responsibilities. It is found that many deputies are taking duties on board that once belonged to the head; more schools are establishing a senior management and middle management system; and incentive allowances are often being awarded to teachers to develop administration and financial systems. Thus in many schools staff are involved with budgeting, auditing, ordering, personnel, human resources and staff development, on similar lines to large companies and businesses. This is quite a change from what happened when we both first began teaching. On the whole, staff are no longer awarded the higher incentive allowances for being responsible for a curriculum area; more often curriculum areas are being developed by groups or task forces, or even in some schools, by individual staff for no extra gain apart from it being 'good for the c.v.'. Indeed the expectation now is that everybody should be involved with the development of curriculum areas, and allowances should only be awarded for wider areas or special projects. This isn't necessarily a bad thing, but it is important to notice the knock-on effects. What it means is that schools are putting a much greater emphasis on management issues, as staff learn how to run a school, and it suggests that there is a growing awareness of the need to develop management skills in our schools for them to make progress. It is important, therefore, that there is a recognition of the way fairness and management are related.

In the rush to think about management it is important to remember the question of where the children fit into all this. What effect do management decisions and changes have on the children? How can the managers of a school ensure that change is both fair to the staff and improves fairness to children? They will need to make sure that the change is being appropriate to the needs of the children both as individuals and as members of social groups. How can they do this?

On a superficial level some people may say: what does management matter? It is what the children are taught and how they are taught that matters – not the management of school. However, this *is* superficial: teaching and the management of schools are intertwined. Decisions made at management level do affect the children and do affect what is taught and how. Indeed on closer examination most, if not all, management decisions will affect the children either directly, or indirectly, whether it is the employment of a new mid-day supervisor, a decision on class sizes, groupings of classes and room allocations, or a decision on which curriculum area is to be developed with staff and children, even down to a decision on who should go swimming. The question about swimming, as we showed, not only involved time and energy, but involved decisions related to who should go, and why: the needs, merits, and entitlements of lower and upper juniors (to use the language of theories of social justice – *see* Chapters 1 and 11). There is also a race, gender and social class angle to this decision, since some children could easily go swimming in out-of-school times, but others could not, given constraints on them of poverty or cultural factors, related to both ethnicity and gender.

We are not saying it is easy to manage a school or to make changes. From the head's point of view, it is impossible to please everybody: the head's place is in the wrong. Michael Fullan, in his excellent book on managing educational change quotes this old joke (Fullan, 1991, p.144):

Mother (calling upstairs in the morning):
It's time to get up for school.

Chris I'm not going to school!

Mother Why not?

Chris Because everyone at the school hates me – the teachers, the kids, the caretaker – they all hate me!

Mother You have to go. You're the head!

We frequently hear teachers say, 'I wish my head was more decisive. I just want to be told what to do!' But then in the next breath the same teachers can be heard to say 'I don't think much to that decision. It's obvious they have been away from the class for ages. Don't they realise that's not appropriate to our children's needs? Why didn't they ask us?' On the other hand, from the point of view of the teachers, senior management may only pretend to consult. They may delegate a particular change to be developed by a group or individual, such as the development of an anti-bullying policy, or of a Record of Achievement – and then may not like the results. Likewise, they may ask for staff's ideas and viewpoints when making changes but have really decided what they want to do anyway. As a result, it can seem hardly worth the risk of putting forward contrary views, and, as a result, the head honestly believes there is agreement and consensus where actually there is none.

However, not withstanding the difficulties of fair management, it is important to try. No matter on what level, or how big or small the decision, it is important that the management of the school take into account how their decisions affect everyone. It is important that everyone makes a contribution to the decisions which affect them, even if on occasion it is quite a small contribution. This is what the empowerment of individuals is about. This is how narrowness of perspective in terms of race, social class and gender can be reduced. As an example we'll consider a recent initiative, of exactly the kind of thing that schools need to respond to, and of the kind where it is easy to fall into the trap of thinking that it has nothing to do with issues of fairness or of social justice. The initiative we consider is the Dearing 20%. The school we describe is Pear Dale.

The 20% solution

The story of 'the Dearing 20%' all began with the publication of the Dearing Report, and the indication of yet more changes to the National Curriculum, hopefully this time to slim it down and make it more workable for schools and class teachers. The implication of this of course was, in fact, *more* work for teachers to familiarise themselves with yet more new documentation and changes, and then to work this into and modify present planning within Pear Dale, possibly a big task involving the school in major changes.

Middleland LEA had to respond as follows to the publication of the Dearing Report. It is an LEA with a variety of schools, some rural and some city, some multi-ethnic and some largely white and monocultural. They had to devise a way of helping this varied set of schools. A meeting for senior teachers was run by the local inspectorate to highlight and discuss the implications of the Report and of the proposals for the new National Curriculum to be introduced in September 1995. The inspectors recommended that schools spent time over the next coming year on a number of issues. These included: an examination of how schools are going to use the 20% of time that will be 'made available' for them to teach subjects that they value, possibly outside of the National Curriculum guidelines; familiarisation with the 'new' National Curriculum; the examination and modification of reports, records and assessment procedures to take account of the changes; and the development of a plan for the future by the whole staff, so that the school 'creates a vision for the future'. This plan, it was recommended, should identify the skills and experiences a school wants its children to have, and be useful in developing a long-term planning structure to ensure this occurs.

This is all very well, but how does such a complex and large task get done in such a way that fairness is observed? It is easy enough to say that what is needed is consultation, trust and respect. It is much harder to find a way of achieving it. All schools hold meetings, but, as we said earlier, only a few of these meetings are genuinely consultative. Some staff just wish that the meeting would be over, and that somebody would tell them what to do. Others think that it is not worth putting forward a point of view if it is only going to be ignored, so they stay silent. Meanwhile the head and senior management know that ultimately they are responsible and accountable for whole school decisions. They also know that they are in possession of all the relevant information, which the rest of the teachers are likely only to have understood in part. Think of the swimming problem. The silence that greeted the original decision on 6 September was broken only on 15 September. What was the cause of the silence? It is a silence that is heard in so-called consultative meetings in schools all over England.

Consultation, trust and respect are as difficult to implement at the level of a school as they were with the children in the classroom during the Fairness project described in earlier chapters. Senior teachers tend to think they know what the rest of the teachers think, just as teachers tend to think they know what the children think, and in both cases they are only partly right. It is not possible to see the process by which Development Plans are being constructed in different schools by looking at the completed documents. It will be easy to see which ones of them have, in fact, been arrived at fairly, by seeing how much real difference they make to the future of the school.

Eleanor, a senior teacher working in Middleland, described what happened in Pear Dale school where she teaches. The school is large with over 400 children and 30 staff. It also has a high percentage of incentive allowance holders and it is therefore able to operate a tiered management structure with senior and middle management. This means it has sufficient staff for planning teams and task forces to be able to work together. She describes the school as having a history of empowering staff to make changes, and to help the school develop forward.

She attended the inspectors' meeting and reported it back to the head and other senior management and went on to suggest that they work this into the development of their 3-year management plan, and that they organise a staff meeting to inform other staff of the inspectors' recommendations. The response to this was positive. The senior management were optimistic about this initiative, and about the chances of implementing it fairly. It was felt that the whole staff needed to know what was happening and what they had to do. It was also felt that the staff as a whole should be part of the planning process, and should be given time to discuss any concerns and opinions they had, so these could be taken into consideration in future development. Although there was optimism, they all felt that it could be a big task. They had all been through the anxieties of the first introduction of the National Curriculum and remembered the rush that it felt. This time there was the feeling that there was a greater opportunity to plan how they wanted their school to be. So they agreed that they wanted to do it properly and not to rush things. They decided to give the staff plenty of advance warning and take up to a year working through the inspectors' recommendations. To be clear about all this, they organised a day just for the senior management team, to put together an outline draft plan for the 3-year management plan and to discuss possible ideas for introducing and developing this work with the whole staff.

At this stage, in the summer of 1994, Eleanor felt that although everybody in the senior management team was reacting favourably and saying that staff should be empowered and a part of the decision-making process, there were some members who perhaps already had a set vision on what the outcome should be. She hoped that they would listen to what the staff had to say. She was also concerned that if the rest of the staff felt as she did, that they would not express themselves openly. She discussed all this with Glyn, another senior teacher on the team, who responded that his fear was the opposite one, that the staff would be so sick of initiatives and changes that they would have neither the energy nor the inclination to participate in the making of the plan.

The senior management meeting took place at the end of June. There was an INSET day scheduled for July, to allow staff to work in their planning teams to plan for the new academic year. It was therefore felt that it would be an ideal opportunity to raise the issues voiced by the inspectorate and to discuss curriculum development and changes that the staff would need to explore over the next year. However, the senior management team were also aware that there were some heavy and difficult issues to introduce, especially at the end of a summer term, so they thought it was important for staff to be given time to think about these. It was decided to introduce the issues and the long-term planning proposals in the weekly staff meeting prior to the INSET day. The July INSET day then went ahead, and was followed by a staff meeting in the September of the Autumn term to discuss the 'Dearing 20%', in which a time exercise, suggested by the National Curriculum Council (NCC), was carried out (NCC, 1993). This involved the staff in working out the total time available in the school day and the time spent on the National Curriculum and other areas such as collective worship and assemblies. Staff worked together in their planning teams and it was indicated to the staff that the intention of the exercise was not to come up with a set number of hours that should be spent teaching National Curriculum subjects and other subjects, as such a system would not match the wide needs of the children in the school. The intention was rather that staff were made aware of how they spent their time at present.

Both Eleanor and Glyn had some of their fears realised, as can be seen by looking back over the processes of the meetings. On the other hand, since the fears sprang from a genuine wish to improve the fairness of both the processes and the outcomes, it was possible to move forward from what happened next and improve the processes of management within the school.

Glyn had thought that the staff would be so sick of initiatives and changes that they would not have the energy to participate in the making of the plan, nor would they want to.

In their meeting the senior management had outlined a timetable of developments that they thought would be appropriate to meet the challenges of the changing National Curriculum. This was to be introduced to the staff with the proviso that it was a flexible structure and would be open to change depending on staff and school needs. However, all this had to be discussed by the staff in an hours' staff meeting, at the end of the school day, or at the July INSET day, which meant doing it on the very same day when the details of work for the next academic year had to be decided.

The staff meeting was difficult in terms of the weight of issues. Moreover, it involved staff having to do a lot of listening on a hot July evening. There was a mixed response. Some staff were ready to go home. Some staff had queries on the format that the changes would take and what the specific requirements were in teaching the National Curriculum. (These were questions that could not be answered until the documents were published 6 months later, in January 1995.) It seemed that they wanted to be told details, rather than discuss arrangements that were still flexible. There were some staff who said they thought it was important that the staff actually took time to discuss the whole complex issue. However, time was hard to come by. During the INSET day there was no time to look at developing the school structure in the way envisaged and recommended by the inspectors. There was also the feeling that it was not worth it because of all the new changes in the pipeline. Instead the staff focused on what to do immediately, even though this would be a temporary stop-gap, to ensure an appropriate level of overlap and progression among classes. To some extent, it was clear that Glyn had been right in his worries about staff enthusiasm and desire for participation.

Eleanor, on the other hand, had been concerned that, although everybody in the senior management team was reacting favourably and saying that staff should be empowered and a part of the decision-making process, there were some members who perhaps already had set ideas about what the outcome should be.

The time exercise which was carried out in the September staff meeting showed that some of her worries were justified. When the planning teams who had been working came back together and were asked for comments for discussion as a whole school, the response was very disappointing. The animated discussions from the group work fell into silence and very little was said. Eleanor later reflected that the discussion had been flowing freely in the teams because the staff had been working in the same teams for at least a year, longer in some cases, and therefore they had felt secure to reflect and discuss areas of weakness and areas to be improved. It is something else to talk about these issues in an open forum in front of the whole staff. She realised that her worry was two-fold. Not only might the management have set ideas prior to the consultation process, but also the staff might not feel confident to discuss weaknesses or to question management decisions. Moreover, they needed to know that their ideas were genuinely wanted and would be listened to when making changes and that it was not just some sham exercise.

Eleanor found herself in the same position that we had been in relation to the children in the classroom during our project. There is a question of trust when consulting with staff, even in a school like hers, where, as she described it, there is a lot of commitment, co-operation and a tradition of working together to move the school forward.

At the end of the July meeting she asked if people minded her feeding back some of the comments she had overheard to the rest of the senior management, without saying who had said what. Staff were happy for her to do this. She also indicated that the purpose of the time exercise was not to get at the staff about time-keeping, or any other related issue, and she re-emphasised that it was to explore how they spend their time at present so they could look at the 20% question and ensure they did not fritter away time but used it effectively.

As she reflected on the process over the summer holiday, she became further concerned that there were several questions that needed answering as a result of the July staff meeting, and that staff views were needed so that the next step forward could be made. With the thought that many of the staff might need to feel safe before expressing their views openly, she decided to give the staff a questionnaire in early October, which she hoped would allow them to express their opinions. The questionnaire was anonymous and staff were told that their ideas would be discussed by the senior management and taken into account when designing the next phase of development. There were four questions and space was allowed for any other comments. The questions were related particularly to the 20%, but, in fact, were inevitably also about the curriculum in general. They addressed the following issues:

1. How formalised/flexible the school should be (i.e. should all year groups cover the same subjects and qualities?).
2. Ensuring coverage and progression.
3. How structured teaching programmes of study should be (e.g. should there be a 2-year plan of programmes of study?).
4. Ensuring that time is not wasted, but used valuably.

The survey was very successful. The staff had just one day to complete the questionnaires, but only one member of staff failed to return any comments. Eleanor then collated the information and had it typed so that handwriting could not be recognised. This proved to be useful when one of the senior management team, clearly upset by one of the comments, asked if Eleanor knew who had written it. Eleanor remained concerned that some members of the senior management had felt either threatened or been unhappy with some of the staff's comments and had taken them personally. So the exercise had been useful in demonstrating the real need for confidentiality, and safety too, when building trust. Equally, she remained very concerned that some of the senior management may have read what the staff said but would still push for development of their own ideas with the mistaken belief that as part of equal opportunities it is sufficient just to go through the process of listening to staff without having to take the comments on board or show evidence that they will be acted on.

So what came out of this for Eleanor and Glyn? They saw more clearly than ever that their two sets of anxieties were linked. The staff indeed wanted to give their views, but only if they were safe in doing so, and if something came out of it – and if it did not involve them in too much work, and too many meetings. Fairness to staff could be improved just by giving them a voice, and empowering them through listening and responding to their voices. The similarities with the classroom situation we described in earlier chapters are striking.

Nudged along by Glyn and Eleanor, the school took some further steps in the direction of managing fairly. The issues of confidentiality and of *real* input were raised in the senior management meeting. As a result, in staff meetings in January and March staff were enabled to put their points of view about the management of the school, the ways in which the school was working and how the development plan could work (*see* Figure 7.1). It became clearer to everyone that taking on the question of the 20% was just a small part of getting clearer, as a whole school, about values, and ways of working fairly. The teachers saw that the new

Getting the plan right (2): Where to go next
(Fill this in groups of two or three, or individually)

Staff and school	Myself	Whose job is it to do it

Figure 7.1 Proformas for anonymous feedback

The process of managing the school
(Do this in groups of three or more)

	What helps us feel involved	What stops us feeling involved
All of us think		
One or more of us think		

Figure 7.1 (continued) Proformas for anonymous feedback

National Curriculum might actually be able to be used in such a way that it did not conflict with their educational values.

What had happened is that Pear Dale school had gone some way towards making the curriculum its own. Focusing just on the 20% would have meant taking over someone else's definition of the innovation. The solution to the issue of the Dearing 20% turned out to be a thorough look at the wider issues of curriculum and management.

As Pear Dale school makes the curriculum its own, it is also becoming more effective. A number of misunderstandings have been straightened out. Planning teams are pulling together better. There is less energy spent on grumbling and on mutual suspicion. As we pointed out earlier, fairer management is also more effective management. Michael Fullan's careful study of the effectiveness of change processes in education shows this very clearly. He points out that any top-down initiative is likely to fail, because of the continuing power of teachers to subvert it. He has also shown that an innovation will only succeed if the following principles are taken seriously (Fullan, 1991, pp.105–7):

1. Do not assume that your version of what the change should be is the one that should or could be implemented.
2. Assume that any significant innovation, if it is to result in change, requires individual implementers to work out their own meaning. Effective implementation is a process of clarification.
3. Assume that conflict and disagreement are not only inevitable, but also fundamental to successful change.
4. Assume that changing the culture of institutions is the real agenda, not implementing single innovations.

School management should pay attention to all the principles of fairness. There is one aspect that we have not yet remarked on. The first principle of fairness includes not only working toward the empowerment of individuals and also dealing with structural injustice, due to race, social class or gender. It is necessary for school management to be aware of groups who might be systematically excluded, even if unintentionally. Any school includes groups of people who feel less central to the processes of decision making than others. These may be groups based in the structure of the school: Section 11 staff, classroom assistants, support staff, cleaners, dinner staff. They may also be groups, often overlapping with these, marked by social class, race and gender. Section 11 staff and classroom assistants are more likely to be from ethnic minorities. Cleaners and dinner staff are more likely to be from working-class families. Teachers on lower scales are more likely than senior management to be female. A school needs to be alert to whether it is failing to hear these groups of people, unintentionally but systematically.

Leading questions

We have emphasised the importance of fair processes and of managing fairly, even when the focus of a particular initiative is not obviously on issues of fairness. However, there is also the possibility of acting directly on issues related to race, gender or social class. In Chapter 5 we discussed achievement, first discussing how to improve learning and raise achievement through fair process in classrooms, and then going on to describe various projects for improving learning and raising achievement for groups of children defined by gender and race. Likewise, we have now discussed ways of improving educational management in terms of fair processes of management, and we now go on to look, briefly, at how educational management can be used to improve schools in relation to gender and race.

In this section we focus on heads, rather than on other levels of management. Teachers who are less senior can have a lot of influence in their own classrooms or areas, but whole-school change is difficult for individual teachers to achieve without the backing of the head or another senior person.

In Chapter 6, we introduced Springfield school where Jacqui is head. We described how they have started to change gender stereotyping and to challenge children's attitudes about gender by introducing a variety of new sports activities. Jacqui had arrived in the school, as a new head, knowing that she was interested in issues of gender. This posed a problem for her about the best ways of getting change. It is obvious to anyone who has tried to deal with issues of social justice or equal opportunities that it is a mistake to appear too crusading and committed. Helen, whose literacy project we described in Chapter 5, had this to say:

> I think, particularly with something like Equal Ops, it's not something that you *can* impose from on high. You can say, 'Right, this is what we will do!' But you actually don't change any attitudes, anywhere along the line. So I think it's much healthier that we are proceeding in a more low-level way. In my last school I had responsibility for Equal Ops and I did the classic thing of 'I'm really enthusiastic and committed, and I'm going to have an INSET day', and in I went. There was a *lot* of hostility, and a lot of people felt threatened: 'There's no problem here! Why are we wasting time on this, when we should be sorting out the latest dictats on the National Curriculum?' So I've learnt a lot from that; that this low-level approach, this kind of drip-feed, is a more effective way.

What she meant by drip-feeding was this:

> We've had just little things crop up, that I or somebody else can take up and raise. All sorts of little things: about behaviour in the playground, adult stereotypes. And there happens to have been something on television about gender and education, and people who have previously said, 'This is a waste of time: a load of rubbish!' have come in and said, 'Oh did you see that programme? It was really interesting because it made me think about what we were talking about yesterday.'

Jacqui had exactly the same view. Morwenna had asked her, tongue in cheek, if she had arrived in the new school as head, saying 'I'm particularly interested in gender'. She replied:

> No! I didn't say anything like that! My goodness me, never! Oh, no! No, no! Don't be silly!

So what did she do? To begin with, she had a clear commitment to the importance of the staff working as a team; to the value of learning from each other's ideas and views; to the importance of respecting the professional judgements of her staff; and to consensus. In view of all this, she was asked how she set things going in a certain direction. She said:

> I don't always. In the case of the sports I just picked up on what I heard one of the staff talking about: how they were worried about the attitude of the boys who played football. And I just thought, how, um, it's coming from them. It doesn't have to come from me. But once it comes from them, if I am skilful, I can actually use it. So I said, 'Hmm, are there any other things they would enjoy doing instead of the football? Then we don't have to worry about that so much. Couldn't we get them going on some other games?'

A different approach worked for addressing racism and sexism in books that were to be bought for the library. Firstly, it had already been established that the library needed refurbishment. Even before Jacqui had arrived at the school the teachers, as a staff, had taken advice from the library services about getting rid of materials that were outdated, both from the point of view of history and from the point of view of unacceptable stereotyping. After she had arrived, they all agreed that if a large sum of money was to be spent on books, they would have to agree, as a staff, about what they were going to buy. Jacqui explained:

> It wasn't *me* buying them. We all went up to Warwickshire, and every single member of staff chose books, including the nursery nurse, and the classroom assistant. We chose books for the school, allied to the particular topics that we knew they were going to be doing during the next year.

It was arranged that all ten staff together – the head, the classroom teachers, the nursery nurse and the classroom assistant – would agree on a Language Policy which would give them criteria for choosing books. This happened through a process which gave pre-eminence to the ideas of the language co-ordinator, but which also took into account everyone's views, through discussion and through individual voting in a secret ballot on relative priorities. The first stage was in a staff meeting. It began with a brainstorming meeting in which the language co-ordinator put forward her ideas, and then all the staff contributed their own views. These were collected and typed out and then presented to the staff. The next stage was individual. Everyone privately marked the list of statements to show their own personal priorities. The resulting list was circulated (*see* Figure 7.2), and made the basis for the Language Policy. The Policy was then used as a starting-point for a similar exercise setting the criteria for choosing books. These were largely focused on literary and aesthetic considerations, such as 'good illustrations', 'lively, good use of vocabulary' and 'unusual style'.

It is noticeable that although there are general statements in the list in Figure 7.2 about the importance of the needs of children, and about providing a positive environment for children, there is nothing about sexism or racism. The same was true about the final

WHY HAVE A LANGUAGE POLICY?

Priorities:

First
To inform and give direction for staff, governors and parents/ All Staff involved together/Consistency throughout the school / First and foremost to be based on the needs of the children, not the likes and dislikes of the staff/Whole school coordination.

Second
To improve the quality of learning for all pupils/To identify and provide support for pupils with Special Needs/Positive/ Someone to take a clear overview/Everybody sticks to what has been decided, like it or lump it/To be rooted in actual practice, what is actually being done with children in the classroom, not just theory/Skills / Handwriting/IT – extension of language skills through IT/Dictionaries – Spelling / Assessment – Recording - Reporting.

Third
To provide a positive environment for all children / Involve children, parents, non-teaching staff in decisions - inform them / Gradual implementation - not too ambitious - flexible / Every stage leading to better integration through the school / Success criteria and review built in / Everybody should be able to see results / Use of outside help and resources / Money and resources to be prioritised and allocated appropriately / Speaking / Writing, developing writing / Reading, reading comprehension, reluctant readers / Grammar / Special Needs, differentiation, extension / Visual imagery.

Figure 7.2 Language policy priorities

list of criteria for book choosing. However, in the event, the books chosen did not include books which were offensive.

Here the ethos established by the head becomes apparent. She has established a co-operative venture, in which individual views can be expressed. Also, she can rely on the atmosphere that has been established to assume that harmful stereotyping will be avoided – and that any anxieties on this score could have been raised. However, also, as she explains, she is aware of fail-safes within her system. She been careful to see that the draft Language Policy had included a section stating how the approaches ensure equal opportunities. She was then able to add confidently:

> We didn't particularly make remarks about books that would have either stereotypical genderism or stereotypical racism in them because we all accepted, as a professional group of people, we would not choose books like that anyway. And anyway, because we were going to a reputable book company, they wouldn't be there. In actual fact they weren't there, because the books had already been pre-selected as being acceptable in today's primary education. So that's how we assessed and chose our books. Hard work, isn't it!

The process of refurbishing the library gave a voice to the individual members of staff, and gave them a full part in the process. It also devolved responsibility to the language co-ordinator. However Jacqui's commitment to race and gender equality has made a difference to the books the school ended up buying. Thus the process was a fair one in the sense explored in the first part of the chapter. It was also one which addressed fairness issues directly, in that the choice of books contained nothing offensive in terms of race and gender.

Jacqui and Helen's views on 'drip feeding', working from informal discussions, feeding, and on the importance of seizing the moment are supported by Debbie Epstein's analysis of 'changing classroom cultures' working as an 'insider', as head of Infants (rather than as an 'outsider', as a teacher-advisor with the local authority). She says (Epstein, 1993, pp.58–60):

> The first phase in change consisted mainly of the gathering of allies, of informal discussions between certain members of the teaching staff, of getting to know the school and of establishing my own credibility as a teacher. …As I became integrated into the school, most of the influence I had was due to taking the opportunities which arose rather than to a premeditated strategy. ...I used to drive to school each day with two of the teachers. These informal discussions (another example of chance) were extremely important. They ranged over a number of issues in education and often centred on racism, both overt and covert. Such

'backstage' discussions are a key element of micropolitics.

In the following chapters we return to classrooms again, first to look at the curriculum, viewed through the lens of trips and topics, and then to look at ways of involving parents and the wider community in the work of the school.

Chapter 8

CURRICULUM PLANNING: TRIPS AND TOPICS

'Can we go again?' said Aziz – but what had he *learnt*?

It is eight o clock on a Thursday morning in June. Already the classroom is filled with children holding their bags and comparing the snacks that are packed in them. Parents and other adults stand around self-consciously; some of them know each other and begin chatting. The teacher is also self-conscious. She is holding sheaves of photocopied papers which she is distributing to the adults, while keeping a wary eye on the buzz of excitement that fills the room, while liaising with colleagues who appear from time to time to make last-minute arrangements, and to wonder out loud if the buses will arrive in time.

Soon there are about 120 children holding onto their packs and bags sitting quietly in the hall, while the head gives a pep talk about behaviour. They are to be on show, he says. The reputation of the whole school is at stake. Teachers, parents and other adult helpers look suitably serious. No one is left in any doubt that today is to be special and memorable.

The buses have arrived. This news sweeps through the room, even before the teachers issue instructions. Partners are chosen. The seats fill up. Bodies are counted and we are off. A day out of school. Instead of getting on with the maths scheme, instead of wondering what to write and how to spell it, instead of sitting quietly and listening when the teacher tells you; instead of *all* the normal routines, the children and teachers head out of the city. It is all right to play clapping games and tell jokes. It is all right to sit dreaming and looking out of the window. The teachers will only stop their own conversations and walk back through the bus when the buzz of noise is punctuated by a shriek, or if the children's games take them out of their seats.

Along the motorway, down the country roads, through the villages: 'Is anyone going to be sick?' 'Can we eat our sweets?' 'Can we have a drink?' 'Will it rain?' 'How far is it now?' At last, the buses all pull up and we are all there.

Last instructions are given. Each adult has four or five children to keep company. The parties set off towards the gatehouse of Warwick Castle. A long time later, after we have all seen the dungeons, found the armoury, climbed the walls, admired the furnishings, eaten our picnics, played by the river, walked through the gardens, taken photographs, bought our souvenirs, and fallen asleep in the bus on the way home, we finally arrive back at school. Waiting adults claim their sleepy children. The buses drive off. The teachers go home. Another school day is over.

This was a school day. What has been learnt? The trip will at least be memorable. When we asked some children what they remembered from last year, the trips stood out as special. Adults too. When we told people the subject of this chapter we unlocked a flood of memories.

When we look back over our own teaching careers, the same thing happens. Carol really enjoyed her trip taking children to the Eureka science museum in Halifax: the music room with the musical stepping stones, that entice you to jump backwards and forwards making tunes; the body section with the big noses you can look into; the 'factory' where you can make things. It was of this trip that Aziz said, 'It was the best trip we've ever been on. Can we go again?' The trip to Mablethorpe was another teaching highlight for Carol. The first time they travelled from the city in the middle of England to this Lincolnshire seaside resort, there were children on the trip who had never seen the sea. They were amazed at it. They were so excited at seeing it that they ran straight into it – still dressed in all their clothes. Morwenna has vivid memories of taking children to Bristol Zoo, where groups of children sat spellbound, drawing the waterfowl. Another time she took a groups of excited, noisy, inner-city children to quiet, genteel Bath. Let off the bus in front of the Abbey, they immediately ran off, whooping, to investigate Woolworths, leaving a group of startled citizens behind them.

What is being remembered here? The answer is: the excitement, the day out, the laughs, and the accidents. But if these are the things that stand out in the memory, why is a day trip regarded as a school day? We ask again: what has been learnt?

The Warwick Castle trip was part of Carol's topic for the half-term. For weeks, the classroom for these Year 6 children had looked like a castle. The entrance had been turned into ramparts and a gateway, using sheets of card painted to look like stone walls with arrow slits. Medieval shields took pride of place on a display board. The story of King Arthur had been read aloud. The class had designed period costumes for themselves. But it was the trip which was the focus for all this work. The trip may have 'come out of' the work. Equally, the work was planned round a suitable trip.

In one sense, then, it is not difficult to identify which parts of the curriculum have been covered. Warwick Castle is a suitable trip for Year 6 children. The trip was part of a topic, of which the trip was an important focus. A large number of national curriculum programmes of study were covered, especially in the areas of history and language.

Planning the curriculum round topics and trips is, as it has always been, a widespread feature of classroom life. It even has the sanction of Government, even though some of the documents avoid the term 'topic'. The words have changed more than the practice. The curriculum is now most often described in terms of curriculum areas, but on any day of the week, a visitor to most primary classrooms could tell at a glance what the present topic is. The 1993 NCC document, *Planning the National Curriculum at Key Stage 2*, says well-planned topics 'can be an effective way of organising the curriculum' and that 'opportunities of linking aspects of different subjects can be explored.'

So topics and trips are good for covering the curriculum and keeping up motivation. They are more than this, though. While they are vehicles for the teaching of facts and skills, the learning of those facts and skills is always accompanied by the more imperceptible learning of values and attitudes. One of the children drawing birds that day at Bristol Zoo spent the rest of the academic year pursuing an investigation of birds, drawing them, writing about them, reading up about them, and observing them. His parents reported that since going on the trip he had joined the Royal Society for the Protection of Birds, and was spending his weekends following up this interest. Deciding to teach school subjects through topics is not just a class management decision about the efficient use of time and resources. It is also an educational decision about the importance of teaching particular values and attitudes.

An example of how a topic can be set up specifically to teach values is given by Jeff. When he was working as a multicultural advisor, he was asked to do some work in Wood End school. Wood

End school is situated between the inner city and the suburbs. The neighbourhood is largely Asian, and would be regarded as working class by most measures; but as Jeff says, it is Asian working class, which is different from white working class, as shown, for instance, in the aspirations of the parents and in their attitude to education. Jeff feels that the culture of the neighbourhood is strongly reminiscent of the culture of his own English white working-class grandparents, who grew up in the city at a time 'when there *were* working-class aspirations and there was a culture where education was seen to be important.'

Jeff spoke enthusiastically about a topic which he worked on with the deputy head. It was planned around the teaching of attitudes and values related to social justice, and also, around the basic maths curriculum. Jeff explains how this topic was set up and why it was so exciting for someone like himself, committed to social justice and also interested in teaching maths:

> We went and we said to the children, 'Right, what are your problems? What are your main problems in school? Do some problem solving!' They said, 'The way that groups are arranged is a problem; toilets are a problem to us; name calling is a problem to us.' We said, 'Right, divide into groups depending on which of those problems you are interested in working on, and then you need to devise a questionnaire for everybody.'
>
> That was the beginning of the topic. But by the end a lot of mathematics came in, because the classroom groups had to do things like find out how people would want the classroom. They had to make a scale model of the classroom. They ended up doing a 3-D thing, to see the ways they could organise the desks and how much space children took up. So all kinds of things were happening. We'd said that there needed to be a practical response and that we'd need a practical report.
>
> The name calling thing was: they broke the name calling down into different sorts of name calling. Then they went round and they interviewed children in different years, to find out if it was the same in each year. Then they could come up with some kind of recommendations. So much maths happened. We didn't have to think, we are going to teach bar charts today. And it was never a case of they are all on different study plans and can't ever talk to each other.

Teachers aim to teach values and attitudes, as well as skills and knowledge through topics and trips. However, it is always easier to say what has been *taught* than what has been *learnt* by any individual pupil. This is never more true than in the case of values and attitudes. Given the variety of children that are found in

English primary classrooms, attention needs to be paid to the variety of ways in which they might respond to the rich experience of teaching through topics and going on school trips.

There are two issues that we are going to talk about in relation to the curriculum and fairness. In the first place there is the question of the *content* of the curriculum, including the curriculum of values and attitudes; and in the second, there is the question of *access* to it. We shall stay with the trip to Warwick Castle to discuss the first of these questions – content – and move on to a discussion of a trip to York in order to discuss the second – access.

The topic of the curriculum: what gets taught

Morwenna

The topic related to Warwick Castle certainly fascinated the children. They entered into it enthusiastically. It fascinated me, too. I remembered all over again the pleasure that I had in childhood from learning about knights in armour. I was a colonial child, brought up in Africa, only coming permanently to England after my primary schooling was over. At the age of 8 while on holiday in England, I was taken to the Tower of London, where I was knowledgeable about all the armour I saw. I had spent hours playing with home-made shields and swords. I was absorbed in the fantasy of being a medieval knight at the court of King Arthur. The memory of my early interest and fascination, together with my adult understanding of my own social class, gender and culture (i.e. white middle class, female, from a family of migrants, rather than black or male, or rooted in a single place), made me wonder just what I had been learning about myself and my place in the world. More importantly, I asked myself: what were these inner-city children learning now?

The topic also made me remember my own reactions to school history. Thinking back to my childhood, I found that place was as important to me as family links. When I was child, growing up in Tanzania, I was in a position a little bit like the Asian or African Caribbean children we teach in Nottingham. Of course I was part of the colonial ruler culture, and my school was all white. White people were rich and powerful in comparison to the black African population and all schools were fee paying – so no wonder there were no black children in the school. Still, I was born in Tanzania, of parents who were British in some sense, though they too had both been born in Africa. We – young immigrants to Africa – learnt English history in primary school, and very dull I found it. When I was 10, for the first time we learnt Tanzanian history and I found it riveting. The place where I was growing up was important in a way that 'my' culture as defined by adults was not. On the other hand, I also had a romantic attachment to the idea of being Scots: my grandmother was Scots, though my father was born in Africa. I had, in fact, never known her, since she lived half a continent away in another part of Africa.

Helping the children in Carol's class carry out various activities about castles, made me reflect on the contradictions and dilemmas inherent in a topic focused on medieval English history. Children need to learn history, so a topic based round medieval history is entirely appropriate. What is more, this particular one, focused on the trip to Warwick Castle, engaged the children's interest and imagination. It also taught them a significant portion of the National Curriculum. Similar contradictions and dilemmas appear in any historical topic, as we point out later in this section.

The Year 6 class included middle-class and working-class children. Some of them had very poor parents struggling on benefit, while others had parents wealthy enough to own a second house in France. There were children with grandparents in the Punjab, others with grandparents in the Caribbean, and yet others whose grandparents had lived all their lives a few miles from the school.

It was an afternoon spent in the classroom, helping children design heraldic shields, that first made me think hard about some of the contradictions inherent in the activity. For the white children putting a cross on the shield probably signified nothing very much. Like most whites, including myself, most of the children come from secular rather than religious backgrounds. (In fact, as it happened, very few white children chose to put a cross on their shields.) However, there were contradictions inherent in this symbolism for Muslims (as there would have been for Jews, or Hindus, if there had been any in that particular class.)

One Muslim child, Asad, put a cross on his shield. Should we have suggested to Asad that he and other Muslims used the Islamic symbol of a crescent? (And where would that have left any other religions?) Plainly this would not have been a good solution. Zafar, who is a devout Muslim, consciously and explicitly refused to put a Muslim symbol on his shield, in case it was accidentally put on the floor. Moreover, making an issue of the symbolism for the 'Christians' and 'Muslims' in the class would been to mark them as different from each other, especially so, since the historical period they were studying was the time of the Christian Crusades against Islam. We would have been running the risk of encouraging an 'us' and 'them' to develop – the crusades re-enacted in the classroom – rather than helping mutual respect and understanding to develop. On the other hand, Islam today is the focus of continued attacks in the press. More than the other religions of England it is labelled 'fundamentalist' (rather than as including orthodox and liberal wings, like any other religion, like Christianity or Hinduism.) To be a Muslim in England is not, therefore, easy. It is not that this one afternoon in the classroom matters so much. The point here is that Asad and Zafar will, presumably, meet similar situations again and again, requiring them to pretend to be something they are not, or to mark themselves as 'the enemy'.

The issue that we are raising here is grounded in the third of our principles of fairness: the value of the individual, and the recognition of how individuals and their identities are always rooted in the communities from which they spring. Here this principle results in a dilemma in history teaching, and, indeed, in teaching most of the curriculum. On the one hand, (a) education is about teaching a *common culture* for all children being educated in this country (in rural Berkshire as well as inner city Bradford, for instance); and on the other hand (b) good effective education requires that teachers make sure that children can relate to the education they are being offered, that it does not require them to forget who they are at home – their *self-identity*. Children of all races and religions need access to all the curriculum which has been sanctioned as proper by a white Christian culture, at the same time as they participate in re-defining what is important. Here we see the issue is one that is important for the future of multicultural/anti-racist education. And it is just as important in gender-neutral/anti-sexist education, not to mention in education in which either different social classes are acknowledged as valuable members of the community, or which, on the other hand, challenges the basis of the social class divisions in England.

This issue is not confined to medieval history and the Crusades, even if this historical subject provides a particularly rich source of dilemmas. To show this we may look at the way the topic was introduced – a way that would be good for any historically based topic. The children were asked to go back in time, in their imagination on a time-line, and think what their home might have been like then. They were taken on a guided fantasy round their house, noticing, for instance, that there was no television in the corner, and no telephone. They then imagined leaving the house and going to the market and to the castle. They were also asked to make a time-line of their own life, and to interview their own families about what they remembered of the past.

Surely this was a very valuable introduction to an historical topic. The concept of time is difficult for children, even in the upper juniors. It is important to start with the knowledge and experience of the child and work from that to more distant times and places. However, any such introduction needs to come to terms with the fact that only those children with one or more white parents could imagine that it was their own great, great, grandparents that they might encounter in any guided fantasy that took them back to earlier times in England. The Asian and African Caribbean children were being asked to go back in time, but staying in England. The same would have been true for many Jewish children, or for others who remembered forebears from the rest of the world, if there had been any of them in the class. There is nothing wrong with that, but these children and grandchildren of migrants were undertaking a different exercise from their white classmates. Anyone with mixed parentage – which may be a sizeable minority – were acknowledging only parts of their parentage.

There is a richness here, in the diversity of experience which the children in an inner city can bring to the classroom – but it is one where the effect of the differences is not evenly distributed with respect to the curriculum. Would white school children in rural Lincolnshire be asked to fly back in time to a place where everyone looked different, and they had no relatives? Well, yes they would, but only for a topic on a 'foreign' place like Ancient Egypt. It would not be an analogous exercise.

Everything we have said so far about cultural diversity applies to social class and gender, too. The issue here is difference: not just religion and ethnic background, but social class and gender too. Part of the pleasure of history is imagining yourself to be very different people, and part of the pleasure of places like Warwick castle (for us) is *exactly* that ordinary women, like us, are no longer excluded from the beauty and riches of such a place, on the grounds of social class and gender, and that we too have access to it all.

Had it done Morwenna or Carol any good as children to imagine that they were part of the ruling class, rather than of the peasantry (where their own families must have come from)? Morwenna remembers asking teachers about 'ordinary people' only to find that there was little knowledge about them available in school books for primary age children. Carol remembers that at her primary school, history always seemed to be only about 'important' people – except for the Egyptians, and that one historical topic she related to and remembers particularly well. They 'did the pharaohs', of course, but they also learnt about dress and every-day life.

But history is not only written by the rich and powerful; it is written by rich and powerful *men*. These men write about other men – particularly rich and powerful ones. The point here is that imagining that you are anyone who counts in history tends to mean imagining that you are a boy. This is only partly to do with the position of women in society. It is also to do with the way history has been written so that the lives of women and girls are largely invisible.

In short, it was a very different thing doing this topic for Thomas, a white, middle-class boy, son of a struggling single parent; or for Suzie, a white working-class child of unemployed parents; or for Zafar the son of an Asian, Muslim taxi driver, who had middle-class aspirations for his children. What is the effect on Thomas, who can more straightforwardly identify with the people he studied? We wonder if it is, in fact, more difficult for him in some ways, just because he was not asked to identify with people who appear to be unlike him. He had fewer opportunities to see the range of ways of being a human being and to try them out in his imagination. Suzie and Zafar, on the other hand, can try out extensions of their sense of self, as long as it is not being crushed (as I hope it was not). Thomas is learning and re-learning what it is to be a white man in this culture, and may have a harder job expressing his own (quite gentle) personality, which does not match the stereotype for him.

What lessons about teaching can be drawn out of all this? Teaching a history topic should be both about establishing a common culture and also about responding to differences of self-identity including differences of religion, ethnic background, gender and social class and respecting them. There are two main points here.

Firstly, because education is teaching a 'common culture', a topic on Warwick Castle should be raising the same issues in rural Sussex as in Toxteth. However, even though the same issues are raised, the topic needs to be different in the two places in relation to how it is related to the children's self-identities. In rural Sussex, the self-identity of pupils – where they think they belong, where they 'are coming from', who they think they are – is likely to be less complex for most of the children. They are likely to be white English people in a setting which has been white and English for generations, and people like them are the kinds of people who appear in most school books. In Toxteth, there is a diversity of peoples, including black people who have been settled in Liverpool for generations, and others whose grandparents were born and brought up in other countries. They are not the kinds of people who appear in most school books.

Secondly, the common culture of Britain today is one in which there is diversity. Therefore, in any setting, be it rural Sussex or Toxteth, it is important to try and get behind the all-male, all-rich, all-white view of history, whatever the particular topic being studied. For instance, it is important to focus on the role of women in Viking times as well as on the fire and pillage image which is so widespread. Children can consider how the Vikings brought new languages, and no doubt felt the difficulties and pleasures of migration, just as migrants do today. Other large-scale migrations can be used to compare with theirs, using Africa, the Caribbean or the Indian subcontinent as examples. In short it is important to acknowledge the variety of ways that children can relate to a topic. Everyone needs sometimes to be in a position where they are marginal and, at other times, to be in a position where they are central.

There is no need to be paralysed by the difficulty of responding to diversity. It is possible to go a long way through responsiveness to the children's own concerns – having established enough trust and openness for them to make those concerns felt. This responsiveness is based on the second principle of fairness, the importance of process. In this case, having concern and valuing people is more important than particular pieces of knowledge related to gender, race, or social class. After all no one teacher could possibly be expected to know it all. And teachers are themselves drawing on their own, relatively narrow, education.

We have discussed a history trip and topic. Like all trips and topics it contributed to cross-curricular themes like PSE and citizenship. It gave powerful messages to children about appropriate relationships between teachers and children. It was a chance to develop the trust and openness that we have argued are necessary to improve teaching and learning. It also gave children powerful messages about what is important in the common culture, and what experiences are thought valuable for all children to have. These points are all implicit in trips like the one to Warwick castle, but in ones to the seaside or to the park, they become explicit.

Carol

As a teacher I have found that visits out with the children are an opportunity to learn about the children in a different setting. They provide the chance to see the children interact with each other outside the confines of school and how they behave with other adults or in new situations, all important factors for the Primary school teacher who is involved in educating the whole child.

They also provide me with a unique opportunity in getting to know the children better. And there's the chance for the children to see the teacher as a human being who will jump about on musical stepping-stones, build sandcastles, paddle in the sea, put their head in the stocks and do countless other silly things. I also become aware of some of the fears and insecurities of the children. You can't improve a situation or difficulty until you are aware that it is problematic. Working with children all day it's often hard to remember that they are children and not the little adults that I try to think they are. It's a question of expectations. For instance, at Warwick I discovered that Manzar and Amir were scared of heights and I was able to show respect and reassure them that this was normal and later in other situations I was able to ensure that this issue was dealt with sensitively. Strategies were discussed to overcome and milestones were recognised (milestones that may remain private with the teacher and the child).

The trips give the teacher a chance to learn about the children in a different way and this helps the teacher respond to children's individual needs and assist in their overall development. I am reminded of the work we did on exploring effective learning and teaching in the Fairness project. We found the children were more concerned with their social needs than their academic ones, and these had to be dealt with and explored before an improvement in learning and teaching could take place.

What about trips to the seaside and the park? Why did we all go? It was a nice end-of-year social activity. Is this all? Many of our children have never been to the sea, except on a school trip, so every few years the school ensures that this activity is offered to give the children the experience. This crosses a variety of backgrounds, culturally and socially. Trips therefore can provide children with experiences they may not normally get, but which are part of British experience. The visits to the Mosque, the Gudwara and the Asian dance workshop are like this too.

We have said that trust and openness are crucially important if children are to be able to raise the concerns which let them bring their social differences into a topic. However, there are some obvious problems with relying on the children and their communities to raise most of the issues. The main problem is to do with who raises the gender, social class or race issues. In a school like Riverside, there is an ethos which allows such things to be mentioned. For instance, as we showed in Chapter 4, the anti-racist policy is in force; children know they can complain of racism, and they do. The ethos of the school also constrains how these issues are mentioned. As we said in Chapter 3, children could more easily openly discuss the way they viewed each other as girls and boys than they could discuss the way they viewed each other in racial terms. In another school assumptions might not be challenged at all, especially if it is an all-white one or one which has no mix of social classes.

Even in Riverside there are problems about the more deep-seated assumptions of gender, race and social class. For instance, it is so much taken for granted that the masculine is the norm that neither children nor staff would consider it odd that girls are often asked to empathise with men, but boys are rarely asked to empathise with women. Similarly, even in schools with relatively high proportions of children of ethic minorities, both black and white children are used to seeing the white as the norm. So it does not occur to them to ask questions in a way which would allow Carol to introduce it into her teaching. And if this is true for a school like this, how much more true must it be for other schools with a less sympathetic ethos, where the children are less diverse in background.

So teachers cannot only rely on the children. Teachers themselves need to be sensitive to the issues in all-white schools or in schools with no social mix, so that they can raise them, when the opportunity presents itself. This is, of course, partly because racism, sexism and class-prejudices need to be addressed in all schools. Partly, this is to be fair to the few individual children in every school who are different in some way, who are there in nearly every school, and who need support without having the spotlight turned on them. We are not saying this is easy. A variety of strategies have been tried, including pairing schools, special trips, bringing in visitors, and working with colleagues from schools with a different social mix.[36] And, to repeat, we are not asking the impossible. No single teacher can know everything about all the different communities the children come from, and nobody is asking them to.

Access to curriculum: who's going on the trip?

Mala is 7. Her mother hovers anxiously in the classroom. She has all her stuff for the trip ready and packed, including her insulin, some emergency sugar, and her snacks. She is good at managing her diabetes, but it is hard for small children to remember the rules, day in and day out. Will she be all right? Of course she will. Her mother will be there, after all. But naturally she is going on the trip. So is everyone else. Even Joseph and Billy are coming, though some teachers would like to leave them behind. Even Dilip and Lorraine will be there, though it has taken a lot of work behind the scenes to ensure this. Aslam will be there, no doubt viewing the day as a chance to do nothing much, as usual.

This is the first trip of the school year for this class of Year 3 and 4 children. The class is 'doing the Vikings', and the trip is to York where the first stop will be the Jorvik museum. In Jorvik they will sit in a 'time train' and be taken back in time to see a life-size model Viking village. Some of the children have been there already, and are explaining what is in store to anyone who will listen.

Joseph and Billy find themselves in rather small groups led by teachers. This has not happened by chance! Joseph has a love of obscenity and takes a delight in pushing the bounds of acceptability until he discovers the limits. It is a game that he has taught to some of the other boys. At this moment, at the start of a rainy October morning, this highly intelligent, unhappy boy is torn between living out his habitual fantasy that he is a rattlesnake, and enjoying the game of daring to annoy the assembled adults so early in the day. Billy is in a different small group from Joseph. He is quiet enough at the moment, but only last week he broke a school television set in one of his rages. It is almost certain that he will express the unhappiness of his short 8 years of life by throwing a spectacular tantrum, at some point during the day.

Dilip and Lorraine are ready and waiting. Dilip is quietly taking everything in. She is well behaved and easy to overlook among the more boisterous children. She tells Morwenna that she is looking forward to the day. A few years ago there was a chance that young Asian girls like herself would not have come to school today, their parents anxious about the tiring effects of the long day ahead, for what seemed to them to be dubious educational benefits. Lorraine is her usual energetic self, chattering away at the centre of her group of small girls. We are glad to see that she has remembered her glasses, which have shown a tendency to get left behind, all term. She has a lot to remember, being aware that even at 8 years old she has serious contributions to make to her family household: her father has lost his job, and her mother picks up work where she can find it. Lorraine gladly helps out with a paper round, taking it over from her elder brother, without the newsagent's knowledge. She also does her share of chores. Money for trips to expensive museums many miles away is not easily found. However, here she is.

Aslam, as we said, is not expecting to do much work today. But then he rarely does. He is not badly behaved, exactly, but is always being badgered to get back on task. He finds himself in the same group as Billy, with the class teacher. She will have a chance to begin to establish a relationship with him based in mutual interest and enjoyment. She hopes that he may begin to change his attitude to school work as a result.

The trip to York was a great success. The rain held off most of the day, and even though the toilets at the usual half-way stop were closed, the *Happy Eater* was kind enough to let 120 young children use their toilets in groups of five at a time. The Minster shop proved an excellent source of souvenirs. Neil felt ill most of the day, but otherwise nobody was hurt or got lost. The swings and the bags of chips to be found near the car-park were a source of widespread delight. In other words, everything passed off as you might hope for a school trip.

It was also educationally valuable. The children came back enthusiastic about what they had seen and done. They had learnt a lot more about the Vikings and were able to put what they had already learnt into context. Time and place in history came together for these 7 and 8 year olds; it would have been hard to achieve this so well in the classroom. Links had been made 'between aspects of different subjects' (NCC, 1993).

What of the children who might have been a problem? Mala was fine. Nobody really expected otherwise, but we were glad to see that her confidence increased; just as important, so did the confidence of her parents. Joseph and Billy had not made life easy for the adults who were with them. Billy had had his tantrum: his teacher had not enjoyed holding on to the screaming child, while tourists from other parties stared curiously. It was a relief that one kindly couple commented to her: 'Rather you than me, duck.' Joseph had relieved himself of most of his obscenities during the ride in the little cars in the museum itself. It was a nuisance, but no more, keeping the adult on her toes, but not preventing the other children in the party being thrilled by the special effects round them. By the time Joseph was out again among the York crowds he was back to being a rattlesnake, which was exhausting to the teacher with him, but containable. Lorraine, Dilip and Aslam just enjoyed themselves, joining in with everything just like everyone else.

That Lorraine, and others, might have had a problem bringing lunch – or owning up to being one of those entitled to a free school meal – was effectively masked by the large number of extra packed lunches provided by the school. It was obvious that anyone feeling a bit peckish, or just wanting a bit of chocolate slab, could come and get some – without being conspicuous. There was also a strictly enforced limit on spending money. Souvenirs were compared on the way home, but there was little opportunity for pupils to outdo each other on grounds of wealth.

Thus the trip was a success on three separate counts. First, it was an enjoyable, human mode of learning, which involved parents as well as teachers, and which touched the imagination deeply enough to make the experience memorable. Second, it had helped the teachers teach and the children learn a significant portion of the curriculum. Third, and most importantly, it had been fair. No one had been left out of either a human, convivial experience on the one hand, nor been denied access to part of the curriculum on the other. Both of these are matters of fairness.

Questions of access are, like those of the content of the curriculum, matters of fairness, with answers rooted in the principles of fairness that we have been explaining. It is unfair to individuals to deny them access to some parts of the curriculum. It is particularly unfair if some children are denied access to just those parts that are enjoyable, special, and which touch the imagination.

Parents can miss some of these points, especially if the trips are expensive, or if they have not been in enough communication with the school to understand the value of topic work and its associated trips. Morwenna will not forget the awfulness of leaving 8-year-old Emily behind on a trip to a nature centre in the South of England. Her mother said, 'She's been there before,' and that was the end of it. That school did not have a tradition of involving its parents; the result of that lack was that the child missed out on an essential part of her whole education: PSE as well as science. Not only was she excluded from the pleasures of a day enjoyably spent pond-dipping and looking down microscopes, but also it was made more difficult for her to benefit from the rest of the education on offer in school. This is in marked contrast to Dilip. The Asian parents at Riverside now support school trips, no doubt because of real and serious consultations with them, over the years.

Emily was not marked out from the rest of the class by race or by social class. However, if she had been, all the problems she would have been facing would have been magnified. As we said, children are at risk of being left out because of a range of reasons related to race, gender and social class. Sheer poverty can get in the way. Parents may be worried about their girls being out for long days, and getting overtired. Social classes and cultures which expect a formal education for their children may not see the value of trips at all, except in so far as they are a treat. For Emily the situation was one in which she was experiencing unfairness, as an individual. The situation would have been unfair with respect to the other strand of fairness, if the matter had been made worse by there being a socially structured reason for her being left out – as would have been the case with Lorraine or Dilip, if the school's policies had been less effective at making sure children did not get left out for reasons of poverty or culture.

The same issues are there in relation to the topic in the classroom. For some children with special educational needs, 'the basics' can take over and narrow the curriculum to the detriment of motivation, imagination, values and attitudes as well as to knowledge of subject areas. Such narrowness is also to the detriment of a child's chance of using knowledge gained in one area to help build up knowledge in another. They are denied the obvious delight that children often take in the products of work which are not 'basics': the pictures, the models, the experiments. And finally, they are denied the possibility of being valued for such work even if they know that they will always be toiling away behind the rest of the class with respect to 'the basics'.

Children with special educational needs are particularly at risk in this respect, but they are not the only ones. Race, social class and gender can combine to narrow the curriculum for some children, if the teacher is not alert to the issue. Who is able to bring things into the classroom that are relevant to the topic? Who can get dirty and join in wholeheartedly? Who needs language tuition that can crowd out other areas of the curriculum? Who finds that their own experience and cultural knowledge is made use of – and who does not? Teachers need to be continually alert to these questions, and to ways of answering them that will include parents, children and other teachers, rather than leave them out.

Chapter 9

GETTING CLOSER TO HOME: IMPROVING COMMUNICATION BETWEEN HOME AND SCHOOL

Worlds together

> *Q:* Do the parents come into school to potter about in the classroom much? Are they welcome to do that?
>
> *A:* They are. They are. It's... um.... Well, they're more welcome in some classrooms than others, to be honest. I think teachers are so hard-pressed that even those who a few years ago would have said, 'I'd rather not have them seeing what I'm doing,' are now really just grateful for the extra pair of hands.... We've talked quite a bit about how we are going to involve more parents, and we've tried various things.[37]

It is easier said than done. Almost all teachers agree that it will be better for children if communication between home and school improves – even if it is already quite good. Some parents agree. For some, it seems that there is a strong reluctance to come into school. Here is one head's views about the parents from the surrounding, mostly white, mostly working-class area:

> *Q:* Have the parents been to talk about the home reading scheme booklet with the class teachers?
>
> *A:* Not an awful lot. I think there's still a feeling that 'This is something else we've got to do,' in stressful and busy lives. They are not awfully clear that it is very valuable, and they believe it is our job to teach the children to read. So I think the difficulty is getting parents in, because they feel quite threatened by the school, and actually getting to talk to them about it is hard.

For some parents it is a waste of time pursuing such links in the face of what they feel are patronising and arrogant attitudes from teachers. Lou is a member of a team of social workers on another, similar estate in a neighbouring town. The team works with parents on a number of problem areas, including home–school links. Lou thinks that part of the difficulty is that parents, who are probably fairly anti-school anyway because of their own experience, usually go up to school when there is trouble: they do not, therefore, hear very positive things about their children. But this is not the whole story, as the following incident shows:

> When I first started working on the estate, I went down to the Nativity play at Christmas, because some of the kids said 'Oh, can you come?' So I went down. I was absolutely appalled. The head who was there has retired now. She talked to all the parents just like you talk to a group of 5 year olds. She said, 'Now, the children have worked *very* hard on this, so I want you to be very quiet. To *listen*.' I couldn't believe it. I think it is because of where the school is. I've never heard that sort of thing when I've been to school as a parent, because, I suppose, my kids have been to fairly middle-class schools.

Any parent who is not close to the system can find it off-putting. Jean, a competent and confident working-class woman, who was born and brought up in the same city as her children, says she is frightened by going up to visit her children's school. She says that she doesn't know what to say; she doesn't know what to do. In her case, she makes the effort, and she has the time to do it. Lou used to have a similar reaction, as a parent:

> Even for me, I have to say when I first went back into school with Pip when she was 5, when she first started school, I went right back to how it was when I was at school. You get the same feelings, don't you? There was this antique headteacher who was just like the woman we had when we were small.

Jean and Lou who find it difficult are, at least, using their own first language. Not surprisingly, many of those Asian parents who are less at home in English and the English school system, find it harder still to make useful contacts with their children's teachers. Nor is it all plain sailing in schools with middle-class catchment areas, where the parents want to be in close contact with the school and to influence it. Here is a head from such a school talking about a display in the hall:

> The parents helped us with that, so it's not just down to the staff. They enjoy the creativity of it. I like them to come in. Well, you saw us: parents all over the place. ...But it doesn't always go well I'm afraid. It's

> very difficult, with the best will in the world.[38]

And here is a head, who works hard at keeping home–school links in good shape, talking about the behaviour policy. The school is situated in quite a wealthy area, and the discipline problems are 'low-level':

> Slowly, it's working. We still have days when it disintegrates. We do involve parents as well, sometimes, again, really so that we can present to the children a united front. We need that support.
>
> We've written to the parents. We have explained. We have mentioned it over the years. We included it in an Open Forum we had in lieu of an open evening, which was well attended.

In Riverside school, there has been a whole-school policy for over a decade to involve the parents, and it seems to be working. Parents are welcome in all the classes, and the teacher with special responsibility for home–school links abounds with ideas and enthusiasm. In the next chapter, we explain how the links are extending outwards into the wider community too.

For our part, we are sure that links between school and home provide a vital element in improving fairness for children. Good relations, where there is real communication and interaction between school and parents, make the school a better, fairer place for the children. Good relations can be established at school level by the head and also at classroom level between individual class teachers and parents. We do, of course, recognise how hard it is to make the best use of contact with parents. It can all too easily get to quarter to nine on Wednesday morning and there is Jane, Sarah's Mum coming through the door, and the maths work sheets still haven't been photocopied. Or there is Akbar's Dad bringing him in this morning, and at last you can get a chance to talk to him – if only there wasn't a steady stream of children urgently giving you notes from home, and the teacher from the next class wasn't waiting for a word about the next stage of the topic work.

Helen, the Acting Head of Green Park, whom we introduced in Chapter 5 in connection with the gender and literacy project, describes the importance of an interview with a parent. The point was that he was not just being asked into school to hear the school's perspective on his stepson's bad behaviour. More importantly, he was hearing that the school valued his intervention, as a parent and as a man:

> In fact [for people on this estate] children are women's work, and all things pertaining to children are women's work. School is one of them.

I had a father in this morning. I'd had to send a letter home because his son had been abusive, and he'd spun a yarn about it wasn't him, it was somebody else. ...His stepfather came in and he was quite shocked. He said, quite apologetically, 'Well, normally, his Mum sorts anything to do with school.' He was apologising for his own lack of competence in this area. I thanked him for coming in. I said how pleased I was, and how helpful it would be to the boy.

Jacqui, the Head of Springfield, whom we met in Chapters 6 and 7 working on gender and games, explains how important it is to have good relations with parents, not just for dealing with behaviour problems but also when going through the upsetting business of statementing a child with special educational needs:

What upset us about the new code of practice [introduced in 1994] is there seems to be an emphasis in it that the parent and the school would be at odds with each other and the LEA would be there to pick up the pieces. In actual fact, we find that ourselves and our parents are together on most things of this nature. We always see the parents, right at the beginning, and an interview takes place, not just with myself, as head, but with the class teacher, the support services teacher and anyone else – like the occupational therapist – who might be involved And the code of practice doesn't seem to support that at all.

Good – or bad – relations with parents can have dramatic effects in the classroom for individual children. Ten-year-old Alan benefited from somebody else's parent. He was a child with specific learning difficulties. Kath, whose child was in the classroom opposite, would come every day and spend 10–15 minutes with him, listening to him read, before she went to work. This really helped Alan. He started every morning in a positive way, having read and achieved something. Being given one-to-one attention helped set him up for the day. Another child who was helped by somebody else's mother was James. He was one of the very few black children in his suburban school. He was used to being the only black child in his class, taught only by white teachers. His work was transformed when Akua, a black primary school teacher from West Africa, came to spend time in his school, working with his teacher. Not only did he form strong personal links with her, but also his status in the class changed, now that one of the high-status adults in the room was also black.

Seven-year-old Tundi believes that she cannot do very much: or, perhaps, she feels that she gets more attention this way. However, on the day her mother came into school and gave her time in school to learn spellings, she got ten out of ten on the test. She had a great day. Moreover, as her teacher observed, Tundi was able to begin the difficult task of constructing a new concept of herself as able and capable. Paul was another child whose view of himself was strongly affected by the quality of relationship with his teacher. This quiet, 8-year-old boy had lots of social problems within the class, often finding himself with few friends. Some of this seemed to stem from the previous year when his mother and his teacher did not have a good relationship. This year, with a new teacher, that relationship has been transformed. His mother comes into the class, where she spends time working with the other children. They like working with her, and Paul's image in the class is being raised as a result.

We have told these stories to show how improving home–school links leads to the breaking down of stereotypes on both sides, to working together in the interests of the children. The stories also show how such links help teachers to see each child as springing from their home – but not defined by it. In short, home–school links are essential for the development of all the elements of fairness: to the building up of trust and openness; and to teachers building up a view of children both as individuals and as members of the community.

All the schools that we know of try hard to involve the parents and the community. All of them know that there is no room for complacency. There are ways of setting about reaching out to parents that help the school in working towards fairness and justice. Throughout the book we have been emphasising that fairness is more about ways of finding your way through the fog than it is about thinking there is some sure way of escaping the fog altogether.

Robin Alexander's (1992) report on primary schools in Leeds shows the range of ways that schools try to link with homes. He points out how difficult it can be for teachers working without clear policy guidelines from LEAs or government. His list of the wide range of strategies adopted by Leeds primary schools is helpful as a starting-point: they include transmitting information through booklets and meetings; involving parents in school life through home visits or coffee mornings; enlisting parents' help in class with reading or running the school library. He also explains the source of some of the difficulties that arise (Alexander, 1992, p.92):

> The report [the third report to Leeds City Council] also examined the very real difficulties which sometimes beset home–school links, suggesting that a clash of basic objectives between teachers and parents

> may sometimes lead to a confrontation between widely differing models of home–school links. We identified four pairs of complementary roles commonly adopted by teachers and parents in their encounters with each other: consultant and client; bureaucrat and claimant; equal partners; casual acquaintances.
>
> Problems arise when there is a mismatch between the models adopted by the teacher and the parent – when, for example, one wants to make a complaint while the other wants to give advice. ... Both may leave the encounter bewildered and disappointed.[39]

Each school has to start from wherever it is, and move forward in the best way possible. One such is described in this chapter. We report on the efforts a nursery school has made to encourage the Punjabi speaking parents to become more involved in their children's nursery education.

In the nursery

Janet is one of three teachers at Pinebank, an inner city nursery school. She has worked there for 4 years now. (The head, Nicola, has been there nearly 20 years, a third teaching post is a job-share, and there are three other members of staff. Together they are responsible for 52 children, most of them attending part time.)

Approaching Pinebank just before it opens, you can see groups of Pakistani parents – mostly mothers – and their children walking companionably towards the school. Inside the long low room (shored up at one end by hastily erected scaffolding, after it was discovered to be unsafe) are all the usual nursery activities. There is a home corner, with two children comfortably in bed. At the neighbouring table Jamie and Omar are both poring over jigsaws. At another table a group of little girls are thumping and pinching at lumps of playdough. Outside, even though it is not a warm day, the children are playing with the large toys and on the climbing frames with one of the Asian assistants. The well-established garden stretches up a small hill into shrubbery. The peaceful scene is momentarily shaken as a father begins shouting angrily at Nicola. He is leaving one child at the nursery for the afternoon session, and his younger child, frustrated at the time he is taking, is beginning to yell. Nicola, meanwhile, has reminded him that they had arranged to discuss the child's progress report this afternoon. This upset is a pity – but, paradoxically, it is a symptom that home–school links have improved over the last couple of years. He and the teachers are, at least, in communication, and in spite of this temporary setback there is every hope that the communication will improve his young children's chances of a good education.

Eighteen months ago the teachers were not achieving the degree of communication with the parents – especially the Asian parents – that the staff would have liked. While all is not yet well, the situation has been turned round, as a result of the school beginning a careful process of reflection, information gathering, tentative actions and evaluation – a process which takes all perspectives into account. To the teachers in the thick of it change feels frustratingly slow. Yet, looking back, it is possible to see the extent and speed of the changes, not least in attitudes and ethos in the nursery.

For some time it had concerned Janet that very few of the Asian parents came into the nursery to see what their children were doing, or to help their children or the staff. The shared record system that they used did mean that the parents had a little contact with the staff, but generally this contact was minimal and only as a result of the staff requesting it. They did have contact in as much as they saw an adult from most families every day, when the children were brought to and collected from the nursery; but the parents did not join in their child's play, nor did they appear to appreciate that their children were learning through play. This was seen by the kind of clothes the children wore to school: very elaborate dresses for the girls and often expensive shirts or suits for the boys. When these clothes got wet, or paint was spilt on them, the parents were not pleased. They expected the staff to keep the children away from the messy activities.

Before Janet started teaching in the nursery, the school was already inviting parents into the school for a parent and toddler session. This was held one day each week during the morning and the afternoon session. An hour was set aside for the parents to bring their younger children into the entrance hall area of the nursery. There were suitable toys set out for these children and they could play while the parents talked. A member of the nursery staff was with the group, but the group was separated from the nursery by a curtain. The parents and the children could have a drink during their time in the parent and toddler group and a member of the nursery staff made it for them. For some time this had been quite successful for the mothers who used it, but it was not used by very many families. At one point there had been a group of Asian mums who wanted to learn to knit and someone used to help this group and it was very successful. But at no other time had there been many Asian families attending this parent and toddler session.

One of Janet's duties was to develop the parental involvement in the nursery and so she looked at this parent and toddler session to see how more families might be encouraged to attend. She felt that the timing made it difficult for some families to attend, as they were expected to bring their child to the nursery for 9 a.m. or 1 p.m., and then return for the parent and toddler session at 10.30 a.m. or 2.30 p.m. Also, as the group met in the entrance hall, it became very congested when the parents came to meet their nursery children. To overcome these problems an area of the nursery was set aside for the parent and toddler group. This was set out with suitable toys and there was space for the very young babies, and for the parents where they could make their own drinks when they wanted them. This area was separated from the rest of the nursery so that the parents knew their children were near them and were safe. A member of the nursery staff was with this group, as before. The timing of this group was altered so that the parents could stay when they brought their child to nursery and could stay in the group for the whole length of the nursery session.

This seemed to be a success at first, as more parents attended and brought their friends with them too. So there were more parents and more toddlers in the nursery, and there was a good feeling in it because the staff could become much less formal in such a group. Yet there were still very few Asian families attending these sessions. Some did attend once or twice but none seemed confident enough to mix with the white parents. The nursery always made sure there was a bilingual member of staff present if there was little English spoken by the Asian families attending. But even the Asian parents who were fluent in English did not attend these sessions regularly.

Janet decided to look at other ways of involving the parents in the nursery. Two avenues were explored. First the staff looked at what other, neighbouring nursery schools were doing. Second, Janet herself decided to explore the views of the other workers in the nursery and the views of some of the parents, by interviewing them.

Each member of Pinebank nursery staff was given time to visit other nurseries which held 'community days' of some kind. Then they all reported back to the whole staff what they had seen, how it had been implemented, what problems they might have had to overcome, and how they felt it might be useful for their own school. As a result of all these visits and discussions, they planned what was to be called a 'Toddler Day'. Every Wednesday afternoon the only children attending the nursery were to be the older children who would be transferring to the Infant school, the few full-timers who had been given places at the school because they had problems of a social nature, and those toddlers who would be attending the nursery the following term.

For some time the nursery staff had visited any families who were to be offered a nursery place for their child and had explained a little about the nursery and had given them a starting date for their child. Now these visits were to be used to offer parents a place for one of them alongside their child and, at the same time, to explain about the importance of the Wednesday afternoon sessions. To place some obligation on the parents to attend – to build up links with them and to involve them in their child's education – the parents were told that their child would not be offered a place, unless they, themselves, attended the sessions. (Six sessions attended regularly was the minimum before a child would be offered a place.)

Pinebank nursery staff felt that many of the families viewed the nursery only as a child-minding facility. If the families were to value the nursery as a place of education, and were also to see the importance of the home–school partnership, they needed to make a commitment. They would therefore have to make appropriate arrangements, even if this was difficult in terms of juggling child-care arrangements for any younger children. Not surprisingly, some parents did not easily adjust to the new system. Some of these were families who had seen their older children through the previous entry arrangements, and they did not think it necessary for their children to attend on a Wednesday afternoon, with a parent staying with them. In fact one or two did not attend the first term. Either they came one Wednesday and not the next, or they came one week and said they could not stay themselves but expected the child to be able to stay. The nursery made no exceptions, explaining gently that the new system was for the child's benefit in the long run. By the second term of the new arrangements no parents expected their child to begin at the nursery without first attending the Wednesday sessions first.

It was hoped that the parents understood the value of the sessions, but of course it was always possible that they only went along with the system to gain a place at the school. Janet felt it was important to explore the views of everyone concerned with the new system. She decided to see if others shared her and the head's view of the value of the new sessions – that the parents and new children would become familiar with the nursery routine, and that the parents would have the opportunity to observe the value of play. She decided to interview the staff and six (out of a possible 12) of the parents of the children attending the Wednesday sessions to see how they felt. All the parents interviewed were Asians. She asked a bilingual member of the nursery staff to ask the questions for her in Punjabi, when necessary, and to translate the answers for her to record. She assured everyone that only those people immediately involved would be able to identify them (and this promise has been honoured in this account).

The members of the nursery staff (three nursery nurses, the bilingual instructor, and the bilingual, welfare assistant) were asked two questions: 'What do you expect the parents and children to gain from attending the "Toddler" sessions?' and 'What do you expect to gain from the sessions?' The parents were asked 'What do you expect you and your child will gain from attending these "Toddler" sessions?' The questions were kept deliberately simple and open-ended not to 'lead' the answers – and also to be non-threatening.

All the nursery nurses thought the session would allow the parents and the children to become more at ease in the nursery. This would lead to the children being able to settle more quickly and easily into the nursery routine when the children began coming without their parents. The same staff were expecting the sessions to allow good relationships to become established between the parents and the nursery staff. One nursery nurse thought that these good relationships could allow the parents to develop the confidence to approach a member of staff if they had a problem. The nursery nurse thought that parents would expect benefits of a social nature.

The words 'familiarity', 'comfortable', 'settle the children', and 'feel more secure' were used to describe the benefits these visiting children would experience. One nursery nurse thought that ideally the parents would begin to obtain an insight into what the staff were trying to achieve in the nursery, although she also said that some of the parents were only attending the sessions so that their children gained a place at the nursery. She saw this as parents looking for a safe place to leave their children, thinking that these sessions were necessary merely to achieve a nursery place. There was a hope expressed by these nursery nurses that parents would look at the nursery activities and begin to realise that their children could be, and would be, learning through play, but there was little expectation of such an outcome.

The bilingual welfare assistant thought the sessions were to help the children to settle more easily into the nursery routine and for the parents to be more at ease with the members of the nursery staff. The bilingual instructor seemed to view these sessions only as a way of allowing the parents to see inside the school. She gave no indication that the parents could learn what their children were doing in the nursery and then help their children to learn at home.

The six parents – all Muslims – felt that Wednesday session helped their child to settle in the nursery. One said it would have taken two or three weeks to settle her daughter in the nursery if she had come straight into it without the Wednesday sessions. This same mother thought there would have been a lot of crying if her daughter had not become familiar with the nursery before being left on her own. The parents' answers were all concerned with their child becoming more settled in the nursery, and being less upset when the parent left – and this was true even when the adults were asked directly what they *themselves* had gained from the sessions.

Janet concluded that the parents that she interviewed saw the nursery as a safe place where their children could learn to mix happily with other children. This view was confirmed by watching what the adults did during the Wednesday sessions. If the children were upset, the parents tried to settle them by joining in their play. But otherwise they did not participate in the children's activities unless a member of the nursery staff joined them and encouraged them directly.

Janet had hoped to go forward from this situation by encouraging the staff to participate in such play, then they could go on to explain to the parents what their child was learning and how an adult playing with the child could help to extend the child's experience, knowledge and understanding.

However, she could see that it was not going to be as straightforward as she and the head had first thought. The answers that the bilingual staff gave to her questions indicated some of the complexities, especially as these two staff were the main point of contact for many of the Asian parents. Neither of them saw how the parents could begin to learn the value of play. To make sure that all the staff were aiming for the same relationship with the parents, there would have to be some discussions about the nursery staff's aims for the 'Toddler' group. This would mean that they would all have to sit down and list some of the knowledge, skills, attitudes and concepts that the children were acquiring while they were playing with each activity that the nursery offers them.

The nursery was moving steadily towards a different kind of relationship with parents. It felt like a long slow road. The road has been described in some detail, partly to show how long and slow it feels – even though, in fact, all this activity only took a year. As we said in Chapter 1, an important principle of fairness is attention to process as well as to its end result. Treating people fairly is an important part of enabling fairness to flourish. What this means is that establishing fairer schools takes time. Janet was careful not simply to establish procedures, but to try them out, evaluate them, and, most importantly, to do that time-consuming and exhausting thing: explore the views of other participants.

The long process produced some results which contributed to greater fairness. Care was taken to hear the voices of the parents (and so, indirectly, the children too, since so much of their identity springs from their homes). It is all to easy to guess at what parents think. It is much more difficult – and much more rewarding – to ask them, as was done in the early stages of this project. Similarly it is all to easy to assume that colleagues share our views. Again, it feels more difficult, but is actually more rewarding, to risk hearing what they really think. All this led to greater trust and openness, and to a sense of ownership of the aims of improving home–school links – as became evident in the next stage.

An overriding aim of the project was to improve the achievement of each individual child, in a way that did not require any of them to compromise their sense of identity as Asian – or white – girls and boys. This continued to drive the project forward, even though it took an unexpected turn.

Unexpectedly, money became available to the nursery as a result of a governmental initiative channelled through local government and business consortia. This money was given to schools as a result of competitive bidding. The bids had to be drafted in a particular way (for instance 'target' groups of children had to be identified). Money was only obtainable for certain named areas, of which one was literacy. The nursery put in a successful bid for money to help in literacy work. Three thousand pounds was made available, together with staff supply cover for the equivalent of 2 weeks. Meanwhile, of course, as we have been describing, the nursery staff had become very much more aware of the importance of home–school links to all their work. The bid, therefore, was targeted at the 'leavers' group' – the group of children who would be moving up to the Infants school the following term. The money was to be used for the nursery to work with them and their parents.

A room was set aside for the parents and furnished invitingly, with new curtains, chairs and carpet. It had a two-way mirror down the length of one wall, overlooking the body of the nursery. A thousand pounds was spent on the leavers' home-loan books. This was a scheme that had been in operation before, but could now be extended. It was important to find books that had no text, since the local Asian parents spoke Punjabi at home but read it in Urdu script; frustratingly, all the available Punjabi books were written in Punjabi script. The school records were made more visual, with the various skills portrayed partly in pictures, and filled in using colours (*see* Figure 9.1).

The full booklet covered the following range of skills, social and emotional, self-help, gross motor, fine motor, reading and writing, language, mathematical, scientific (*see* Figure 9.2 for the first of these).

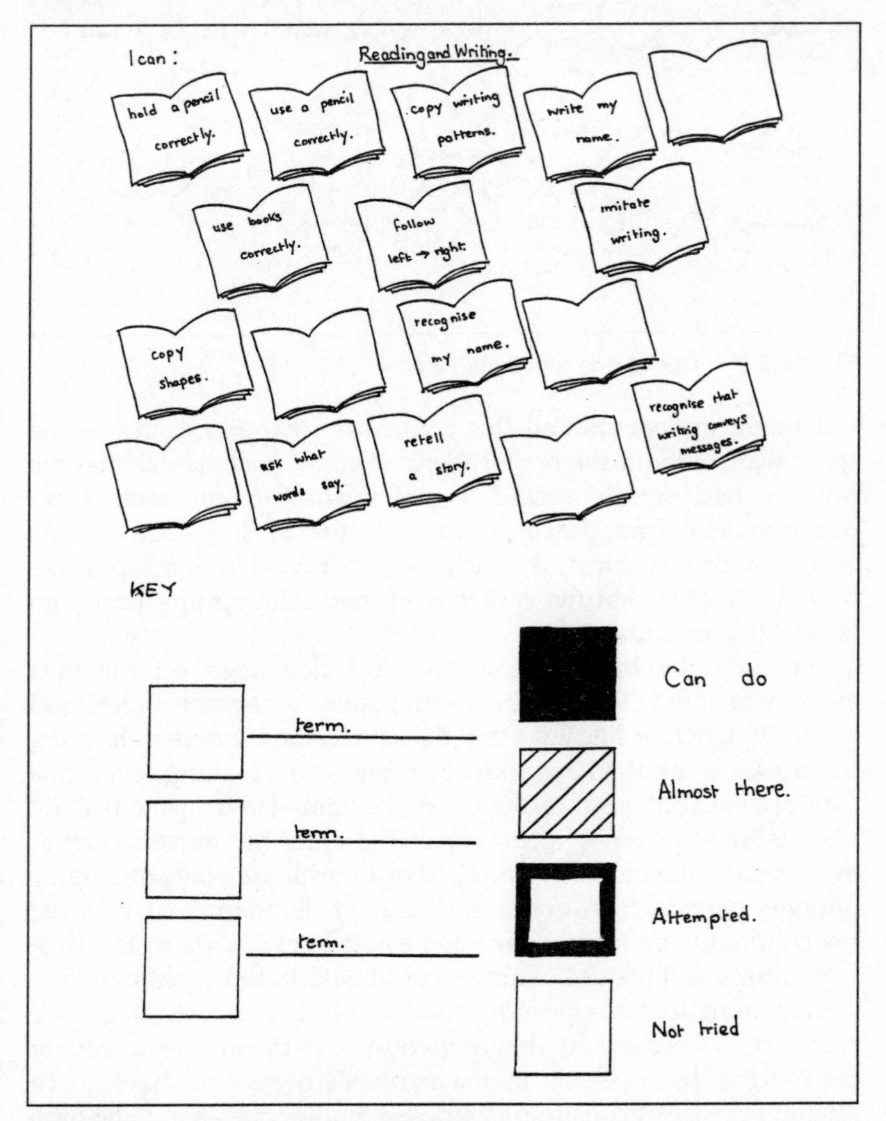

Figure 9.1 Reading and writing skills

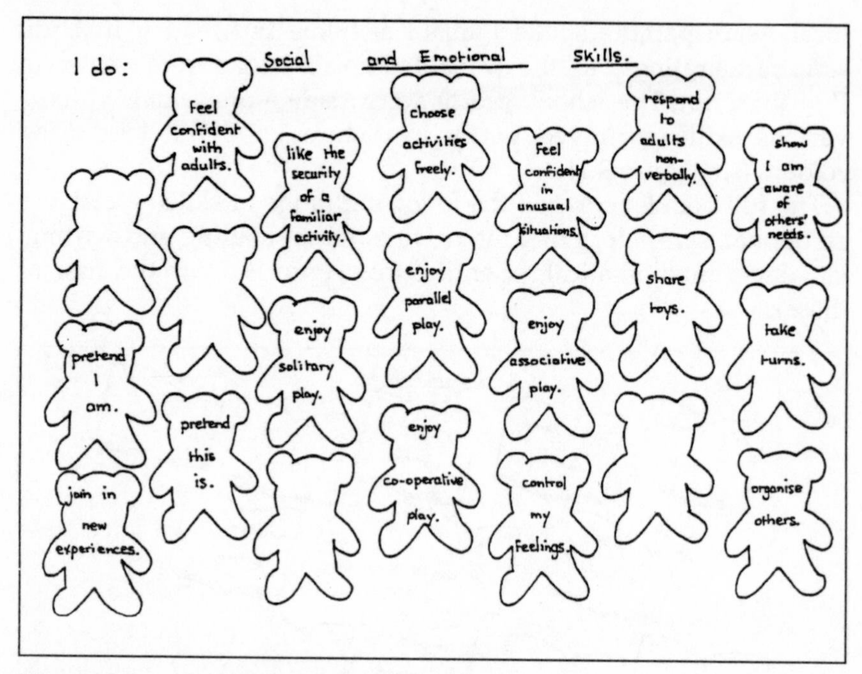

Figure 9.2 Social and emotional skills

It might appear that all this could have happened, in just the same way, without the earlier work. It could well appear that the nursery had simply seized a rare chance to get some extra resources. However, the coherence and value of all this activity was clearly made possible by the earlier work. It was also made possible by the attitudes that the earlier work had both sprung from and helped to consolidate.

The way the bid was put together depended on the new awareness of how to build links with parents. Everyone understood the importance of finding ways that overcame barriers to forming the links – and so, to improve ways of making everyone comfortable, but also to build on the knowledge gained about parents' perceptions of good reasons to enter the nursery. Just as importantly, the bid was put together to facilitate ways of helping not only parents, but also the staff as a whole, to understand what the children were learning and to be able to articulate it. The two-way mirror and the use of new record books both helped in this.

Everything that has been done so far is still at an early stage. The record books are already being revised, and the arrangements for the Wednesday sessions in the parents' rooms will have to be altered because of constraints imposed by the timetable of the local infant school. However, already there are clear improvements. This is what Janet has to say about it now:

> More parents come more easily into the nursery. We had a lot of them before would just step over the threshold and push them towards the cloakroom. I think more of them come in. I think the sharing of the records has helped, and when that has gone right through that will make them more aware of what the children are learning, what we are talking about.
>
> The bilingual assistants have another language sheet if the home language is Punjabi. It's exactly the same sheet. She just fills it in for Punjabi. And if I've got a child who hasn't got a great deal of English, sometimes it's difficult to really assess whether they can do these things, so then we ask one of the bilingual members of staff to check.
>
> It's very difficult when you're there, it's difficult to appreciate when things are changing. One of the nursery nurses who used to do quite a bit of supply for us, and hadn't been in for quite a while – she came in not so long ago and she said, 'Oh! It's so different!' I think she thought that the staff pull much more as a team, much more working as a team. I think that's true. I don't think we weren't before, but for somebody to actually say it, it must have been noticeable. But it changes gradually when you're part of it, and you hardly notice.

In the next chapter we look at an attempt to move even wider than the home and school, to make links with the local community. We show how Riverside, like Pinebank, was able to use a little money to great effect.

Chapter 10

RIGHT UP YOUR STREET: DEVELOPING COMMUNITY LINKS

In the Autumn term, 1994, Riverside school carried out a small project to try and enhance community links. This was a natural extension of the Fairness project, because it has been becoming clearer to both of us just how important home and community links are to a school which is trying to work in fairness to children. The project is called 'Right up your Street'. It is described in this chapter in a set of extracts from letters written by Carol to a friend of hers who teaches in Denmark, and extracts from the report she wrote to the Greater Nottingham Business Partnership which funded the project.

A letter to Denmark

June 15, 1994

Dear Bente,

Thanks for your last letter. The start of your next school year sounds as if it will be exciting – especially the exchange visit to Holland. I wish we could do something like that. I doubt we could ever afford it, but it would be a treat to bring our kids to Denmark and of course nice for me to visit again.

I think I told you that Riverside school is in the inner city? Well most of the children are from either an Asian or White background and only a small percentage are from a Black background. Well I've got four Black children in my class, one of whom, Shaibu, is a Rastafarian and he's really conscious of his culture but does tend to have a poor self-image, probably not helped by the fact that I know very little about Rastafarianism, and not wanting to use it as a total excuse, but there isn't that much on different cultures and History in the National Curriculum or even very much time because of the constraints of the National Curriculum to cover it. Anyway the other day his Mum came in and talked to the children about what it meant to be a Rastafarian. It was brilliant! The children were really involved. They could ask all those questions that adults with all our hang-ups may have wanted to know, but would have been too embarrassed to ask and Shaibu beamed with pride. I suppose it's important that we don't stop there and that I do more and raise more issues of Black awareness through other areas of the curriculum.

It got me to thinking though about how much we can learn from others and how important it is to actually value areas of the children's life rather than just paying lip service to it and saying we do it when actually what we are doing is saying we believe in it, including it in our philosophy and as a result think it is happening when it plainly isn't.

Sorry Bente! I hope this isn't getting too deep, but it really made me think of other areas of the children's life that we don't tend to consider at school. Take the community for instance. Save for the occasional walk round to look at the buildings or plant and animal life or pollution, how often do we really acknowledge that this is where the children live, and then value it ? And how much do we actually use all the knowledge and expertise that is available to us in the community? I mean there's really so much we could do. It's such a huge resource: take just the shops and local businesses around and about. There's a lot we could learn about them and I'm sure they could gain a greater understanding of us. But I suppose it's like everything else, it needs time and money, but perhaps I'll see how some of the others think.

Anyway I'd better close. I've got to make some folders for the parents coming on the trip to the seaside. I hope it's a sunny day again. It'll be chaos if it rains! Hope you are well.

Love Carol

Extract from the 'Right Up Your Street Project' report

Introduction

This paper is a report on a project which has aimed to raise the children's awareness of the community they live in so that they can appreciate its value. The project has been supported by the Greater Nottingham Education Business Partnership (GNEBP). It has involved 130 Year 3 and Year 4 children, four class teachers and a variety of support staff and parents at one of the inner city Primary schools.

A letter to Denmark

July 8

Dear Bente

Thanks for the post card, sounds as if you had a good break. We've got a few more weeks yet before we break up for our summer hols. But, yes, I'm well, and yes the meeting at the TEC was a great success. For a start it was nice to be out of the classroom for an afternoon, and – how civilised! – we were offered tea, coffee, orange juice (in a glass, no chipped mugs) and, wait for it, nice biscuits. Quite a welcome! Anyway they also offered us up to £1000 to put together a project proposal which matches their criteria. This could be an ideal chance to develop links with the business community. The idea is to make a project working with the children and local industry or businesses. I've spoken to Brian and he says that if our planning team is interested we can go ahead. We've got a meeting on Monday so I'll let you know how it goes.

Oh! The other thing is that the people at the TEC have a teacher placement service and they have also offered funds to allow the four class teachers in my planning team to go and work at the businesses that we develop links with. So for example we could go and work in one of the local shops. The idea is that we then share what we have learnt with the kids and staff. I can just see myself working at the local chip shop, but who knows it could be a change of career or perhaps I could do a bit of moonlighting! Joking apart, it is really good because you know what it is like in terms of financing. We would never have the funds to put money into such a project and now, with them, we can have a really good stab at trying to develop community links rather than just saying it's something we should do.

Anyway I'll keep you informed. Sorry these letters are rather short at the moment, but, you know, it's report writing season! I'll be in touch.

Love Carol

Extract from the 'Right Up Your Street Project' report

Objectives

The objectives of the project were for the children and staff working in Base 3 (4 classes of 7–9 year olds) to investigate the local shops and services so that they acquire information and skills that enable them to build their own street of shops that can then be shared with the rest of the school. This would then form a springboard to the school's commitment to develop community links and at a later date develop an environmental trail involving local industry.

Partner Organisations

The area around the school has a large range of businesses and industry but it was decided that the major form of business was the small corner shop or service. These, like the school, reflected the multi-cultural nature of the community, they were accessible for the children and would probably hold more meaning for them. It was from these factors that the idea for the street truly developed.

Project Outline

1. Teacher placement for all four class teachers.
2. Children to walk around on a fact-finding mission of shopping in the community.
3. The children to identify the shops they wish to develop, and market research which would be likely to be most successful.
4. Pupils to visit shops and tradespeople to visit school.
5. Design and make shops, resources and services to sell.
6. Market the new street.
7. Grand opening of the street, with school, parents and VIP guests.

A letter to Denmark

July 30

Dear Bente,

Just a quickie to let you know I will be about during the second week of August if Laille and Jens are passing by on their way to Scotland. I've got a meeting with some of the teachers one day that week to talk about the project and write our schemes of work but apart from that I've nothing planned.

Oh! My new class for September seemed quite interested in it all. I think some of them have already decided the shops that they want. They were so full of ideas. Mind I'm not sure too many understand how to run a business. They certainly haven't got much of a notion about profit. One child thought we could buy some penny chews from the sweet shop and sell them for 1p, and another wanted to go straight ahead and cut hair and didn't think they might need any special training. Oh well I suppose this is where we are at, we've got to start somewhere, especially if we are child centred and all that. Anyway hopefully they'll get a better picture of the business world by the end of the project.

I'll close now so you can get this in time to pass the message on to Jens before he leaves. Anyway bye for now.

Love Carol

Extract from the 'Right Up Your Street Project' report

From Proposal to Practice

We began by planning the topic and subjects to be covered in more detail. As teachers, first and foremost it was important that we covered the necessary and appropriate National Curriculum areas as well as allowed time for an induction period for those children who will have moved from the Key Stage 1 department to the Key Stage 2 department in September. As is our normal practice we shared the planning process between the four class teachers and then met to pull it together and formulate a document of our scheme of work for the Autumn term. This included subject-specific areas as well as a weekly breakdown of topic-related activities so we could ensure that we would complete the topic on time. A copy of this was forwarded to the GNEBP.

A letter to Denmark

September 15

Dear Bente,

Well the new school year has begun and there's good news and bad news. The good news is my class aren't too bad, although they do seem a little young and immature, and we've heard from the GNEBP people and they've accepted our project proposal, and wait for it, offered us £l,200 because they think it's a really worth while idea. The bad news is that life in a Primary school is never straightforward despite the best laid plans as Eve was off ill for 2 weeks. It's a pity as it happened right as we were introducing the topic to the children and it will probably delay some of our teacher placements. Oh well it can't be helped. I suppose it's a good job we are a flexible lot, us primary school teachers.

Anyway despite the setbacks the project is going well. Eve, Kelly, Ruth and myself all had a meeting and decided on which shops and services we would contact. It's a good job we've all got different interests. I decided to go and try and link with the florists and the hairdressers (well mine had been so keen on cutting each other's hair). Eve is going to the local café. I think she wants to fulfil her ambition of having a little tea shop somewhere. Ruth is going to the newsagents and a picture framing shop and Kelly is going to one of the Asian supermarkets owned by the family of a child in my class.

I must admit though it had all sounded alright when we were writing the project proposal, but it was quite nerve wrecking going out into the field as it were to talk to people about the project and trying to sell it to them. Kelly and Eve came with me on my first visit for moral support and also so they could listen to what I said. I think we were worried that the small shop keepers might just say no, but they didn't, so it did get easier. The hairdressers was easy because a lot of us have our hair cut there so at least she knew us. Mind for some it did take time and we had to have some class release time as it was impossible to talk between customers at lunch times.

I'm really not sure what the tradespeople think about the project though most have seemed positive and offered to help, and really only two shops have been a little apprehensive. The pottery shop only wanted very small groups of 'good' children (whatever these are!) to visit and didn't want a member of staff to work there and I'm not sure the local newsagent really understands that Ruth really wants to work in the shop.

Still we've managed to link with six shops who are prepared to let us work in their shops and will support the project in whatever way they can, so that's a positive sign, and, when I think about it, the people at the sandwich shop were keen and thought it a good idea. They even suggested that one of them would come and talk to the children before they were asked. Anyway we'll see how it goes. We've got a meeting tomorrow to discuss it all.

I'd better close I've got all my maths books to mark and it's my assembly tomorrow. I'll keep you in touch.

Love Carol

Extract from the 'Right Up Your Street Project' report

The placements did not necessarily take place according to our original outline plan. We really had to fit around the tradespeople and balance this with school needs and any staff illness. Because some of the classes were not very settled at the beginning of the academic year we decided to space out our placement visits. This meant the children were not unduly disrupted and also we could go to our placements on days and times that were convenient to our hosts.

All the teachers found the placements to be a great success. There was the opportunity to learn something new and see outside beyond the classroom into the business world. The information that was gained was disseminated to other staff at regular weekly meetings and through the general school weekly diary meeting. Staff also shared the information and the experience they had with the children, that is children in Base 3, as well as others in different year groups through assembly times. Many of the older children from Base 4 became very interested in the project. They would talk to teachers about their 'different job' and come with suggestions and ideas for the street. Indeed, when the street opened, a group of other children from different classes, not involved directly with the project but who had shown great interest, were invited to participate and help.

A letter to Denmark

October 2

Dear Bente,

Thanks for the letter, you sound really busy with the 10th class project. I hope they enjoy their first experiences of 'real work'. And talking of work I've been on my first teacher placement. I went to work in the local florist shop last week. It was great, I didn't really want to come back to the school. Mind, I was scared stiff when I first arrived. I thought I would make a right mess of things but everyone was so friendly. The boss had quite a sense of humour so kept pulling my leg about being a teacher and giving me nasty jobs etc., but he couldn't have been more helpful.

Anyway it was all really interesting. When I arrived the boss had just returned from the early morning flower market so I had to first make the coffees (which was really stressful; I was so worried about getting everything right I got really confused with the sugars and amount of milk taken. Luckily I didn't poison anyone). Then I had to help unload the van and was shown how to prepare the flowers. I mainly worked with two of the girls, one in the shop and one in the back preparing flowers and making up the orders. I thought it was great. I was shown how to make a basket and a bouquet and I even learnt how to gift wrap a plant. I can't say my efforts were too successful. It was all a bit like being on the Generation Game, you know where contestants have a minute to make something that an expert has just demonstrated. But I really enjoyed it all. Some of the kids came to see what I was doing and they seemed impressed with my little display in the shop and they took some photographs and a video of me trying to look as if I knew what I was doing. They even had a little go themselves. (In fact Vicky has said she will come and do some workshops on making arrangements and gift bows.) I actually hadn't realised there was so much work to running a flower shop, we never stopped, what with customers popping in, telephone orders and deliveries and long-standing contracts to hotels and firms, and amidst this, all the preparation and care of the plants and flowers, not to mention awkward customers!!

Anyway when I returned to the class the kids had made me a lovely scrap book all about my time at the flower shop. But I don't think I'll be giving up the day job for a while yet.

Well I must go. Bye for now.

Love Carol

Extract from the 'Right Up Your Street Project' report

A Fact Finding Mission by the Children

The real start for the children began when they were asked to explore the local community to examine the types of goods and services available or indeed missing from the locality. To develop the children's skills and to cover the large area three activities were planned. The first was a walk along Riverside Road to look at what they noticed about the street and buildings. It was really an observational activity but did raise the important issue of how it could it be improved and what would they like to do to make it better. The second was a walk around the Cloomber area to carry out a survey of the shops and services in the area and the third was a walk around the South Gate area using a historical trail looking at buildings and what they were used for and whether there had been a change in the use of the buildings over the years.

On returning to the classroom the children recorded the information that they had gathered in charts and graphs. They noted that there were some large businesses in the area but the ones closest to the school were smaller shops.

The children became quite skilled at observation work, some counted up the number of similar type shops while others discussed which were attractive and why. The next stage was for the children to identify the shops that they wished to develop.

Pupils to Visit Shops and Tradespeople to Visit School

The children were able to visit the teachers at work on their placements and they were involved with taking photographs and making a video of the project. The children designed questionnaires and interviewed the tradespeople and some interviews were taped although the quality of the recordings were not brilliant with the Dictaphone the children used. The children did tend to ask more searching questions when they actually visited the shop than those they wrote on the questionnaire. For example, many children wrote 'What is the name of your shop?' or 'What do you sell?' which in some circumstances was a little obvious, but once there they would ask questions like 'How do you make a bouquet of flowers?' 'What is this for?' 'Why do you have to be nice to customers?' 'What do you do if somebody does not like their new hairstyle?' Questions were stimulated by being in the environment of work.

Several businesses also allowed the children to return so that they could try working in the shop. Children phoned the order for staff sandwiches through to another group of children at The Crusty Cob Shop who then made up the orders and another group of children styled each others hair at the hairdressers. This was valuable as it made the project more real and the children were able to put into practice some of the information and skills they had acquired through talking with their teachers and the tradespeople. It was noticeable that children were beginning to gain a greater understanding of how the business world operates. They began talking about the importance of making a profit, about ensuring that goods were of good quality so people would buy them, and about how to make a welcoming and attractive environment for their customers.

Some of the tradespeople also came into school to talk to the children about their job and demonstrate some of the things they have to do. All the children were involved in a flower arranging workshop and some were shown how to make a basket of flowers and a ribbon bow for a bouquet.

A letter to Denmark

October 20

Dear Bente,

Hello there! Perhaps we are in the wrong jobs after all. The community work experience project for the 10th class seems to have been a great success. Our project is developing but probably not as quickly as we had originally planned.

I think we are feeling time creeping on. We have had to commit ourselves to an opening date for the street so we can fit in all the different Christmas activities at the school in the hall, and also so we can book a local councillor to come and open it.

Anyway we've decided that that's life in a Primary school so we are going to have to be a bit flexible with our plans. We had hoped the children would carry out some market research to find the types of shops that would be most likely to be successful, but we haven't really got the time. And I suppose we've got to be practical and work within the children's capabilities. And of course now we are getting worried as to what the shops are going to be like; we've got less than 6 weeks now and we are not sure how professional and polished they are going to be. I suppose we are at that crisis stage when we think we've bitten off more than we can chew. At least I hope so!

Anyway, because there are quite a few children in each class that will need some kind of adult support, we've decided to limit the number of shops that we have, so there aren't too many different activities for us to cope with. We've each decided to develop one shop, although some may have different departments, and we've decided to try to keep the community feeling by trying to re-create the shops in the locality, particularly the ones where we've been on placement, so the children can make their own street and develop it how they would like to see it.

We did discuss all this with the kids. They are quite happy to develop the shops they've visited so there's no problem there. And they also seem happy with the department idea. In fact Jordan in my class who has been desperate to have his own joke shop said that was alright we could have a flower shop and he could still design a joke flower.

So I think we will end up with five main shops as the nursery nurse has said she'll organise a sweet shop. So I'm going to do the flower shop, Ruth is going to be the framers, Kelly will do a sort of gift and pottery shop and – you've guessed it – Eve will do the café.

I just hope it all works out. I think I'm expecting a few sleepless nights ahead of me. Anyway I'm going to try and get some rest now. So bye for now.

Love Carol

Extract from the 'Right Up Your Street Project' report

As the project progressed and the children worked on their own street the link with the business community seemed to strengthen. A local food shop helped with the order for the bridge rolls in the café, the supermarket let the children use their ticket pricing machine, the hardware shop made up the frames for the shop fronts for the cost of the materials used and a local firm supplied some extra large sheets of cardboard for the shop design.

The children invited all the host businesses and other people within the community to their grand opening. As it was near Christmas not everybody could attend but a few people have said they will come and visit the classrooms and share the video with the children in the New Year instead. However three of the shops were represented as were members from the religious community,

It is now hoped that these links will continue to grow. The signs seem positive as staff, children, parents and tradespeople have all commented on the positive nature of the project. Already we have had the owners of the local café come to help with the Christmas party, and play Santa. Many staff teaching other year groups have said that would now feel more confident in contacting shops and using the local community more. We have decided to keep in touch with our business hosts through regular cards and invitations into schools. Indeed the children are maintaining the link in a natural way by going to the shops to buy things, and having a chat with the people who work there.

A letter to Denmark

November 12

Dear Bente,

Nice to hear from you again. Yes you are probably right about the panic stage when you have doubts that a project will be successful. And yes things are going quite well. I'm not saying it's been easy but we are beginning to produce things for the shops and the shops themselves are beginning to develop.

The kids have had a brainstorming session to think about names for their shops and have voted for the one they liked the most. And I think they are beginning to feel that it is more real. We've had some quite business-like meetings to make decisions about the shop. I think my class will be running some large corporate business soon!

Anyway what has been good has been the fact that not only have the local businesses been helping out, but also we've had a large number of parents and other relations coming in to help. Some of the parents have seen us working in the local shops and this has really got their interest. Even parents whose children aren't in the class have been stopping us and asking what it's all about and how things are going. So yes we are feeling much more positive about it all and if the end result is not as polished as we hope it doesn't matter as much as the fact that we've managed to get so many people working together and involved with the school.

Well I'll try and find something suitable from the flower shop to send you.

In the meantime, bye for now.

Love Carol

Extract from the 'Right Up Your Street Project' report

Once samples were made, each class decided on what products and services they would eventually sell and set about discussing who would make the products and when. Again classes worked different systems, with some children working in teams to make specific products, while others worked a rota system with children involved in a number of activities

Once products and shop names were organised, the children turned their attention to the actual design of their shop and how to organise it. Children drew up plans for the front of their shop and worked with the nursery nurse in making them. The street had to be held in the dining hall because of pressure of space at Christmas time, so the children decided to make a shop front which could be portable and which could later be used in different classes.

A letter to Denmark

November 25

Dear Bente,

Well I know I was beginning to feel more positive about the street project last time I wrote to you. Well now it's really taking off and getting a lot more businesslike, I think. I'm quite amazed at what the children have been doing and most of it has been coming from them.

They've designed logos for staff uniforms and put them onto a tee shirt. Ours is 'The World of Flowers' so we've got a flower with the centre of the flower being a drawing of the planet Earth which I thought was quite clever.

The kids have also listed the jobs that are needed to run the shops and they've had to apply for the different posts. All the managers have had to write a letter of application, some have even provided references. I thought I'd send you copies of two of the applicants I had (*see* Figure 10.1). I was really impressed. As they were so keen I got them the day after we'd talked about it in school. The kids then drew up a list of questions to ask the managers at an interview. It was all done properly. The candidates had to wait outside. Lots were drawn to see who would go first and then they came in to be questioned by the class. And the questions weren't easy! They were asked what they would do if someone wasn't working hard enough or if a customer had a problem or was difficult – even what they would do if they caught someone stealing or there was a crisis such as a robbery or fire. I told you I was impressed and to think how immature I'd thought they were in September! Anyway, after the interview, the children voted for the candidate they most wanted. I've actually got a manager and a deputy manager now.

Not all the jobs had to go through an interview. It was decided the accountants would take a maths test. I had quite a mixed bag of children apply for this but I was really pleased for the child who got it. She's got quite a low self-image of herself and she spent much longer than the other children working through the sums, only to burst into tears at the end saying that she wouldn't get the job because other children who she knows are brighter than her worked quicker than her, and therefore stood a better chance. But what was really nice was that when I marked the tests she was the only person with all the sums correct and those children with perhaps higher mathematical abilities had made silly mistakes so the class decided to give her the job. You should have seen the look on her face!

I was actually quite surprised at the jobs the children wanted to do. I thought they'd be a rush to be a manager but it wasn't so. So we've got waiters and waitresses, sales assistants, distribution and delivery teams, first aiders, health and safety personnel, a quality assurance inspector and cleaners. I had quite a laugh with mine over this as Nazar, who has real difficulties with English as a second language, was desperate to be a cleaner, why I don't know. But anyway he was full of delight to get the job, but then I thought it may be politically incorrect to use the title 'cleaner' so I suggested possibly 'hygiene technician', only to be told by Nazar, 'No they wanted to be cleaners as that was what they did'! So who could argue?

Anyway the managers are now making rotas for the times children have to work when we open the street. They are even allowing for breaks. I think it's brilliant as it's all coming from them. They've even suggested writing a code of conduct and guidelines of what to do if certain problems occur in the shop. Mind, I think they may stand the chance of meeting a difficult customer, but an armed raid or terrorist attack is perhaps a little unlikely!

I'll let you know what happens we open in little over a week. I'll be in touch.

Love Carol

Extract from the 'Right Up Your Street Project' report

The shops were now beginning to feel like a shop and the next stage was to market the opening of the street.

Marketing the Street

It was decided that a grand opening ceremony would probably

attract parents to come and visit the street so a programme of events was arranged. The children wrote letters and designed invitations and posters which were then delivered to local shops and old people's homes to advertise the event. More personal invitations went to the host businesses and people from the religious community and a letter was written to the local councillor who is on the Board of Governors asking him if he would open the street. The children also put posters around the school and wrote a letter which was sent to every family in the school so that they would know about the street. Teachers helped by giving regular reminders at assembly times and giving the children an idea of what would be on sale.

The advertising seemed to be going well but by now there was a snowballing feeling and it was felt that other activities should be available at an opening ceremony. It was decided that it would be nice to have some street artists and the steel band. Several children came up with suggestions and as a result parents came to help with juggling and face painting, the headteacher's daughter came to draw portraits and several of the Section 11 staff were drafted in to help with badge-making, face-painting and *mendhi.*

A letter to Denmark

15 December

Dear Bente,

Well at last we made it! The street opened and was a great success. We had all 130 children involved in some way. There was Indian dancing, the steel band and carol singing. Some children had written speeches and others presented our host businesses with a thank you present. The street was opened by the local councillor ringing the school bell. You can imagine how we felt, it was a sort of mixture of pride and relief.

Anyway the turn-out by parents and tradespeople was excellent. It was really standing room only. I don't think we've ever had so many people attend an event at the school before. It was quite a squash to get the children from other classes into the hall to visit the street.

One of my parents volunteered to take photographs and the technician helped make a video, so when we are all sorted I'll send you copies. We even had a photographer from the local paper here taking photographs so, who knows, we may be famous. But there was a tremendous feeling of success and achievement and the day really did belong to the children. You should have seen them. They really took their work seriously and it was amazing to hear them talk to their customers. It was all 'Can I help you? Is there anything else you would like? Would you like it wrapped?'

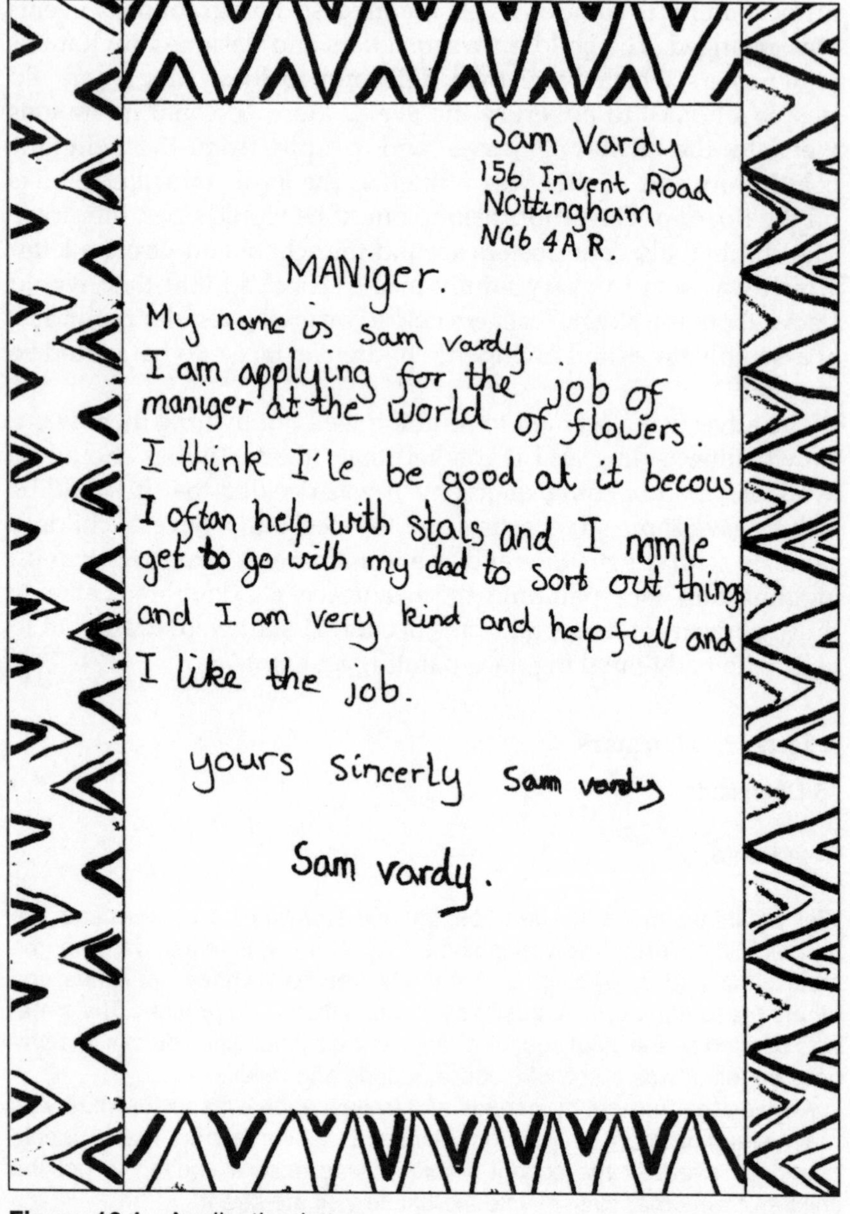
Sam Vardy
156 Invent Road
Nottingham
NG6 4AR.

MANiger.

My name is Sam vardy.
I am applying for the job of
maniger at the world of flowers.
I think I'le be good at it becous
I oftan help with stals and I nomle
get to go with my dad to Sort out things
and I am very kind and helpfull and
I like the job.

yours Sincerly Sam vardy

Sam vardy.

Figure 10.1 Application letter

Mind, by the end of the day I think a few children were beginning to realise that it was quite stressful being a shop-keeper, particularly when the shop is busy.

I think what was really nice was that the children and staff really did pull together. The children took it on themselves to do their job properly. We didn't have to go and ask children to clean up. When they saw a mess or

265 St. John's churchall Road
Mapperly
Nottingham

Dear Sir/madam

I'm Joesphine Smith and I'm applying for the Managers job at the world of flowers. I'm 98 years old and although I do not have a great deal of experience. I think that I will be good at this job because I'm a very responsible and sensible person. I am also Very hard working freindly, and I will always try to be as helpful as possible when dealing with customers and staff problems. I am very artistic and a creative person who is willing to do this job as best as I can.

yours Sincerely

J. Smith

Figure 10.1b Application letter

a problem they went and dealt with it. And probably the best thing for me was the feedback from the parents and local traders who were really impressed and thought it was great. Perhaps the most satisfying was the parent who at the beginning of the week told us she didn't approve of the shop project, as it was teaching the children about commercialisation etc. Anyway she still came to the street and did make some cakes to help us, and at the end of the day she came to apologise as she said she hadn't realised that the project was so community linked, and she was impressed with the results.

Anyway I'm really pleased with how it went but I think now I'm going to have a rest and perhaps a little well deserved tipple. So cheers for now.

Love Carol

Extract from the 'Right Up Your Street Project' report

Evaluation and Conclusion

It has to be said that a project like this does require a lot of hard work from staff and children and it is important to remain flexible to work around problems and accommodate other people, particularly the host businesses. Careful planning is important but it is essential that it is not too rigid, especially when working with young children, as it is vital that you work at their level and adapt plans accordingly. Of course it does not always have to be done at this level, and several staff have talked about small groups of children linking with particular shops to find out about jobs, health, safety and hygiene and at present the nursery have expressed some interest in carrying out such a link. It is now hoped that the school will develop the link with local businesses to develop an industrial trail around the school.

Looking back at the original project outline it would appear that most of the objectives have been successfully met. The teachers worked in the local shops, the children found out about the local business community, pupils and tradespeople visited each other, resources were made and shops designed, they were then marketed and advertised and the street opened. The work has been shared within school and the local community and photographs have been taken and a video made. The only slight hiccup was the market research to see which type of shop would be likely to be most successful, and even then this was covered in a slightly different format to reflect the ever-changing needs of the children and the project.

However, probably more important than whether we achieved the project outline, was the effect the project had on the children and the school as a whole. The children have really matured over the term; they have gained a greater understanding of the business world; and they have learnt how to communicate and work together. Indeed in the week of the street there was a strong feeling of togetherness throughout the school. The older children were proud of Base 3's achievements; and other staff, children and parents were offering their help and support in whatever way they could. On top of this, there was the feeling of truly belonging in the community. Links have been successfully established and the plan now is to maintain these through further activities.

A final comment

We were lucky to have the support of The Greater Nottingham Training and Enterprise Council, their help and funding were an obvious advantage and did spur us on to make the project successful, especially as there was a certain amount of accountability. What we have learnt from this project has been the possibilities open to us in establishing links with other members of the local community and the business world. We were able to bring a lot of skills, knowledge and experiences into the school from outside that we simply didn't have, we have managed to motivate the children and given them a feeling of success for whatever level they are at and we have been able to highlight the value within their own community.

Figure 10.2 shows what one of the children had to say about the educational value of the exercise. It also shows the children were reflecting on the kinds of community they lived in, in terms of jobs and the environment.

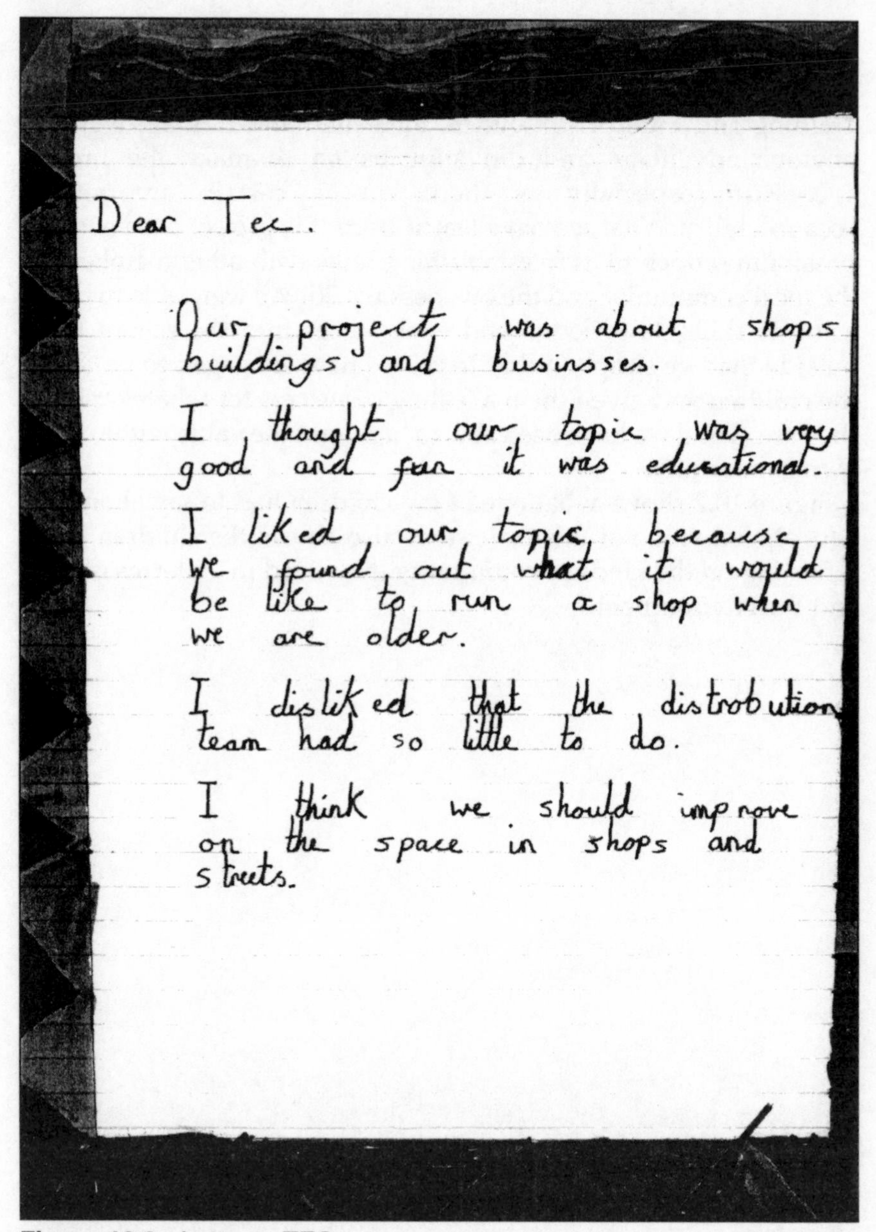

Dear Tec.

Our project was about shops buildings and businsses.

I thought our topic was very good and fun it was educational.

I liked our topic because we found out what it would be like to run a shop when we are older.

I disliked that the distrobution team had so little to do.

I think we should improve on the space in shops and streets.

Figure 10.2 Letter to TEC

Chapter 11

A FRAMEWORK FOR CHANGE

We began this book by asking how far primary schools are fair to children. We wrote the book, we said, in the hope of improving fairness to children. We have now discussed a number of case-studies of children, teachers and schools to show how fairness can be improved. It is time to look more closely at some principles that underlie what has been said: what is meant by fairness, what kind of change will lead to improvement. It is also time to draw together out the lessons of the case-studies and summarise what is needed if schools are to be fair to children.

So what is meant by fairness and social justice?

Justice is based on a sense of what is fair and right. People agree with laws – the laws of the land or the rules of a school – only if they think they are fair, if they accord with their sense of justice. The phrase 'social justice' is meant to catch this sense of rightness in a society. Social justice is the justice that goes beyond the law. As David Miller says, 'To describe a state of affairs as just or democratic is to pass favourable judgement on it' (1976, p.7). Of course, we in Britain do not all agree on what is just or democratic – or fair. The Britain we live in now, in the 1990s, is a plural and multicultural society. This is most obvious in racial terms but it is also true of the two sexes and of social class relations (as maps of voting patterns show). The people on the two working-class estates mentioned in Chapter 1 will not agree closely either with people living a few miles away in the inner cities, or with those living in the rural communities and dormitory suburbs a few miles in the other direction. It is also likely that within each community the women will not agree closely with their menfolk about what a just society would look like, or how to get one. Though how far women – or men – would agree with each other *across* communities is hard to say.

These differences need to be acknowledged but they should not be exaggerated. There are strong similarities too. Firstly, in Britain, there is a widespread recognition of certain core values of tolerance, respect, care, the importance of educational achievement, and of individuals being rooted within family and community and, simultaneously, of individuals' rights to work out their own destinies. Secondly, children will not grow up to be carbon copies of their parents. They need to be given conditions in which they can work out their own ideas of what makes a fair and just society, first in classrooms, then in schools, and finally in the wider world.

The idea of social justice was expressed well, 70 years ago, by Hobhouse. He does not specifically mention educational institutions, but it can be seen that his words certainly apply to schools (Hobhouse, 1922, p.13):

> Social and political institutions are not ends in themselves. They are organs of social life, good or bad, according to the spirit which they embody. The social ideal is to be sought not in the faultless unchanging system of an institutional Utopia, but in the lore of a spiritual life with its unfailing spring of harmonious growth unconfined. But growth has its conditions and the spiritual life its principles, the sum of which in the relation with which we are here concerned we call Social Justice.

Hobhouse's words show that social justice is not an optional concern either for teachers or for senior managers in school: its presence – or absence – is part and parcel of the ethos of any school. Education is only undertaken and delivered because of a widespread belief that it is good both for individuals and for communities. This 'being good for' is exactly what is aimed at in social justice: it is the good of the whole community which respects what is good for each of the individuals within it.

The movement for equal opportunities in schools was a movement for social justice. However, most equal opportunity policies assume that identity in the form of race and gender is the basis for intervention. It has become increasingly apparent that social justice or injustice cannot be simply described in gender, race, or class terms: all of these are complex descriptions which interact with each other to form a multiplicity of possibilities for each individual.

Some examples of real children will show the kind of thing we are thinking of. In Chapter 1, we mentioned Mosiah and his complex identification with Caribbean and Black British culture. Another child, Claudine, is a particularly good examples of the complexities of being British. She has Guyanese parents but was born in the UK.

Her best friend at school is Araya, whose parents are from Africa (Eritrea) and the UK, and who was also born here. Her friends in class are mostly white, and so are the social circles she moves in at home – except for her childminder who is African Caribbean, and who is strongly conscious of her black ethnicity. Recently Claudine wrote a complex story which involved her visiting several continents, including Africa, and ending up in Peru. Attached to the story was a free-hand map of the world with the countries recognisably marked on it. This child is only 7. She is clearly making sense of the complexities of her self-identity in racial terms and, no doubt, in social class terms too, living in a socially mixed part of an inner city as she does. We are suggesting that working for fairness in schools takes account of children's race, gender, class, and learning difficulties, but that it needs to go further than 'equal opportunities' in taking account of the multiplicity of ways that individuals create their own lives, and the ways that schools can empower them to do so.

Social justice has traditionally been thought of in terms of needs, merit, empowerment and entitlement. These ideas are helpful to teachers, but only to a very limited extent, as we said in Chapter 1. We agree with the significance of such ideas, but we also emphasise the importance of trust, safety, and of teachers working closely with parents and their communities. We ourselves began with the intention of working towards equal opportunities and have moved to thinking of it as fairness and social justice, as we have worked together on the Fairness project. Our explanations of fairness and social justice are rooted in the experience of working in real classrooms.

Nothing grand! Making schools fairer

The aim of achieving fairer schools – social justice – can seem very grand. Even the three principles first put forward in Chapter 1 can look rather ambitious for a busy primary school, when they are stated formally. But all schools need a vision, and these principles should underpin it. Here they are again:

1. Social justice in education is made up of two strands: one deals with the empowerment of individuals and the other deals with the righting of structural injustice, due to race, class, gender and special needs. These strands are interlinked, and both are essential.
2. There is no one right answer – teachers need vision, principles

and some methods to try to realise them. Process is not just a means to an end, it is part of the end.

3. There is no conflict between individual excellence and social justice. On the contrary, teaching which improves social justice is good for all children.

And here is Jacqui discussing them:

> That second principle, I think, is as near to what we are trying to do in our very small way as we could possibly get. Not that we're doing anything grand! Because we can't! But, it's like, just an ongoing attitude, and an engendering of attitudes, isn't it? That just going on, all the time, in everything that we try and do.

This idea of doing things in a small way, but with a passionate commitment to the principles involved, is a central theme for us in writing this book. Small steps are more effective in the long run than grand gestures. As we have been at pains to emphasise, single grand gestures are far less likely to result in increases in fairness than steady persistence. The journey will be a long one. Just as important, it can start from anywhere. How far it gets is more important than the starting position. We have deliberately used ordinary children, teachers and schools for our case studies. To return to the metaphor of walking through a fog, which we first used in the Chapter 1, we have not used the bright clearings, the beacons of excellence (though we do think we have described some excellent things going on). Rather, we have focused on what can be done from each situation as it appears, whatever its present problems and opportunities.

Joining in with others rather than telling them what to do is another central theme. As the Fairness project progressed we understood increasingly that the children should be involved as much as possible, not only as informants but also at the stages of setting the questions, devising the methods, and using the results. In other words they should be treated as partners rather than as patients.

Respect for the views and feelings of all individuals is an essential part of being fair to them. To quote Freire, the famous Brazilian educator, 'We cannot enter the struggle as objects in order later to become subjects' (Freire, 1972, p.44). It is important to point out that there is no pretence that all partnerships are equal in power. For instance, children are not being asked to re-invent the wheel, or to disregard their teachers' greater experience and knowledge – we are not advocating 'discovery methods' in a new guise. Rather, children are given the opportunity of sharing something of our greater experience and knowledge but also – and this is the point – of using it for their own ends or even rejecting it altogether. The importance attached to the idea of joining in with others, rather than leaving them extends beyond children. In the chapters on management and links with homes, there is an emphasis on inclusiveness and dialogue, with all concerned.

The case studies discussed in the book show how effective partnership can be. Fairness means good, effective teaching, and good, effective management, as we have kept on saying. Whether the participants are children or adults, the better each one of them understands the reasons for what they are doing, the better each one of them is able to join in and help.

Setting out on a journey towards greater fairness means change. The model of change that was used in all the case studies of projects we described is called 'reflective action-research'. As it is a model of change which includes research, it can be thought of as 'research and development'. This method of research and development is distinguished from a range of other kinds of social science research and development by its emphasis on small-scale action, which is planned and evaluated by the people *within* the situation, rather than by those researching *on* it, or trying to change it from the outside. In this respect, it is different from large-scale research, which tends to use the physical sciences and engineering as a model. Action research is not trying to identify large-scale causal laws and 'teacher proof' methods of delivering the curriculum, which can then be applied to all schools and classrooms. Instead it focuses on the rigorous examination of a single situation, using knowledge drawn from experience and research findings to illuminate it, in order to improve it. The purpose is always to improve practice on the ground, rather than to find the exact truth about a particular situation, let alone about education in general.[40] Helen's gender and literacy project is an example of how a piece of small-scale research can give enough information for improvements to begin.

Action research proceeds through a continuing cycle of action, observation, analysis, evaluation and planning (*see* Figure 11.1). The people who carry out the research are reflecting and acting on their own work and their own work situations, rather than coming as experts from 'outside'. As far as possible, all the participants contribute to formulating the research questions and collecting the data. Whenever possible the work is explained to colleagues who can criticise it constructively. The way that action, observation,

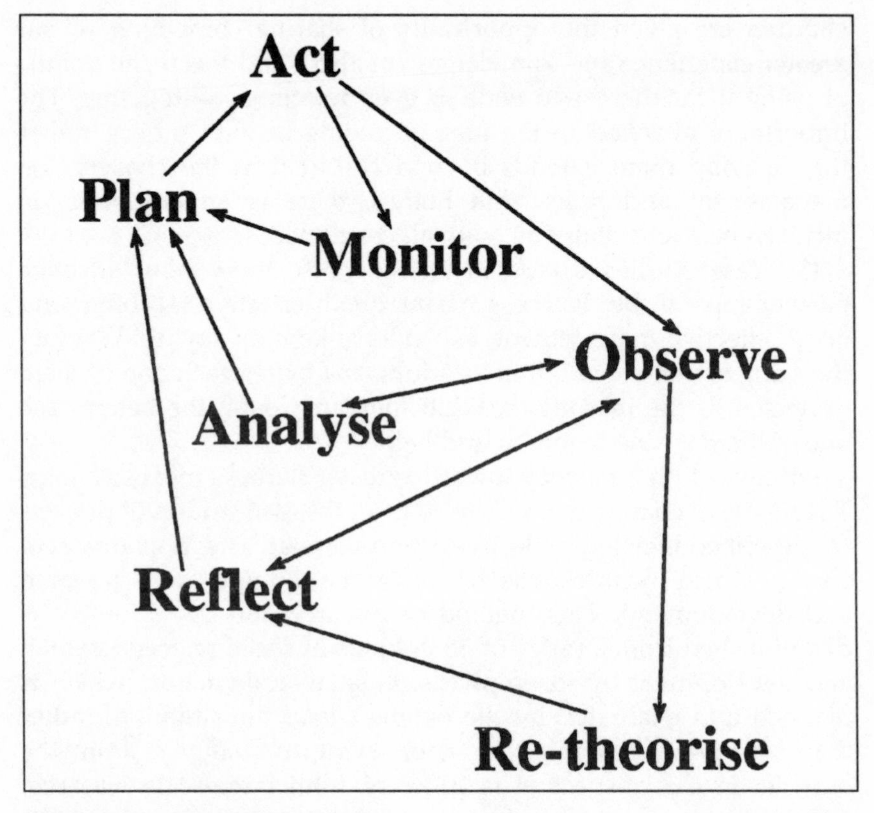

Figure 11.1 Reflective cycle

analysis, evaluation and planning are all necessary, but rarely follow each other tidily is discussed in Griffiths (1990) and Griffiths and Tann (1991). Often the very fact of observing affects the next actions, and so it should, if improving the education of the particular children in the class is taken to be more important than a controlled, careful, experiment.

Moreover, as we found in the later stages of our project, there was a need for a kind of 'pre-wash cycle', before the action–research cycle could get under way. This was the stage of building up sufficient trust and communication with the children, which we described in detail in Chapter 3.

Reflective action–research can feel quite unsettling. Because the process is responsive to the views of others and to the changing situation, it is impossible to keep in tight control of what happens. This is in contrast to the idea of rational action in more 'scientific research and development' where it is important to stick to pre-determined aims and objectives.

In the Fairness project we were engaged in finding the questions as well as in answering them. Then, as the project progressed, we realised that we would do better to involve the children in finding the questions, so even the identity of the 'we' of 'we were engaged in finding the questions as well as answering them' was re-assessed as the project went along. We also took account of comments from everyone who came into contact with the project. They included not only the children, but also teachers in Riverside school, support staff, parents, teachers from other schools, local inspectors, academic colleagues at the University and in other Universities, and Morwenna's students on her courses. All of them helped us broaden our ideas and perspectives.

A second, unsettling, aspect of it being 'own work' is that the real world keeps intruding on plans. Since action research takes place in the real world, there are practical constraints on it. In particular, everything else does not stop for the project. A more formal research and development project would require the school day to be fitted round it – needing a small group of children to be available, or for a class to be engaged in a particular activity at a certain time, for instance. In contrast, this project had to fit round the normal life of a school with all the attendant interruptions. (There were plenty of them, ranging through unexpected visits from television crews; the removal of all the chairs from the classroom for the Harvest Festival assembly; the arrival of new furniture; an externally imposed experiment re-organising the children by ability in certain subjects; and illness of children and staff.) Moreover, the changing circumstances of our professional lives also altered what we did. (These circumstances included preparing reports, the availability of particular sources of funding, reading new theory, working on other projects, and taking up new responsibilities or planning to do so.)

While having to work round all this disturbance was frustrating, it meant that there was much less distortion of what is actually normal teaching and learning. In Carol's class it was interesting to contrast the effect of a single visit by the local inspectorate, which considerably changed the normal reactions of the children, with the ordinariness of Morwenna's visits to work on the Fairness project. In other words the practical constraints on the project could also be regarded as a strength. Any actions and conclusions that come out of it are rooted not in the 'hard high ground' of scientific, laboratory research, but in the 'swampy lowlands' of the complex real world, to use a metaphor made famous by Schon (1983). To extend this metaphor, the high ground may look impressive, but things actually grow and flourish in the fertile lowlands.

What we have not included in one short book

There is a great deal that has been left out of this book, although we recognise that it is still very important. We were sorry to leave it all out. All we have space to do is to list some of it.

Firstly there are a number of areas in which schools should act on the principles of fairness which we have not discussed at all. They include: curriculum planning and the 'basics', teachers' careers, teacher education, play and dinner ladies, OFSTED inspections and requirements, primary–secondary transition, assemblies, governors, bilingualism, and special schools. We could have been more explicit about how to weave fairness into all of these areas.

Another thing that has got left out is much of our background reading and knowledge of research. We have mentioned some books along the way, but they are only a fraction of those that have influenced us. Still their ideas have influenced us one way and another. Some of them appear in the notes (page 203), but there were many more, as the list of references shows.

Getting fairer schools: lessons for teachers and schools

Throughout the book, from the classroom where we begin in Chapter 2 to the streets where we end in Chapter 10, the same themes emerge. We have discussed a range of case-studies, including projects and individual children and teachers. The same themes appear in all of them: valuing individuals, using the lens of social groups and cultures to understand them, trust, safety, sharing and kindness, choosing and solving things for oneself, and effective behaviour policies. Sometimes one of these themes comes to the fore, and sometimes another. However, we pointed out that all of them are needed all the time. In the part of the Fairness project where we focused on trust, we were simultaneously remembering the diversity of the pupils and we were developing trust partly through enabling them to choose and solve things for themselves. In the case-studies on bullying and harassment, where safety and the importance of social groups were emphasised, the importance of supporting individuals in making their own choices was also emphasised. The themes apply to adults as much as to children. In the chapter on safety we pointed out that effective behaviour policies, such as harassment policies, apply to teachers as well as to children. In the chapter on management the importance of trust and allowing individuals to solve things for themselves underpinned all the efforts to improve fairness.

These themes are very much the same as the children in Carol's present class came up with in a discussion about fairness. We give them the last words on the matter, in an edited version of what was a long talk. We have only included examples of each idea, and left out all the discussion that went on round the various ideas. The discussion also inspired some children to produce lists of their own of how to improve school (*see* Figure 11.2).

School Improvements
By Claudine

1. Grass in the playground.
2. Some climbing frames. Because we don't get enough exercise.
3. No more name calling.
4. More P.E.
5. More apparatus.
6. No bullying.
7. A bit more staff.
8. Longer lunch hours.
9. Safety.

Improving School
by Rose

1. Drawing pictures of things which you want to have in the play ground like haunted houses and things and going round houses and asking if they'll help - but that might be a bit expensive.
2. Having grass so if you fall over you don't hurt yourself so much.
3. Dinner ladies don't sort things out very well.
4. To have more trees.
5. A bit more benches in the middle of the yard.
6. I think on toy day we can take roller skates and skate in the Gym.
7. I think we should have more P.E.
8. More education.
9. No bullying.
10. More safety at school.
11. Longer lunch hours.
12. More videos.
13. Choosing topics.
14. Black history.
15. More trips.

Figure 11.2 Improving school links

Carol You know Miss Griffiths and I are trying to write a book which is all about to do with making schools fair for children. We want to get some of your ideas, so that other teachers will read it and see what children think. We think it is valuable to listen to you. You're going to help other teachers. We won't put in anything personal of yours. If we do want to use something of yours, we'll ask you. We've made some questions. It doesn't necessarily mean we're going to stick to them. You may have better ideas. What do you think should happen to make this school a better school to live in?

Leku If you could choose your own dinners...

Gwen Get grass in the playground. If you fall over on concrete you'll hurt yourself more than if you fall over on grass.

Tundi Make sure that the places at dinner time are clean. They never clean up anywhere.

Talib We could have more things like roundabouts and things on the playground.

Mala No more bullying.

Tundi You choose when you go into assembly.

Liza On *Sesame Street* they had these pictures of people saying 'Would you help us make our new playground?' and they'd drawn pictures of what they should have in their playground and they looked to see which one was the best and then made it out of wooden things.

Craig We could put these cameras in the wall and see children, if they're being naughty or not, in the playground.

Grace I think we should let all the children in the big yard and have sports in the other yard.

Leku I think that all the little children and the big children should go in one yard, and then the little children could learn.

Liza I think we should have more education. ... In maths and spelling. ... And PE and drama.

Rose I think we should have a bit of black history.

Carol Where?

Rose Well we can have it in clubs...

Carol Because we've got a black history club.

Rose ...Or just study about it in class.

Leku More culture. Like religions and all that.

Aidan I think all the good children can go out and all the bad children should do the work.

Leku I think that all the good children shouldn't suffer from the bad.

Morwenna Our book is about being fair to children. What do you think 'being fair' means?

Leku When one person gets something good, the rest of the class should get something good.

Philip Sharing. We should share

Carol Teachers or children or both?

Philip Both. If the class got something unusual for Christmas, or something, then someone was playing on it, and someone else wanted to play on it, then the person who's playing on it should let them.

Shakir You shouldn't snatch off people when they've got something. They do that with the Lego.

Talib It would be better if people look after the books and not leave them dog-eared.

Shelly I think children should have a say in a topic.

Carol Can I just ask about the National Curriculum? Sometimes I've got to teach things because they are in the National Curriculum.

Shakir I know! We choose and then you say if it's all right or not.

Leku I think that people should, when they are playing, should let other people play with them.

Danny It would be better if you had a school bus.

Aidan It would be better if we look after the school better.

Katie I think, like, yesterday lunch time, only some people were being naughty, and if some people are naughty today, all of us will have to miss their playtime. Just the people who are being naughty should miss their playtime.

Leku I think that there should be more dinner ladies, because there are nine dinner ladies and more than 300 children in the school, so they can't look after them all at the same time.

Craig I think on the topic you should have more trips out.

These children understand what fairness is. They have shown that for them a fair school is one in which there is an ethos of no bullying, sharing, choosing, looking after each other, and being looked after themselves, a decent environment with enough playthings, a rich educational experience, attention to all cultures, and fair discipline procedures. It sounds good to us, and we think it can be done.

NOTES

1. When one of us is speaking for herself, the part of text is marked off from the rest by a heading and a change in font. The name of the person is indicated by the heading.
2. In his book on primary education, Robin Alexander refers to a large body of research which talks about the reasons behind 'schools locked into a cycle of self-reinforcing inadequacy': reasons which include 'a consistently noted pattern of underexpectation and underachievement in primary schools' (1992, p.23).

   This book is a report of a report. Leeds City Council asked Alexander and his colleagues to evaluate its Primary Needs Programme initiative. As he carefully explains in Chapter 2, 'needs' were identified in the following groups of children: those with special educational needs; ethnic minorities; girls; those having social and material disadvantage; and those having high abilities. Alexander argues that any policy directed at meeting children's needs should specify how to identify a need, diagnose it and provide for it. This is an argument for differentiation. He remarks that there are no clear policies for differentiation. For instance at classroom level (1992,p.21):

   > At any given point in time, selectivity of teacher attention is an essential response to the demands of the task. However, if it leads to the persistent neglect of some children then the consequences are likely to be serious, and the strategy must be called into question, especially if, as we found, there is a tendency for 'undemanding' children to be given undemanding work.

   While the research is centred on Leeds, there is every reason to believe that similar patterns would emerge in other areas (p. 164).
3. In his Leeds study (*see* note 2), Alexander comments that there were some teachers and heads who did not recognise how they could improve the education of all children if they were to pay more attention to equality, and equal opportunities in the areas of ethnic minorities and of gender (1992, pp.15–I6). In her case studies of primary schools in a large industrial city in England, Debbie Epstein comments on some of the reasons that a minority of governors and teachers were opposed to anti-racist work in their schools (1993, pp.59, 73, 82).
4. All names of schools, teachers, children and LEAs have been changed. The only exception is that the two main authors are Carol Davies and Morwenna Griffiths, and they both work in Nottingham.
5. With hindsight, and with more time to reflect, Morwenna might have

written something different in her Journals! However, since the point of these case-studies is partly to show processes, they have been presented exactly (well, almost exactly!) as written.

6. We use 'they' and 'their' rather than the more clumsy 'he or she' 'his or hers', when appropriate. We would point out that this usage is not only found in the speech of everyday, but also in the great works of English literature through the centuries. According to Leonard (1929, p.225; quoted in Bodine, 1990, p. 171):

   > Quite as many cases of reference of 'they' and 'their' to words like 'person' and 'one' and 'everybody' could be discovered in an equal number of pages of Jane Austen or Walter Scott as of Addison or Swift....There is good evidence that British usage is still about equally unfettered in the matter.

7. We have taken care to disguise them not only in the case of these contracts, but also by changing names and personal details about the children all through the book.
8. There have been a number of research programmes on the effects of primary education, which all point to the same conclusions: the quality of teaching a child receives at pre-school or primary school will affect them both academically and socially into their teens and beyond. The findings on pre-school are summarised in The Commission on Social Justice's Report (1994, p.125). Fullan summarises international research which shows that it is the quality of extra early education which has a lasting effect; simply providing more education does not make such a difference (1991, p.229). In Britain, a follow-up of Peter Mortimore's junior school project on effective teaching in London schools, has shown that the quality of a primary school has a significant impact on pupil achievement and attitudes (Sammons, 1994).
9. Being valued means belonging to a group which values you, and which also values the other groups to which you belong. We say more about this is Chapter 6. A more philosophical discussion of the educational issues can be found in Griffiths (1990). A more lengthy philosophical discussion, which is less educationally oriented, is in Griffiths (1995b). It is never too early to start: Siraj-Blatchford outlines some of the practical ways in which teachers can show they value children of all ethnic backgrounds (Siraj-Blatchford, 1994, p.62).
10. Andrew Pollard gives the example of his own children who negotiate rules with him whatever he might wish, when for instance trying to get them to school: 'I appear to think that my children will learn to get ready with coats on if I instruct them to do so and if I tell them off when they don't. Some chance!' (1990, p.58). This is consistent with their behaviour in classrooms. Drawing on his earlier research (Pollard, 1985), he summarises the situation, 'children do not passively experience the routines, rules and structures of schools. They constantly act so as to get the most enjoyment from situations' (Pollard, 1990, p.25).
11. Such as Reid (1981), Holt (1982) and Pollard (1985). (See note 10).
12. Willes (1983) and Pollard (1985) provide evidence of this. In their book, Elizabeth Grugeon and Peter Woods describe Abbas, a child for whom English is a second language, 'becoming a pupil'. In his ninth week at

school, he has become competent enough in basic English to begin to learn how to respond to his teacher's expectations about appropriate answers (Grugeon and Woods, 1990, p.38). More recently, the contributors to 'Learning through talk', Section 4 of the report from the National Oracy Project (Norman, 1992), have gone beyond a description of children giving the answers they think teachers want, by suggesting strategies teachers can adopt in classroom discussions to help them move out of 'the expert role' (Corden, 1992, p.174).

13. There are recent overviews of some of this research, paying particular attention to primary education, in Skelton (1989), Grugeon and Woods (1990) and Tizard *et al.* (1988).
14. Alexander (1992) reviews a number of strategies that teachers can use to deal fairly with a range of children. Also see Norman (1992) for a series of studies of such strategies. The data collected by Alexander and his colleagues are presented in the terms of large-scale surveys, while the contributors to Norman's book present their data in the context of particular teachers, children and classrooms.
15. For instance, see case studies presented by Debbie Epstein (1993) about working for race equality in city schools. Also see Skelton (1989) about gender equality. The case studies from a number of different primary schools in Claire *et al.* (1993) cover hearing-impaired children, travellers, and sexuality as well as gender and race equality.
16. This is true even of work in which there is a strong commitment to seek out the perspectives of pupils, like Pollard and Tann (1987), Grugeon and Woods (1990) and Claire *et al.* (1993).
17. We come back to Kelly's work later on in this chapter. See note 21 for some references to Elinor Kelly's work on bullying and harassment.
18. It may be helpful for white people to put Yusuf's reactions into the context, familiar to most visible minorities, of facing widespread harassment. A recent survey by Leicester Racial Equality Council showed that eight out of ten households in the Asian community 'had experienced racial attacks in the past 2 years with over half of those questioned adding that racial abuse is a constant element in their life. Only 9% of reported complaints to agencies resulted in a satisfactory outcome for the victim' (*Asian Times* 12 November, 1994)

    It is not only children and teachers who need to be included in school policies on racism and name-calling, but also parents, as Iram Siraj-Blatchford argues (Siraj-Blatchford, 1994, especially pp.100ff.).
19. This African Caribbean child cannot bear to actually say the word which offends him so much.
20. Although we only discuss Besag, our criticism also applies to other work, which is otherwise excellent and helpful, such as that of Maines and Robinson (1992, 1994) and Kidscape, 152, Buckingham Palace Road, London SWIW 9TR.
21. Her ideas can be found in Kelly and Cohn (1988) and Kelly (1991).
22. Richard Hatcher (1995) gives a thorough account of the different reasons that children use racial abuse to each other, even when they are not themselves racists. How much such language has power to hurt was

vividly explained in Fanon's ground-breaking book 40 years ago (Fanon, 1952, 1986).

23. We should emphasise again that we have been careful to hide the identities of the children involved.
24. Wolfendale (1992) provides a useful overview of the issues of parental involvement in reading, within the context of a more general exploration of the role of parents in schools. David (1993) also discusses literacy and is also one of the few studies to examine the gender issue which we are pointing to here, that 'parent' often means 'mother'.
25. Useful overviews and explanations of this research can be found in Ryckman (1992) and Deaux *et al.* (1993).
26. Solsken (1993). Bronwyn Davies (1989) discusses how young children can and do negotiate their own sense of being masculine or feminine by the way they interpret stories, regardless of the intentions of the teacher. Ferdman (1990) is an academic's analysis of the relationship between literacy and cultural identity in the multiethnic society in the USA. More practically, the Runnymede Trust (1993) examines how cultural diversity can be integrated into the English curriculum at Key Stages 1 and 2.
27. A brief, useful overview of the history of Section 11 until the beginning of this decade can be found in Wallace and McMahon (1994). Other information came from 'Lost for words in an unequal world', *Times Educational Supplement* 9 September 1994; 'Baffled contestants in the regeneration game', *Times Educational Supplement* 14 October 1994; 'Campaign forces Home Office climb-down', *Asian Times*, 3 December 1994.
28. For instance, Mortimore *et al.* (1988) show that Year 3 children who spoke Bengali scored lower than the average in mathematics, while children who spoke Gujarati scored higher. In contrast, the report of Nottingham's Inner City Project (unpublished) shows that Bangladeshi boys score higher in mathematics than Indian boys, and much the same as Pakistani boys.
29. A useful overview of such figures can be found in MacGilchrist (1992). Nehaul (1995) provides a thorough overview of research on African Caribbean achievement. Studies of primary schools in London which include data on gender, social class and race include Tizard *et al.* (1988) and Mortimore *et al.* (1988). One of Tizard's co-authors, Ian Plewis, explains some of the subtleties of gleaning information from figures in a useful article about defining underachievement (Plewis, 1991). Paterson and Goldstein (1991) explain some of the statistical methods available for analysing data in terms of multilevel modelling, that is, in studies which have more than one variable, such as gender, social class and race.
30. See, for instance, Tajfel (1978), Milner (1983), Verma and Pumfrey (1988), Coultas (1989).
31. More suggestions for ways of working with the idea of identity can be found in the Runnymede Trust (1993).
32. The first person to use the term 'stuck' about schools was Rosenholtz in America. She says that in 'stuck' schools 'teachers talked of frustration, failure, tedium and managed to transfer those attributes to the students about whom they complained' (Rosenholtz, 1989, p.208; quoted in Fullan,

1991, p. 123). In Britain, David Hopkins and Mel Ainscow say that schools often get stuck in early implementation 'when the change hits the "wall" of individual learning or institutional resistance' (1993, p.292).

33. The distinction between 'truth' and 'fiction' is always blurred in autobiography (Griffiths, 1995a). Teachers working on INSET courses at Nottingham University have found it useful to fictionalise their experiences, often, as here, using other works of fiction to do so. Also see Convery (1994).
34. People find it difficult to explain why they act as they do to explain their personal theories accurately (Griffiths and Tann, 1991). Martha Nussbaum, the American philosopher explains:

    Most people, when asked to generalise, make claims that are false to the complexity and the content of their actual beliefs. They need to learn what they really think, through work on the alternatives and through dialogue with one another, so that they arrive at a harmonious adjustment of their beliefs, both singly and in community with one another.

35. This trend is discussed in McHugh and McMillan (1995) and Webb and Vulliamy (1995). There is some evidence that in some schools the opposite trend occurs, as heads take on teaching under pressure from tight school budgets.
36. See Antonouris and Wilson (1989), and Grugeon and Woods (1990) for some of these ideas.
37. Several senior teachers and heads have been generous enough to be very frank with us. We protect their anonymity in this quotation and in the next one!
38. Again (*see* note 37) these heads have been generous enough to be very frank with us. We protect their anonymity in this quotation and in the next one!
39. John Bastiani also lists a number of 'sharply felt contradictions, or dilemmas' (1989, p.14) which, sooner or later, will have to be tackled by schools developing a whole-school approach to the improvement of home–school relations.
40. Discussions of action research and reflective practice can be found in a number of books, of which the most accessible are probably Kemmis and McTaggart (1982), Carr and Kemmis (1986), Pollard and Tann (1987) and Winter (1989). The particular model used here is described in Griffiths and Tann (1991).

REFERENCES

Alexander, R. (1992) *Policy and Practice in Primary Education*. London: Routledge.
Alexander, R., Rose, J. and Woodhead, C. (1992) *Curriculum Organisation and Classroom Practice in Primary Schools: A Discussion Paper*. London: DES.
Antonouris, G. and Wilson, J. (1989) *Equal Opportunities in Schools: New Dimensions in Topic Work*. London: Cassell.
Bastiani, J. (1989) *Working with Parents: A Whole-School Approach*. London: Routledge.
Besag, V. (1989) *Bullies and Victims in Schools*. Buckingham: Open University Press.
Bodine, A. (1990) 'Androcentricism in presceiptive grammar: singular 'they', sex-indefinite 'he' and 'he or she',' in Cameron, D. (ed.) *The Feminist Critique of Language*. London: Routledge.
Carr, W. and Kemmis, S. (1986) *Becoming Critical: Education, Knowledge and Action Research*. Lewes: Falmer.
Casdagli P. and Gobey F. (1990) *Only Playing, Miss!* Stoke-on-Trent: Trentham Books.
Claire, H., Maybin, J. and Swann, J. (eds) (1993) *Equality Matters: Case Studies from the Primary School*. Clevedon: Multilingual Matters.
Commission for Racial Equality (1987) *Learning in Terror*. London: CRE.
Commission on Social Justice (1994) *Social Justice: Strategies for National Renewal*. London: Vintage.
Convery, A. (1994) 'Developing fictional writing as a means of stimulating teacher reflection: a case study', *Educational Action Research*, **1 (1)**.
Corden, R. (1992) 'The role of the teacher', in Norman, K. (ed.) *Thinking Voices*. London: Hodder and Stoughton.
Coultas, V. (1989) 'Black girls and self-esteem', *Gender and Education*, **1 (3)**.
David, M. (1993) *Parents, Gender and Education Reform*. London: Polity.
Davies, B. (1989) *Frogs and Snails and Feminist Tales*. London: Allen and Unwin.
Day, C. Hall, C. Gammage, P. and Coles, M. (1993) *Leadership and Curriculum in the Primary School*. London: Paul Chapman.
Deaux, K., Dane, F. C. and Wrightsman, L. S. (1993) *Social Psychology in the '90s*, (6th edn.). Brooks/Cole Publishing Company.
Department for Education (1994) *Bullying: Don't Suffer in Silence*. London: HMSO.
Drummond, M. J. (1994) *Assessing Children's Learning*. London: David Fulton.
Elliott, J. (1991) *Action Research for Educational Change*. Buckingham: Open University Press.
Epstein, D. (1993) *Changing Classroom Cultures*. Stoke-on-Trent: Trentham.
Fanon, F. (1952,1986) *Black Skin, White Masks*. London: Pluto.
Ferdman, B. M. (1990) 'Literacy and cultural identity', *Harvard Educational Review*, **60 (2)**.
Freire, P. (1972) *Pedagogy of the Oppressed*. Harmondsworth: Penguin.
Fullan, M. (1991) *The New Meaning of Educational Changes*. London: Cassell.
Gipps, C. (1995) 'Teacher assessment and teacher development in primary schools', *Education 3 to 13*, **23 (1)**

Gipps, C., Stobart, G. and Lawton, L. (1993) *Assessment: A Teacher's Guide to the Issues*. London: Hodder and Stoughton.
Griffiths, M. (1990) 'Action research: grassroots practice or management tool?', in Lomax, P. (ed.) *Managing Staff Development in Schools: An Action Research Approach*. Multilingual Matters.
Griffiths, M. (1990) 'Self-identity and self-esteem: achieving equality in education', *Oxford Review of Education*, **19 (3)**.
Griffiths, M. (1995a) '(Auto)biography and epistemology', *Educational Review*, **47 (1)**.
Griffiths, M. (1995b) *Feminisms and the Self: the Web of Identity*. London: Routledge.
Griffiths, M. and Davies, C. (1993) 'Learning to learn: action research from an equal opportunities perspective in a Junior school', *British Educational Research Journal*, **19 (1)**.
Griffiths, M. and Tann, S. (1991) 'Ripples in the reflection', in Lomax, P. (ed.) *Managing Better Schools and Colleges: An Action Research Way*. Multilingual Matters.
Griffiths, M. and Wells, G. (1984) 'Who writes what and why', in B. Kroll, and Wells, C. G. (eds) *Explorations in the Development of Writing*. Chichester: Wiley.
Grugeon, E. and Woods, P. (1990) *Educating All: Multicultural Perspectives in the Primary School*. London: Routledge.
Hatcher, R. (1995) 'Racism and Children's Cultures', in Griffiths, M. and Troyna, B. (eds) *Anti-racism, Cultures and Social Justice in Education*. Stoke-on-Trent: Trentham.
Hobhouse, L.T. (1922) *The Elements of Social Justice*. New York: Allen and Unwin.
Holt, J. (1982) *How Children Fail*. Harmondsworth: Penguin.
Hopkins, D. and Ainscow, M. (1993) 'Making sense of school improvement: an interim account of the "Improving the Quality of Education for All" project', *Cambridge Journal of Education*, **23 (3)**.
Kelly, E. and Cohn, T. (1988) *Racism in Schools – New Research Evidence*. Stoke-on-Trent: Trentham Books.
Kelly, E. (1991) 'Bullying and racial and sexual harassment in schools', *Multicultural Teaching*, **10 (1)**.
Kemmis, S. and McTaggart, R. (1982) *The Action Research Planner*. Deakin University Press.
Lomax, P. (ed.) *Managing Staff Development in Schools: An Action Research Approach*. Clevedon: Multilingual Matters.
Lomax, P. (ed.) (1991) *Managing Better Schools and Colleges: An Action Research Way*. Clevedon: Multilingual Matters.
Macdonald, I., Bhavani, R., Khan, L. and John, G. (1989) *Murder in the Playground*. Longsight.
MacGilchrist, B. (1992) *Managing Access and Entitlement in Primary Education*. Stoke-on-Trent: Trentham.
Maines, B. and Robinson, G. (1992) *The No Blame Approach*. Bristol: Lame Duck Publishing.
Maines, B. and Robinson, G. (1994) *If It Makes My Life Easier.... To Write a Policy on Bullying*. Bristol: Lame Duck Publishing.
McHugh, M. and McMillan, L. (1995) 'Training and development of headteachers', *School Organisation*, **15 (1)**.
Miller, D. (1976) *Social Justice* Oxford: Clarendon.
Milner, D. (1983) *Children and Race: Ten Years On*. London: Ward Lock.
Mitchell, A. (1984) *On the Beach at Cambridge*. London: Allison and Busby.
Mortimore P. Sammons, P. Stoll, L. Lewis, D. and Ecob, R. (1988), *School Matters: the Junior Years*. Wells: Open Books.
National Curriculum Council (1989) *An Introduction to the National Curriculum* York: The National Curriculum Council with the Open University.

National Curriculum Council (1990) *Equal Opprotunities for All*. York: National Curriculum Council.

National Curriculum Council (1993) *Planning the National Curriculum at Key Stage 2*. York: National Curriculum Council.

Nehaul, K. (1995) *Schooling of Children of Caribbean Heritage*. Stoke-on-Trent: Trentham (in press).

Nias, J., Southworth, G. and Yeomans, R. (1989) *Staff Relationships in the Primary School*. London: Cassell.

Nias, J., Southworth, G. and Campbell, P. (1992) *Whole School Curriculum Development in the Primary School*. London: Falmer.

Norman, K. (ed.) (1992) *Thinking Voices: The Work of the National Oracy Project*. London: Hodder and Stoughton.

Nussbaum, M. (1986) *The Fragility of Goodness*. Cambridge: Cambridge University Press.

Paterson, L. and Goldstein, H. (1991) 'New statistical methods for analysing social structures: an introduction to multilevel models', *British Educational Research Journal*, **17 (4)**.

Plewis, I. (1991) 'Underachievement: a case of conceptual confusion', *British Educational Research Journal*, **17 (4)**.

Pollard, A. (1985) *The Social World of the Primary School*. Holt Educational.

Pollard, A. (1990) *Learning in Primary Schools*. London: Cassell.

Pollard, A. Broadfoot, P. Croll, P. Osborn, M. and Abbott, D. (1994) *Changing English Primary Schools? The impact of the Education Reform Act at Key Stage One*. London: Cassell.

Pollard, A. and Tann, S. (1987) *Reflective Teaching in the Primary School: A Handbook for the Classroom*. London: Cassell.

Reay, D. (1990) 'Girls' groups as a component of anti-sexist practice – one primary school's experience', *Gender and Education*, **2 (1)**.

Reay, D. (1991) 'Intersections of gender, race and class in the primary school', *British Journal of Sociology of Education*, **12 (2)**.

Reid, J. (1981) 'Negotiating education', in Kemmis, S. (ed.) *The Action Research Reader*. Deakin University Press.

Richardson, R. (1990) *Daring to be a Teacher*. Stoke-on-Trent: Trentham Books.

Richardson, R. (1991) 'Empowerment, access and the legal framework', *Multicultural Teaching*, **10 (1)**.

Rosenholtz, S. (1989) *Teachers' Workplace: The Social Organization of Schools*. Harlow: Longman.

Rudduck, J. (1991) 'The language of consciousness and the landscape of action: tensions in teacher education', *British Educational Research Journal*, **17 (4)**.

The Runnymede Trust (1993) *Equality Assurance in Schools: Quality, Identity, Society*. Stoke-on-Trent: Trentham.

Ryckman, R. M. (1992) *Theories of Personality* (5th edn.) Brooks/Cole Publishing Company.

Sammons, P. (1994) Ethnicity and achievement in Inner London, Conference Paper, Queens University Belfast, September.

Schon, D. (1983) *The Reflective Practitioner*. Temple Smith.

Sewell, C. A. (1995) 'A phallic response to schooling: black masculinity and race in an inner-city comprehensive', In Griffiths, M. and Troyna, B. (eds) *Anti-racism, Culture and Social Justice in Education*. Stoke-on-Trent: Trentham.

Siraj-Blatchford, I. (1994) *The Early Years: Laying the Foundations for Racial Equality*, Stoke-on-Trent: Trentham.

Skelton, C. (ed.) (1989) *Whatever Happens to Little Women?* Buckingham: Open University Press.

Solsken, J. (1993) *Language, Gender and Work in Families and Schools*. Ablex Publishing Company.

Southworth, G. (ed.) (1994) *Readings in Primary School Development.* Lewes: Falmer.

Steedman, C. (1986) *Landscape for a Good Woman: A Story of Two Lives.* London: Virago.

Tajfel, H. (1978) *The Social Psychology of Minorities.* Minority Rights Group Report No. 38.

Tizard, B., Blatchford, P., Burke, J., Farquhar, C. and Plewis, I. (1988) *Young Children at School in the Inner City.* New York: Lawrence Erlbaum Associates.

Verma, G. and Pumfrey, P. (1988) *Educational Attainments.* Lewes: Falmer.

Wallace, M. and McMahon, A. (1994) *Planning for Change in Turbulent Times.* London: Cassell.

Webb, R. and Vulliamy, G. (1995) 'The changing role of the Deputy Head', *School Organisation*, **15 (1)**.

Wells, C. G. (1985) *Language, Learning and Education: Selected Papers from the Bristol Study: 'Language at Home and at School'.* London: NFER-Nelson.

Wheldall, K. and Panagopoulou-Stamatelatou, A. (1991) 'The effects of pupil self-recording of on-task behaviour on primary school children', *Journal of the British Educational Research Association*, **17 (2)**.

Whitaker, P. (1993) *Managing Change in Schools.* Buckingham: Open University Press.

Whitehead, F., Capey, A.C., Maddren, W. and Wellings, A. (1977) *Children and Their Books.* Basingstoke: Macmillan Educational.

Williams, P. J. (1993) *The Alchemy of Race and Rights.* London: Virago.

Winter, R. (1989) *Learning from Experience.* Lewes: Falmer Press.

Willes, M. (1983) *Children into Pupils.* London: Routledge and Kegan Paul.

Wolfendale, S. (1992) *Empowering Parents and Teachers: Working for Children.* London: Cassell.

Index